In the end, we lead who we are and this pragmatic guidance will be a boon to anyone interested in becoming a fully human leader who can bring out the best in others. Neither abstract theory nor a simplistic "recipe" for success, this book provides clear behavioral descriptions and practical exercises for developing the habitual practice of the Nine Virtues essential for effective leadership. A book for rereading, reflecting, and gifting to aspiring leaders.

—Carol A. Aschenbrener, M.D.
Former Executive Vice President and Chief Strategy Officer,
Association of American Medical Colleges

People seek positions of leadership for a variety of reasons; sometimes they don't pursue leadership but assume it when a need arises. In any case, people are often unprepared for its complexities and can end up damaging the department or organization they are leading and the organization's people—including the leader. It is important for people who are leaders or who aspire to be in a position of leadership to think deeply about leadership and to learn and practice leadership skills. While several authors have written about leadership and the competencies and skills required to be successful, none is as fundamental as *The 9 Virtues of Exceptional Leaders*. Jenkins and Haden have described what is most important in any human interaction: virtue. I highly recommend *The 9 Virtues of Exceptional Leaders: Unlocking Your Leadership Potential* to leaders and aspiring leaders at all levels in any organization.

—George R. Boggs, Ph.D.
President and CEO Emeritus, American Association of Community Colleges, and
Superintendent/President Emeritus, Palomar College

Karl Haden and Rob Jenkins have written a wonderfully motivating book for people in all settings: business, home, school or community. I love the suggestions on how to develop each virtue at the end of the chapters. That changes this from a "just-read-me" book to a "read-and-practice-to-learn" experience. We've included *The 9 Virtues of Exceptional Leaders* as a new resource in our international business etiquette and image development programs.

—Laura Cotton, Managing Director, Pearl Strategies, Ltd.

I can't put it down. *The 9 Virtues of Exceptional Leaders* is a lively text…on virtuous leadership that is both accessible and engaging (quite the page turner) and yet provides all the fodder and support that makes it an exceptional academic read and resource.

Within the first twenty words of Chapter 1, readers will notice the unique approach to the leadership conversation authors Haden and Jenkins invite us to in *9 Virtues*. It is peppered with a plethora of metaphors, analogies, and quotes. Every reader will find something to relate to among the authors' images, examples, and ideas and therefore will feel worthy of inclusion and ready to partake in this conversation on leadership. Readers who haven't yet recognized their leadership potential, those who aspire to be leaders, those who are new to leadership, and those who are seasoned will find gems among the pages of this treasure.

Early in the discussion, the authors introduce us to self-awareness' importance to the development of each of the nine leadership virtues. Allowing for the natural leadership potential in all of us, albeit at different levels, the importance of self-awareness needs to be nurtured to develop leadership to its greater potential. Each virtue has a chapter devoted to understanding its meaning and dynamics. This is followed by invaluable exercises to practice as a means needed to nurture the natural potential in all of us. Of course, the outcome of practice has been taught to us from childhood: "Practice makes perfect."

Most important for the leader is to appear natural, comfortable, and knowledgeable. This indeed is the result of behaviors intentionally practiced to become habits. The authors have been masterful in demonstrating this, for example, in Chapter 5, Humility. They engaged the reader by meeting her where she lives, using common terms, identifying its component parts--listening, being teachable, empathy, selflessness, putting others first, service, and it's not about you. Then each was given specific steps to practice to begin the habit formation process. Key to success is recognizing the import of emotional intelligence in the process.

Haden and Jenkins support the reader's learning by using common language and by recounting, summarizing, and previewing new ideas from the beginning of the book to its end. Rarely, if at all, does a leadership text provide explicit exercise direction on how to develop a skill or talent. This is an outstanding strength of *The 9 Virtues of Exceptional Leaders,* in addition to the attractiveness of a leadership text that is accessible, engaging, and well written.

—Jacquelyn Belcher, J.D.
President Emeritus, Georgia Perimeter College
and the Board Chair of the American Association of Community Colleges

Karl Haden and Rob Jenkins have written a highly important book that contributes to, and furthers our understanding of leadership in a unique, thoughtful, provocative, and clearly written manner. While the shelves are full of books describing the techniques that leaders use in the name of effectiveness, Haden and Jenkins seek to describe the foundation of effective leadership. *The 9 Virtues of Exceptional Leaders* builds on Stephen Covey's *7 Habits of Highly Effective People,* Jim Collins's *Good to Great,* and other books which have sought to describe the principles of effectiveness in leadership.

The premise of *The 9 Virtues* is that virtuous leadership is a habit. Quoting Aristotle, they point out, "We are what we repeatedly do. Excellence (or virtue) is then not an act, but a habit." While the Nine Virtues can be discussed individually—humility, honesty, courage, perseverance, hope, charity, balance, wisdom and justice—the truly virtuous leader practices each of the virtues in all aspects of their life at all times. From the chapter "The Virtuous Leader," they state, "Courage without charity is merely ruthlessness, just as wisdom without humility is arrogance, perseverance without hope is fanaticism, and honesty without justice is cruelty. An individual who appears to display one virtue—or even several of them—without displaying them all, in the end, really has none of them. That person is not virtuous, whatever redeeming qualities he or she may possess."

In their discussion, Haden and Jenkins draw upon philosophy, personal anecdote, collective wisdom, and strong examples of virtuous leaders. For example, Martin Luther King's "Letter from a Birmingham Jail" effectively illustrates the virtue of humility and Viktor Frankl's *Man's Search for Meaning* helps provide depth to the discussion of balance (and other virtues). Each of the chapter's discussion of the Nine Virtues concludes with recommendations on how to practice that specific virtue in order to bring it to the level of habit.

In conclusion, *The 9 Virtues of Exceptional Leaders* contributes to, and expands upon, the conversation of effective leadership by highlighting the habits—virtues—that lie at the core of effective leadership. This is not a "how to" book; rather, it is a deep, yet accessible, exploration of the DNA of leadership—the factors that truly separate the leader from the pretender.

—Hershey S. Bell, M.D., M.S., FAAFP
Vice President of Academic Affairs and Dean of the Lake Erie College of
Osteopathic Medicine, School of Pharmacy

The value of leadership in all realms of civilized society is becoming ever more critical. Haden and Jenkins will make you rethink the essentials of being a leader. Their book guides you on a journey of self-discovery as you learn to practice each of the Nine Virtues.

—Richard W. Valachovic, D.M.D., M.P.H.
President and CEO, American Dental Education Association

The 9 Virtues of Exceptional Leaders offers a fresh approach to one's journey through leadership. This is not just another book on leadership theory. It is a book that guides the reader through some self-reflection to determine whether or not you are truly practicing habits and behavior that can make you more effective. Whether you are an aspiring or a "seasoned" leader, these authors invite you to do a little homework to make the most of your true leadership potential.

—Charlotte J. Warren, Ph.D.
President, Lincoln Land Community College

The virtuous leader is the kind of leader we all want, and frankly we need, to keep our country great. Whether in government, academia, or business, we need this type of leadership! *The 9 Virtues of Exceptional Leaders* is an entertaining and compelling read, the kind of book that helps you understand good leadership and teaches you how to be your best!

—Aaron Gagnon, Vice President and Chief Audit Executive,
Abercrombie & Fitch, and Former Partner, Ernst & Young

Haden and Jenkins bring focus to critical truths about leadership in *The 9 Virtues of Effective Leaders*. Leadership is, in fact, not a natural occurrence. Neither is virtue. One must work at both and both can be learned. By deconstructing Virtue as nine individual virtues that combine to produce the essential personalized core for leaders, the authors challenge us to cultivate and develop these traits. Their premise is simple. These are not simply techniques that are to be acquired as leadership tools, but rather ways to become a virtuous person who will thus be ready to assume the role of effective leader.

—Lawrence Miller, Ph.D.
CEO, Miller & Associates Educational Consulting
Former Director, National Institute for Staff and Organizational Development

The 9 Virtues of Exceptional Leaders

Unlocking Your Leadership Potential

The 9 Virtues *of* Exceptional Leaders

Unlocking Your Leadership Potential

N. Karl Haden, Ph.D.
Rob Jenkins

Deeds Publishing | Atlanta

Published by Deeds Publishing
Atlanta, Georgia
www.deedspublishing.com

Library of Congress Cataloging-in-Publications Data is available upon request.

ISBN 978-1-941165-84-3

Books are available in quantity for promotional or premium use. For information, write info@deedspublishing.com.

First Edition

10 9 8 7 6 5 4 3 2 1

To our mentors, who taught us virtuous leadership.

Contents

The fountain of life is character.
And, from it, in their order, flow forth our actions.

—Zeno of Citium, 334-262 BC

Acknowledgements

THE AUTHORS WOULD LIKE TO ACKNOWLEDGE WITH GRATITUDE THE outstanding professionals at the Academy for Academic Leadership (AAL), without whom this book would not have been possible. In particular, AAL Chief Operating Officer George Weinstein—an accomplished writer in his own right—brought to the project his indispensable knowledge of the book publishing business, along with his unparalleled organizational and editorial skills. Jessica Merrill, also at AAL, served as an early sounding-board and as one of the manuscript's first editors. We also thank Lynn Whittaker, a professional editor and the last in a line of editors, who assisted us in reaching the final draft. The AAL staff and senior consultants constitute a dedicated and wise team. This book, and AAL itself, would not exist without them.

In addition, the authors would like to thank Mark Babcock of Deeds Publishing for his editorial and design expertise, which resulted in the first-class product you now hold in your hands; and publisher Bob Babcock, whose knowledge and marketing acumen proved invaluable.

Writing a book about virtue is one thing, but living virtuously before the people who know and love you is another. First and foremost, Karl thanks his wife Jeannie. As the wife of an entrepreneur she too must persevere with him through the ups and downs of life tethered to a business. She also exhibits the greatest charity in his lifelong pursuit of balance. Nowhere is the virtue of hope better cultivated than in parenting. Karl owes a debt to his daughters, Maggie and Lila, for teaching him about hope. They are a constant source of inspiration.

For his part, Rob wishes to thank his wife Bonnie, as always, for her patience, forbearance, and sage advice, along with his four children—Jennifer, Robert, Michael, and Nathan—all of whom are excellent examples of what can happen when people truly apply the principles discussed in this book. He would also like to thank all of the many leaders he has had the pleasure to observe, to work with, and to work for. Together, they have taught him everything he knows about how leaders ought to behave—and, in some instances, how they ought not to behave.

In addition to examples from the authors' experiences, readers will find references to other contemporary works on leadership. They also will discover the considerable influence of history, literature, philosophy, and religious texts on the authors. We do not (and could not) know many of the leaders, thinkers, and exemplars who gave substance to this book. Yet, they are our daily companions through the work they left behind. If *The 9 Virtues* provides to the reader a different or even illuminating vision of leadership, that perspective should be credited to the giants on whose shoulders we stand.

Introduction

VIRTUE. THE GREEK TERM IS *arête* (AHR-I-TEY). VARIOUSLY TRANS-lated, the concept is more than 2,500 years old—and it is as relevant today as it was when the Greeks first conceived the idea. Virtue is about character. More specifically, virtue is excellence in character: character shaped by actions into habitual ways of thinking and acting. The authors of this book believe that virtue is not only key to personal well-being and the existence of good societies in which citizens can pursue life, liberty, and happiness; it is also the heart of effective leadership and thriving organizations. This book describes what we call *virtuous leadership*.

As we began to write this book, the concept of "natural leaders" came to our minds. We thought about people to whom leadership seems to come naturally, the Michael Jordans of leadership—people such as Dr. Martin Luther King Jr., Margaret Thatcher, and Steve Jobs, to name just a few modern examples. The idea of natural leaders evokes the frequent debate in leadership studies over nature versus nurture, leading to this perennial question: are leaders born or are they made? We think the answer is both.

Everyone has leadership potential; in this respect, there are inborn or natural capacities in all of us. Just as some people have more athletic ability or musical talent than others, we each have different levels of natural leadership ability. This book enables you to build on your natural ability, and places the emphasis on the leadership you nurture through actions and habits. The term we use for this nurturing

1

is "character building." Developing the character of a leader begins with whatever natural potential you have and builds on that potential through action and habit formation. Regardless of how much leadership ability you are born with, as the natural seed is nurtured in you, it grows into virtue. And virtue ultimately produces character.

In the pages that follow, we define the character of a leader using the Nine Virtues. Among these virtues you will find the four often called the cardinal virtues: courage, perseverance, wisdom, and justice. You also will find the traditional spiritual virtues: hope, faith (in the chapter on hope), and charity. In addition, we have included virtues that seem particularly relevant today: humility, honesty, and balance. Are these the only virtues that should define the character of the leader? No, but these nine are based on over two millennia of thinking about virtue and what it means to human character. The nine also reflect our observations of effective leaders, as frequent examples show. Our purpose is to apply these Nine Virtues to leadership—to show how effective leaders embrace and become these virtues through their choices.

Virtue is about making the right choices, over and over again, until they become habits. At the end of each chapter on the Nine Virtues, you will find exercises: suggestions for practicing that particular virtue. We encourage you to give these exercises careful attention. Like any habit, the virtues develop in us through practice. Even a virtuoso pianist, a natural-born prodigy, has perfected her talent through countless hours of practice.

One final word about practice. Effective leaders are not simply people who *know* a lot about leadership. Many of those we admire as leaders may have very little knowledge of the literature on leadership. Likewise, the primary goal of this book is not knowledge, but practice. Study the Nine Virtues; but above all, *become* the Nine Virtues.

1. Why Virtue?

A STORY IN THE NEWS NOT LONG AGO SHOWED WHAT HUMAN BE-
ings are capable of at their best and, at the same time, illustrated the
role that leadership plays in bringing out that potential in ordinary
people.

The story involved a late-season game between two high school
boys' basketball teams in Texas. A young man named Mitchell, who
has an intellectual disability, had served as manager of one of the teams
for several years. Since it was the last home game, the coach decided to
let Mitchell dress out with the team and—unbeknownst to him—decided to put him in the game at the end, regardless of the score.

"So you were willing to lose the game?" a local reporter asked the
coach afterward.

"Absolutely," the coach replied. "To let him have his moment? Absolutely."

With the home team leading by 10 points and under two minutes
left to play in the game, the coach followed through on his decision
and put Mitchell in. What followed could serve as a lesson to all of us
in humility, charity, and perseverance.

Time and time again, with the clock running down, team members
passed the ball to their manager, giving him every opportunity to score
a basket. Unfortunately, he missed each time, then lost the last pass out
of bounds with just a few seconds remaining.

But here is where the story really gets good. A player on the visit-
ing team, Jonathan, whose job it was to throw the ball in, called out
Mitchell's name and passed the ball to him, right under his own goal.

3

As time expired, Mitchell took one last shot—and swished it at the buzzer.

Asked after the game why he had thrown the ball to an opposing player with his team trailing, Jonathan simply said, "I was raised to treat other people like I would want to be treated. I know if I had been in that situation, I would have wanted one more shot to try and score."

Now, that is a great "feel good" story, is it not? The kind that ought to be made into a movie, complete with orchestra crescendo in the background. But what is it about stories like this that makes us feel good? Why do we tell them over and over, celebrate them, turn them into Hollywood films?

Is it that, despite what we read in the newspapers and see on television and the Internet every day, despite what we may witness personally, we desperately want to believe that goodness really exists in the world? That in fact we DO believe goodness exists, and we are constantly looking for evidence to confirm our conviction?

Excellence in character and conduct is what we are talking about in this book when we use the word "virtue." We believe that it exists and that it animates, motivates, and inspires all of us. In fact, in this book we are going to deal with many different virtues—nine, to be exact—which in the end are all aspects of a single, overriding concept: Virtue, with a capital "V." We believe that individuals can aspire to those virtues, work to acquire them, put them into practice in their lives, and model them for others. Indeed, we believe that unless they are put into practice, the virtues, for all practical purposes, do not exist. Virtue, in our view, is not merely a concept; it is a way of life.

Moreover, we believe that virtue has everything to do with leadership. Note the role that leadership played in the story above. Initially, one individual, a high school basketball coach, decided that he was going to do what he believed was right, regardless of the consequences. That decision did not merely require him to think or believe something; it required him to *do* something. As a result of his *action*—in putting his team manager into the game—look how the members of the team were inspired to behave. Because of their coach's example, they too acted out of love for their teammate and a desire to do the right thing, passing up opportunities to pad their own stats in order to provide Mitchell with the memory of a lifetime.

Even a member of the opposing squad was inspired by that coach's actions, and by the actions of the other players, not to mention by the parents who had raised him to "treat other people like he would want to be treated."

Not Just the "Flavor of the Month"

Clearly, virtue is a powerful leadership tool. People who do good can inspire others to do good as well, to perform acts they may not have otherwise, acts that benefit not only themselves but also the larger community. This truism has profound implications for organizations.

Virtue is not merely another fad or gimmick, the "flavor of the month." Someone reading this book cannot just say, "Well, that sounds pretty good. I think I'll try being virtuous, see if I can't motivate the troops. Who knows, maybe I'll get a bigger bonus this year!"

Forgive us for belaboring the obvious, but that attitude is not virtue.

Instead, virtuous living is a habit—indeed, a set of habits—that must be cultivated continuously over a lifetime. Benjamin Franklin, in his *Autobiography*, listed 13 virtues, including honesty, temperance, patience, and humility, that he wished to acquire during his time on Earth (and that he thought the rest of us should strive to acquire as well). He then explained how to go about developing those virtues: by taking each in turn and putting forth the effort necessary to practice it daily until it becomes a habit, then moving on to the next virtue on the list. He even created a chart to track his progress, much like the chart a parent puts up on the refrigerator door to keep up with a child's daily chores.

With all due respect to Franklin, we have developed our own list of leadership-focused virtues (some of which, to be sure, mirror his). And our message is not that you should wait until you have perfected one before you move on to the next. But we do agree with Franklin that the key to acquiring these virtues is to put them into practice regularly, so that they become habits. If you practice them consistently, acquisition or internalization will naturally follow.

Implicit in this discussion is the understanding that, at times and in certain situations, any one of us may not *want* to behave virtuously. One may feel angry or hurt or abused and want to lash out, perhaps even believing that such behavior is justified in light of the way others have behaved. In other words, there may be times when you do not feel particularly virtuous. How can you *be* virtuous when you do not *feel* virtuous?

To address that universal dilemma, consider the teachings of William James, the early 20th-century psychologist who argued that, if you want to *be* something—brave, for instance—then you should *act* as though you already are, and ultimately you will be. As James put it, "If you want a trait, act as if you already have the trait." For a soldier in battle, what is the practical difference between actually being brave and merely acting brave? The person who *is* brave and the person who merely *acts* brave both will *do* essentially the same things.

By the same token, what is the difference between a person who is actually virtuous and one who merely behaves as if she were virtuous? Both do the same things; as far as others are concerned, both act the same way. Moreover, for the leader who may not feel virtuous but who, over time, practices the essential virtues of leadership, the virtues ultimately become fully ingrained habits, genuine character traits.

Virtue, then, is not an approach to management—or even to leadership. It is not a technique. It is not something that simply can be picked up or implemented the way we try out new software. Rather, virtue is a way of living, developed over a lifetime. As you come to understand, work to cultivate, and put into practice the virtues we discuss in this book, you will, over time, become a better person; as a result, we believe this means you also will become a better leader.

That, in a nutshell, is the main premise of this book.

Ethics, Values, and Virtue

Two other words often associated with virtue are "ethics" (which we discuss in more detail in the next chapter) and "values." Sometimes, in fact, those words are used interchangeably with "virtue." For our purposes, we would like to distinguish among those three terms, so that you will understand exactly what we mean when we talk about *virtue*. Virtue is at the very core of the effective leader's being. It is the foundation of moral goodness. Virtues are deeply ingrained character traits that underlie and inform everything we do, everything we say, everything we *are*.

Ethics, as you will see in Chapter 2, has to do with what constitutes morality and moral behavior—how a person will respond in a given situation, what he or she will *do*.

Values determine what we consider important and what we desire. Values motivate. They have a major influence on how we behave or re-act. But what underlies values? That is, where do our values come from? We believe that values arise from our culture, our upbringing, and our personal experiences. For that reason, while people may share values, those qualities remain highly individual. Values are expressed through our behaviors because we usually act to achieve what we desire, what we value. These repeated actions shape character. People who behave in ways that are destructive to themselves and others may, in fact, be *living* their values, but the values are those that foster immoral behavior. If virtue is the core of moral goodness, vice is the corrosive of character.

If one wants to be a better person and leader, the answer is not simply to start with ethics—with simply a theoretical construct. Long-term, meaningful change comes about only when a person fully embraces the concept of virtue and begins working to acquire the various virtues we will discuss in this book. Consciously changing one's behavior is part of that endeavor, as we learned already from William James. But ultimately, the quest is to acquire and internalize the Nine Virtues, so that changes in behavior become organic and permanent.

To understand better the distinction we are drawing, go back to the story about the basketball game. While we could certainly argue that the coach and the players behaved ethically, ethics did not drive them. You could say they were motivated by their values, but we typically think of values as something people decide upon, and the players' actions in this case were spontaneous. No, what truly determined the way those individuals responded when put to the test, we believe, was their virtue. Or to put all of this another way, and perhaps place everything in perspective: ethics is a theory about what you should *do*, and values arise from beliefs that you *have*, but virtue is something that you *are*.

Nature or Nurture?

Hand in hand with our discussion of virtue will be an exploration of how to become a good leader. Of course, we believe the best answer to that question is "by practicing the Nine Virtues," but we also recognize this is a topic that has inspired millions and been a subject of debate for thousands of years. We certainly do not claim to have the final answer. Rather, we are hoping to synthesize the very best answers, from antiquity to the present, into a single, coherent system. We believe the best way to organize that system, in keeping with what the great minds throughout the ages have taught, is around these Nine Virtues.

The essential question is this: are leaders born, or are they made? And that question's corollary: is leadership a matter of nature or of nurture? The best answer, we believe, is a simple one: both. We all know from experience that some people appear to be "natural leaders," often due to some obvious traits. George Washington was physically imposing. Dr. Martin Luther King Jr. was a gifted orator. There's no question those qualities contributed to their success as leaders.

At the same time, we have seen people who, on the surface, did not possess qualities that would mark them as good leaders. Gandhi tended to be self-effacing. Eleanor Roosevelt was a president's wife, not a trained politician. Rosa Parks was a middle-aged seamstress on a bus. Such people may have had fewer apparent gifts, but they became effective leaders nonetheless.

One of the main concepts we wish to explore in this book is the connection between nature and nurture within the context of leadership. We assume that all people, by virtue of being human, have a nature in common. At a minimum, this includes intelligence, emotions, basic needs, and the higher needs for purpose and meaning. Human beings possess not only cognitive power, but also the potential for metacognition—the ability to reflect on our thoughts, feelings, and actions. As we will see in Chapter 14, this aspect of our humanity, of our "nature," is one of the keys to nurturing our development as leaders.

So which is it? Are leaders born, or are they made? The answer is a resounding "Yes!" Some people are blessed with certain qualities that, put to the right use, will serve them well as leaders. But the key phrase is "put to the right use." Never forget that, had Washington not used his imposing presence to inspire his soldiers in their fight for liberty; had Dr. King not used his oratory to promote human dignity; their inherent gifts, however great, would ultimately have been worthless. Whatever their abilities, it was their underlying virtues, their personifying of concepts like honesty, courage, and justice, that made them great leaders.

By the same token, the vast majority of us who lack such gifts, or who do not possess them to the same degree, also can become effective leaders within our spheres. We can do so by embracing, practicing, internalizing, and modeling the same virtues that Washington, King, Gandhi, Parks, Roosevelt, and others exemplify: what we have chosen to identify in this book as the Nine Virtues of exceptional leaders. As we embrace those virtues—as *you* embrace them—over time, the question of whether you were born to lead or became an effective leader through your own efforts will cease to have any significance.

You simply will be a leader, someone whom people willingly follow—just as Washington's soldiers followed him, just as thousands of civil rights marchers followed Dr. King, just as those high school bas-ketball players followed their coach.

That is the power of virtuous leadership.

2. The Concept of Virtue

WHEN WE FIRST BEGAN BATTING AROUND THE IDEA FOR THIS BOOK, a good friend and colleague told us, "You probably shouldn't use the word 'virtue.' It sounds too religious."

We understand that the concept of virtue is, for many of us, deeply rooted in religious faith and tradition. Notions of virtue as a means of living up to our fullest human potential and thereby honoring the Creator, along with descriptions of specific virtues and instructions for practicing them, can be found in all the world's great religions. For that reason, the idea of virtuous living is, for many, inseparable from their daily religious practice.

And yet virtue as an ideal has a long history completely apart from any particular religion and even from religion in general. From the heroic societies of antiquity, through Plato and Aristotle, all the way up to modern times, many cultures and individuals have embraced and promoted the idea of virtue outside of a religious context. Although many religions teach virtue, the concept of virtue itself is not explicitly or uniquely religious. A person can practice the virtues we discuss in this book without being religious at all.

Our purpose is neither to promote nor to question any particular religious faith or, for that matter, faith itself. Rather, our purpose is to explore what we believe are the essential virtues of good leadership. We aim to persuade readers that, by adopting and practicing those virtues, they can become better leaders and better people while helping to create better followers, better future leaders, better organizations, and better communities.

11

Ancient Notions of Virtue

Of course, having stated that our purpose does not depend on religion, we do recognize that the Judeo-Christian tradition relies heavily on the concept of virtue. It is a frequent topic of Old Testament prophets, who defined virtue strictly within the context of what behaviors were acceptable and unacceptable to God—the Ten Commandments, to cite one well-known example. Musings on the nature of virtue also appear in the writings of Hebrew poets like David and Solomon. In the New Testament, St. Paul admonished early Christians that, "if there be any virtue," they should "think on these things."

There is likewise a long history of thinking about virtue in the non-Judeo-Christian world. For instance, in ancient heroic societies such as those described by Homer and Virgil, the concept of virtue was basically indistinguishable from that of duty. To do what was right meant to do what society expected of you, based on who you were and where you stood in the social hierarchy. Virtue was clearly defined and unambiguous, rooted firmly in culture and tradition. As a son, if someone took the life of your father, you were duty-bound to take that person's life in return. Such action was a moral imperative, demanded by the paramount social virtue of family loyalty.

As societies grew more open, philosophers like Plato began to recognize that there may be multiple, and perhaps competing, ideas of virtue. For Plato, the ultimate expression of virtue became tied to the value of citizenship: of peaceful coexistence with others in a diverse society. He identified four essential virtues of the good citizen: wisdom, which for him meant recognizing the greater good; temperance, or self-restraint; courage to promote what is right even when afraid or when it conflicts with personal desires; and justice, which occurs when all three of the other virtues are in balance.

Perhaps the greatest ancient authority on virtue was Plato's student, Aristotle, who brought together previous musings on virtue and added his own thoughts, creating a view of human character that led to "virtue ethics." For Aristotle—and for the two of us—virtue is all about action. He believed that through choice, the potential became actual: virtue is a condition of one's character to be sought, an ideal to be pursued, a goal that we can attain. He also advanced the concept of "practical reasoning," which transforms Plato's virtue of wisdom from a mere attribute into a call for action. Wisdom is not about simply "knowing" but "doing"; it is about making (and implementing) good decisions based on sound moral reasoning.

As mentioned at the start of the Introduction, the Greek word for virtue is *arête,* which often is translated as "excellence." As Aristotle put it, "We are what we repeatedly do. Excellence (or virtue), then, is not an act, but a habit."

The fact that we do not often use the word "virtue" in contemporary parlance may be a result of its religious connotations—the reason our friend advised against putting it in the title. We usually talk about ethics, the study of which has become a focal point of social and political philosophy in the late 20th and early 21st centuries. Universities offer ethics courses in their business schools, their medical schools, their schools of arts and sciences. We formulate Codes of Ethics for doctors, lawyers, politicians, educators, athletes—the list goes on. Businesses and other organizations offer "ethics training" for new employees and, later, follow-up "refresher courses." (We know because we have had to take such courses ourselves.) However, the lifelong pursuit of virtue cannot be encapsulated in an episodic classroom experience.

Beyond Ethics

Inherent to some ethical theories is the belief that, if people simply acquire the necessary ethical knowledge, they can, by an act of will, make the morally correct decision in any given instance. Otherwise, why offer classes in ethics or require employees to undergo ethics training? We seem to be saying, "Here, take this class (or read this manual, or watch this video, or visit this website). Then you should be able to make the right choices whenever you have to."

The difference between that approach and what we are proposing in this book should be obvious. A quick scan of contemporary writing on ethics yields such definitions as "the moral correctness of specified conduct"; "a set of principles of right conduct"; "the rules of conduct recognized in respect to a particular class of human actions"; and "the study of proper business policies and practices regarding potentially controversial issues." Note that all of these definitions focus on conduct, actions, and practices in the context of some theoretical framework. In other words, what constitutes a morally correct action is determined by the ethical system in which or by which it is interpreted.

Virtue, on the other hand, as we define it, has more to do with what a person *is* and with what he or she *does*, inasmuch as actions shape character. Virtue is not a list of rules for living, but rather a way of life: a set of deeply ingrained personal habits that together form a prism through which one sees the world. The virtuous person will act in a morally praiseworthy way because he or she is a good person, not because of knowing a lot about theories of ethics.

In his influential book, *The Seven Habits of Highly Effective People*, Stephen R. Covey discusses the difference between what he calls "The Personality Ethic" and "The Character Ethic." Under the former, he writes, "success [becomes] more a function of personality, of public image, of attitudes and behaviors, skills and techniques, that lubricate the processes of human interaction." The Character Ethic, on the other hand, teaches "that there are basic principles of effective living, and that people can only experience true success and enduring happiness as they learn and integrate these principles into their basic character."

Once upon a time, the word "ethics" might have meant much the same as what we mean in this book when we use the word "virtue." (Indeed, Aristotle's great treatise on virtue is entitled *Nichomachean Ethics*.) In other words, there was a time when ethical behavior was certainly thought to be related to a person's character. Nowadays, unfortunately, what people usually mean when they talk about ethics is something more calculating—something much more likely to fall under the banner of the Personality Ethic. Behaving ethically is viewed as a skill or technique that can be acquired, simply by taking a course or reading a book, and then applied as needed to specific situations.

Virtue, as the two of us use the term, is a concept that goes far beyond modern-day notions of ethics. Virtue, as we noted in Chapter 1, is the foundation of what we consider *true* ethical behavior: behavior that not only is morally correct in any given instance but also genuine, sincere, and consistent over time.

Virtue and Leadership

To understand what these distinctions have to do with leadership, let us return briefly to the story we told at the beginning of this book. What motivated that high school basketball coach to put Mitchell into the game? Or rather, what motivated him to resolve, before the game even began, to put his manager in regardless of the score?

Some could argue that the team was well ahead at game's end and probably going to win anyway, so the coach did not risk much with his action. That may be true. However, the coach made it clear in the postgame interview that he had decided beforehand to put Mitchell into the game at some point, no matter what. While admittedly we cannot know someone's motives for certain, in this case we can only take the coach at his word. Besides, the team was just 10 points ahead, and anyone who understands the game of basketball knows that is not an insurmountable lead. So there was some risk involved, however slight.

The real point is that the coach *did* put Mitchell in the game. He decided he was going to, and he did. But why did he make that decision to begin with?

The first thing the coach's actions tell us is how he felt about that young man. He must have had a great deal of love for Mitchell. He must have admired him greatly—admired the way he had worked to overcome his disability, the way he had persevered through adversity in order to be involved in a sport he enjoyed, to be part of a team, to serve others and make himself useful to society. The coach also must have felt a tremendous amount of personal loyalty toward Mitchell, in return for the loyalty Mitchell had shown toward the basketball program.

Love. Perseverance. Loyalty. Need we point out that those are all classical virtues?

The second thing we learn from the coach's behavior is what kind of person he is. Clearly, he is someone with a strong sense of what is right: it was right to play Mitchell, he decided, even though Mitchell was not a gifted basketball player, and even though it could conceivably cost his team the game, because of who Mitchell was and what he had done for the program. In other words, he believed that there are more important things in life than winning a basketball game. How we wish that everyone who coaches young people felt that way.

Moreover, the coach was a man of courage—the courage of his convictions. He resolved to do what he believed was right regardless of the consequences. He also was a man of integrity, who followed through by doing what he said he was going to do, even though the only person he "said" it to was himself. I think we can agree there is something deeper at work here than mere ethics, a rule- or principle-based choice between doing the right thing and the wrong thing in a particular situation.

Now look at the impact that coach's behavior had on the people he led. His decision to do the right thing was a powerful example to the members of his team and even to a member of the opposing team. They saw someone they no doubt admired who did something they knew intuitively to be right. As a result, they were motivated to do the right thing as well—to pass the ball to Mitchell, even if it meant they did not get to score themselves; even, in fact, if it meant losing the game.

Could other team members have decided on their own to give

Mitchell the chance to score without their coach's example? Of course it is possible, perhaps even likely. The spark of virtue may burn in them as well. But here is the key point: they could not have passed Mitchell the ball if he had not been in the game; and they were not in a position to put him in the game. It took a coach—a leader—to do that.

The virtuous leader, then, is someone who has actively incorporated the virtues into his or her life. This leader's actions are determined not by some calculation of the ethics of a particular situation, but by the virtuous habits of thought and behavior acquired over a lifetime.

The virtuous leader also is someone who sets an example of such behavior for others. We say again that we believe the capacity for virtue is at least latent in everyone; but sometimes people need to see someone else behaving virtuously before they have the courage to do so themselves or before they even think to do so.

The way people typically respond after a disaster is a good illustration of this point. At first, most bystanders seem stunned, unsure of what to do. But all it takes is one or two people rushing in to help, and suddenly everyone in the area is doing the same. Those first few to respond are not necessarily any more virtuous than the rest, but they are the ones who take the lead—and without their leadership, who knows how others in the crowd may react?

Finally, the virtuous leader is someone who creates an environment in which the virtues can be both nourished and practiced. We often hear people talk about a toxic work environment. What do they mean by that? Toxic to whom, or to what? Perhaps what they are really saying is that the environment in which they work dampens their desire to do their best, to excel in their jobs, to do the right things for the right reasons. It is toxic, all right, and what is being slowly (or not so slowly) smothered is that innate spark of virtue.

People tend to overuse the term "natural leader." The two of us use the term to refer only to something people perceive, rather than something that actually exists. We recognize that some may seem to have more in-born leadership attributes than others. But we also believe that *all* of us are born with a certain amount of ability and that anyone can develop and put into practice the qualities, the virtues, that make a good leader. What is often called natural in some leaders, even the best leaders, comes through time, effort, and making the right choices—much as top athletes can make the game look easy to anyone who does not know how many hours they spent in practice.

Perhaps the most important thing we can learn from famous leaders who have made it look easy, from Winston Churchill to Bear Bryant, from George Patton to Margaret Thatcher, is that they create an environment in which people can excel. Not only do they exemplify and model various virtues in their own lives—such as humility, perseverance, and courage—but they enable the people they lead to develop and put to use those same virtues. By doing so, they not only teach and inspire those around them to be better people, but they also create better organizations and, ultimately, a better society. That is virtuous leadership.

3. Learning to Lead

ONE OF THE FUNDAMENTAL TENETS OF THIS BOOK IS THAT VIRTUE can be learned, or acquired, over time. By practicing and acquiring the individual virtues (which we will be discussing in later chapters), one becomes virtuous.

Of course, every person is a unique individual, and everyone is raised differently. Some people may, by nature, be wiser or more humble or more courageous than others. Some may have been exposed to better examples of those qualities when they were young. But all of us, if we so desire, can *acquire* those qualities. Once acquired, they will appear to others to be as "natural" as if we were born with them. They will define us and become a part of who we are.

To the extent that good leadership is a function of virtue—another major tenet of this book—we also assert that leadership can be learned. We do not accept the idea that some people are just born to be leaders and others never will be, no matter what they do. Just as with anything else, there may be those who have more natural leadership ability than others. But anyone who wants to lead well can, over time, develop the qualities—the virtues—of a good leader.

Rob has observed this dynamic in his own children. His middle son, Michael, is what most people would describe as a natural leader. From his earliest days in Little League, he was always captain of the team. He has been elected or appointed to leadership roles in every organization he has ever belonged to. At high school football games, he was the one who decided what color students were going to wear or paint on their bodies, and he always led the cheers (or jeers). He was also the one the school's administrators relied on—as they stated pointedly to him more than once—to make sure school spirit never got out of hand. He has both embraced leadership roles and performed admirably in them.

Michael's younger brother, Nathan, on the other hand, was for many years what most would describe as a born follower—not surprising, perhaps, for a child with three accomplished and strong-willed older siblings. Up until the age of 14, he seemed perfectly content in that role. Then, suddenly, Nathan began to develop an interest in leadership. He began reading all he could find about leadership, attending youth leadership conferences, and talking to people in leadership roles, asking their advice. Within a few months, he was elected to the student council, then to leadership positions on the council, and eventually was nominated to attend national conferences on youth leadership. The "born follower" evolved into a prominent leader, and anyone who did not know him before may well have concluded that leadership came naturally to him. But they would be mistaken: he became a leader because he decided he wanted to be one and was willing to do what it took to reach his goal. Perhaps Nathan always had the potential to lead, but he became a leader when he chose to act on that potential.

Leadership, then, is not merely a quality that some people have and others do not. Rather, it is an ability that can be developed as one acquires the necessary character traits or virtues. By seeking out, coming to understand, and ultimately internalizing these virtues, we believe that people can, indeed, "learn to lead."

The Leadership Studies Effect

This belief on our part is hardly unique. Indeed, it probably sounds familiar to anyone who has read one of the many books on leadership development or participated in leadership training. Obviously, one of the most basic premises of any book or course on leadership is that leadership can be learned. Otherwise, why write the book or conduct the course?

The problem with most of those books and courses, however, is that they approach the issue from the standpoint of what Stephen Covey calls the Personality Ethic, discussed in Chapter 2. In other words, most leadership training materials tend to focus on attitudes, behaviors, skills, and techniques.

Another way to look at this distinction is to compare it to the way ethics is often taught these days. Much of our modern focus on ethics treats it as a set of rules, principles, systems, behaviors, and attitudes that can be memorized and applied to certain situations, much as a medical student learns which drug to use to treat a certain disease. We could refer to this as "formula-based ethics." Likewise, we can describe much of what passes for leadership training these days as "formula-based leadership development." This is modern-day, quasi-scientific reductionism at its worst, taking something as incredibly complex and multifaceted as leadership and boiling it down to a set of easy-to-remember rules.

Clearly, the two of us believe that good leadership entails a great deal more. We agree that good leaders tend to display certain attitudes and behaviors, but we contend that those must stem from something much deeper than a simple cognitive understanding of what a good leader should or should not do in a given situation. That is where our central idea of virtue comes into play: virtue is at the very core of the truly great leader. In a sense, attitudes, behaviors, skills, and techniques flow from and back into character. Virtue is a condition of character. For the best leaders, the behaviors most often associated with good leadership are authentic, not contrived; they are *learned* in the deepest and truest sense of that word and not merely as we often use it nowadays, to mean simply adopted.

Political theorist Jacob Heilbrunn reaches a similar conclusion in his essay "Can Leadership Be Studied?" After summarizing the advances in leadership studies made during the 20th century, he asks, "Is leadership simply an act, a self-delusion projected upon followers?" He concludes that students of leadership will need to examine their topic much more carefully in the coming years and asserts that in doing so, they "may discover that the most important things about leadership lie far beyond the capabilities of science to analyze."

Leadership Learning, Not Leadership Training

One of the most significant advances in educational theory over the last 20 years has been a shift of emphasis from teaching to learning. For centuries, the primary focus in any learning situation was on the teacher, the speaker, the presenter, sometimes referred to as "The Sage on the Stage"—the one who has all the knowledge and whose role is to share that knowledge with students. The latter, in this scenario, play an extremely passive role in the learning process. They are not so much learners as people who are being taught.

The emerging emphasis on learning, however, places more responsibility in the students' hands and makes them more active participants in the process. The instructor, some say, becomes more of a "Guide on the Side," whose job is not to somehow transmit knowledge by spouting information but rather to make sure that students are learning through a variety of means, including discussion, hands-on training, peer tutoring, and so on.

We believe that this new paradigm is well suited to helping people become better leaders, which is why from now on we will be talking about "leadership *learning*" rather than "leadership training." You can bring the best leaders in the world to your facility and have them conduct the most stimulating seminars imaginable, but if the audience in that room is merely sitting and listening, we suggest that very little learning is taking place. How much of what they hear are they taking in? And how much can people improve their leadership skills simply by listening to others talk about personal experiences or theories on leadership?

We believe the leader-learner must be an active, not a passive, participant. He or she must not simply memorize the formula for good leadership, but must learn through experiencing good leadership (and sometimes poor leadership) first-hand.

Thus, our answer to the age-old question "can leadership be taught?" is probably not—but it can definitely be learned.

An Experiential Model of Leadership Learning

Oliver Wendell Holmes once said, "Life is like painting a portrait, not doing a sum." That rather neatly encapsulates our philosophy of leadership learning.

Picture for a moment Van Gogh's painting *The Starry Night*. Think not just of the skill necessary to produce such a work of art, but of how much of himself Van Gogh put into that painting. Can you imagine that haunting canvas as the work of any other artist? Now envision yourself buying a paint-by-numbers set that would allow you to re-produce *The Starry Night* on a piece of black velvet. You simply apply the numbered paints to the corresponding numbered sections of the velvet, and voila! You're a great artist!

Right?

No, of course not. We all understand that you cannot recreate a great painting using a paint-by-numbers set. However much it may look like the original—from a distance, maybe, with the light just right—it is not the original and would never be mistaken for it, even by someone who does not know much about art. However skillful the brushstrokes—however well you "stay within the lines"—the painting is just a copy, and something vital will always be missing.

Much of leadership training is essentially like a paint-by-numbers set. We go to hear a famous leader speak, or we read a book in which that person reveals so-called secrets of great leadership, and then we seek to copy them. We try to make our behavior fit into the lines they have drawn for us. But something is always missing. Authenticity, sincerity, passion—call it what you will. At best, we become a crude and insubstantial imitation of some great person, not a legitimate leader in our own right.

That is not to say we should not seek to emulate great people. There is much we can and should learn from Socrates, Aristotle, and Jesus Christ, from Queen Elizabeth I, George Washington, and Eleanor Roosevelt. Identifying what we admire in others and seeking to incorporate those traits into our own makeup is one of the ways we grow as people—just as Van Gogh learned from the masters who preceded him. But at some point, in order to paint *The Starry Night*, Van Gogh had to become himself. Imitation may be the sincerest form of flattery, but if we want to be truly great leaders, copying others can take us only so far.

What we propose, then, in contrast to the formula-based leadership model, is an experiential model based on lifelong learning, reflection, and self-direction.

Lifelong Learning

Too often when we think of learning, we think of going to school for a certain number of years, acquiring the degrees we believe we need to pursue our chosen careers, and then—what? Once we have earned those degrees and launched our careers, are we done with learning?

Of course not, even if we seem to act that way sometimes. For some, lifelong learning may sound like something retired people do when they take a course in ornithology or poetry or ceramics. Perhaps they need something new to occupy their time; perhaps they are pursuing their passions, something they lacked time for when faced with the daily necessity of earning a living.

Yet, great thinkers—and great leaders—have always understood that learning is constant throughout our lives. We are always learning. The only questions are, first, what will we learn? And second, will learning simply be something that happens to us, or will it be a conscious and intentional act on our part? That is, will we take an active role in our own learning, or merely a passive one?

The well-known 20th-century educator and philosopher Mortimer Adler had this to say about the relationship between formal education and lifelong learning:

No one becomes a generally educated human being in school or college, or even in graduate school....Schools and colleges would be at their best, as they seldom are, if they were to prepare the young for a lifetime of learning after they have completed their stay in educational institutions, fully realizing that the diplomas and degrees they have acquired do not signify that they have completed their education.

This is especially true for leaders—who, to be effective, must constantly learn, grow, and evolve to meet the new challenges they face and will continue to face in an uncertain future. As Aristotle said, "All humans by nature desire to know"; to that, we add "no one more so than the virtuous leader."

Leaders, then, must first of all understand how learning takes place. A good way to begin is by identifying *where* it takes place. Educational innovator Philip Coombs noted that learning occurs in three spheres, which he labeled the formal, the non-formal, and the informal. Formal learning, of course, involves schools and colleges, as well as formalized training and certification courses. This type of learning is highly institutionalized, bureaucratic (remember trying to drop or add courses when you were in college?), and curriculum-driven. Its end results include grades, diplomas, certificates, and other paper-based credentials. In short, formal learning is what we are most likely to think of when someone says the word "learning."

But that is not where learning ends. Coombs also talked about what he called non-formal learning, which occurs outside of the formal education system. Most non-formal learning is short-term and voluntary, and it may well be community-based, sponsored by a club or association or community service group. This type of learning would be that learned in, for example, a dance class or a creative writing or money management workshop at a community center.

Then there is informal learning, which tends to be much more spontaneous and much less structured. This is the type of learning that goes on every day in a professional environment, where people are constantly learning how to use new software or what kinds of things not to say within the boss's earshot. Informal learning also seems to be much more private, in that we often feel we are learning on our own, without the formal constructs of classrooms and teachers—even though we may well have teachers in the form of mentors, colleagues, and leaders whom we emulate or coworkers who provide useful information.

Obviously, leaders must prepare themselves with all the formal education necessary to their profession and then continue to learn in non-formal settings where appropriate. But good leaders also are open to informal learning situations, where they can learn not only from trusted mentors and admired role models but also from colleagues, from subordinates, from clients—and ultimately from themselves. This continuous engagement is the essence of lifelong learning.

Another key to understanding how learning takes place is to recognize just *what* it is that we are learning—in other words, what constitutes knowledge. True knowledge involves more than simply assembling a body of facts; it also means understanding those facts. Aristotle taught that as we seek to understand—asking not only *what* but *why* and *how*—we move away from particular facts toward general principles, causes, and the explanations that underlie them. This movement away from pure fact toward deeper understanding is represented on this continuum:

What Constitues Knowledge?

```
━━━━━━━━━━━━━━━━━━━━━━━━━━━━━━━━━━▶
```

IGNORANCE	KNOWING	KNOWING	KNOWING	KNOWING
	THAT	ABOUT	HOW	WHY=
				UNDERSTANDING

Simply being cognizant of a particular fact constitutes "knowing that," and is only one step removed above ignorance. As a simple example, we all know that if someone drops an apple, it will fall to the floor. In other words, we know that gravity exists. But what exactly is gravity? How does it work? Why? Those questions take us further into the exploratory process of learning and ultimately lead to understanding a concept and how it applies. The exploration never ends.

Lifelong learning, then, is not merely the acquisition of facts; rather, it is the active desire to understand both the world and our individual and collective place in it. This journey of discovery is of necessity lifelong for the simple reason that the world never ceases to present us with new and interesting puzzles, dilemmas, wonders, and opportunities.

Reflection and the Self-Directed Learner

Ultimately, those who would learn to lead must understand that worthwhile learning comes only as a result of reflection and self-awareness. Remember our assertion that leaders must take an active role in their own learning? Of course, that involves seeking out the best new information; but it also involves reflecting on that information and, ultimately, coming to know oneself and one's place in the world well enough to put the knowledge we gain in its proper context.

Psychologists Carl Rogers and Abraham Maslow, among others,

used the term "self-actualized" to describe individuals who are striving to achieve their highest potential. We mean much the same thing when we use the term "self-directed" to refer to leader-learners who have taken responsibility for, and an active role in, their own learning.

If knowing is not simply about gathering facts but rather about coming to understand, then reflection must play a key role in the lifelong learning process. How else is one to move from "knowing that" to "knowing why," without spending a considerable amount of time and intellectual effort getting there? Without reflection, there can be no real learning.

In using the term "reflection," we are really talking about two things. The first is what most readers may think of immediately when they hear the word: basically, thinking deeply about something for a long period of time. This has been a key practice for philosophers, scholars, and artists throughout history. Socrates, for example, famously said that "the unexamined life is not worth living." But what we mean here is not merely self-reflection. Instead, we mean reflecting on the knowledge one has gained in order to achieve some measure of understanding. Emerson called this activity "long logic" and said it is the "procession or proportionate unfolding of the intuition"—in other words, coming to know more fully and deeply what one at first knows only partially or intuitively.

Reflection, in this context, thus means thinking about things; but it does not mean passively thinking. Reflection is more than simple head-in-the-clouds contemplation. It also has an active component, as true reflection leads naturally to exploration—to further research and study and then to additional reflection on what has been newly learned and so on, in a magnificent cycle of lifelong learning and intellectual and spiritual growth.

But just what is it, exactly, that we are supposed to reflect on? What gives us food for thought, and where do we get it? We all face problems and dilemmas throughout our lives, both personal and professional; if we have trained ourselves to be reflective, those questions naturally will occupy a great deal of our thinking. But true lifelong learners do not simply wait for life's mysteries to confront them; rather, lifelong learners actively seek out issues and concepts for further reflection.

One of the ways you can do this is by reading—and not just reading books on management or leadership, but all types of books, including novels, poetry, and books about hobbies and interests outside of your profession. All of those will enrich your life in ways that you probably cannot comprehend, much less anticipate, providing not only information about the world around you but also insights that will lead, through reflection, to deeper understanding.

Karl likes to tell about the time he was reading J.R.R. Tolkien's *The Hobbit* to his daughter, then eight years old. Not exactly on *Forbes* magazine's list of hot management books, right? But in the process of reading a bedtime story to a little girl, he came across the following gem of wisdom:

This thing all things devours;
Birds, beasts, trees, flowers;
Gnaws iron, bites steel;
Grinds hard stones to meal;
Slays kings, ruins town,
And beats high mountain down.

This passage, of course, is Gollum's riddle to Bilbo Baggins, when the two first meet in the pitch-black caves under the Misty Mountains. The answer (spoiler alert) is "Time." But what has that got to do with leadership?

For Karl, as he reflected upon it, that poem produced a kind of epiphany. He saw, with staggering clarity, just how precious and ephemeral time is, both personally and professionally. This realization, in turn, helped him to gain a better understanding of himself, of the world, and of his place in it. It led him to reconsider his priorities and made him, ultimately, a better father, a better person, and a better leader.

And here is where the concept of self-direction comes into play. Lifelong learner-leaders are not people to whom learning just *happens*. They are people who take control of their own learning, who actively set out to seek knowledge and, through reflection and exploration, come to understand what has been learned. Lifelong learners are constantly on the lookout for learning moments that occur throughout their lives, whether they seek them or not, and use them intentionally to further their knowledge and understanding. This is especially true when those moments involve what is called "transformational learning"—learning that changes us forever.

Transformational Learning

Throughout our lives, we encounter experiences that fundamentally change us as people. Up to the moment that experience took place, we were one thing; afterwards, we become something else entirely. You may call these epiphanies or light-bulb moments, but for our purposes in this chapter we are going to refer to them as "transformational learning experiences."

Often, these experiences arise as a result of formal education. At the community college where Rob formerly taught, he once had a student who was drifting aimlessly. This student was enrolled in school only because his parents had decreed he would either go to college or get a job, and he thought the former sounded easier. So he headed to the local community college to register for classes, not having any idea what he wanted to do in life.

Then, one day, while walking through an unfamiliar part of campus, this student came across the automotive technology building. He thought to himself, "I didn't know you could take those classes here." He had always considered himself a "car guy," had always enjoyed tinkering with engines, so he thought it might be fun to take classes in auto mechanics. Before he knew it, his hobby had become a profession and ultimately a well-paying career. The last Rob heard from him, he was working as a mechanic for a NASCAR driver.

The day he took a detour across campus was a transformational learning experience in that young man's life. He learned something about the college, and more importantly about himself, that changed him forever.

No doubt many of us can pinpoint moments in our lives when we realized we wanted to become a doctor, a lawyer, a professor, a business owner. For the lifelong learner-leader, however, those experiences continue throughout our lives. They happen as we seek them out, through self-directed, active learning, and often they happen whether we seek them out or not—as long as we remain open to them. Sometimes we do not recognize such moments for what they are, at first; but eventually, as we reflect, we come to see the transformative power of those experiences.

Much is made in today's leadership-studies literature of the transformational leader, a term coined by James MacGregor Burns in 1978. Burns drew a distinction between what he called "transactional leadership," which "merely ...appeals to the economic self-interest of followers," and transformational leadership, which "alters the expectations of followers." Marshall Sashkin expanded on this idea with his "Visionary Leadership Theory," which took "into account not only the practices of leaders but also the effect of their behaviors on the culture of an organization." He argued that "followers are transformed because they internalize the values of the organization," as embodied in the leader.

No doubt all of these ideas sound great. Many of you probably are familiar with them already, as a result of your previous leadership training experiences. Virtually all leaders want to be transformational leaders, or at least see themselves as such; indeed, the two of us have lost count of the number of biographies we have read in which leaders are described that way.

But how does one become a transformational leader? Not simply by reading about other transformational leaders, surely. Remember that emulating great leaders is fine, but attempting to imitate other people's behavior is not the same as internalizing their values. Nor can one become a transformational leader merely by following a written set of instructions, a list of dos and don'ts.

We believe that, because great leaders are by definition lifelong learners, transformational leadership arises from transformational learning. To put it simply, before a leader can hope to transform others, he or she must first become transformed. This is true whether we are talking about a better way to perform a mundane task or a more sweeping reimagining of the entire organization.

Rob spent several years as a high school and college basketball coach. One of the major trends during the 1990s, when he coached at two colleges, was full-court defensive pressure, of the type favored by Coach Rick Pitino at the University of Kentucky. Rob had never been a big believer in the full-court press, but he heard Pitino talk about it at a coaches' clinic and decided he would give it a try. It was a miserable failure. Coaching is all about getting a team to buy into a system and ultimately do what you want them to do, and Rob discovered he could not get his players to do something that he fundamentally did not believe in himself.

Several years later, after leaving college coaching, Rob was watching his son's middle school team and had an epiphany about how a full-court press might be effective in certain situations. And sure enough, when he came out of retirement not long after to coach as a volunteer at a local high school, he tried what he had learned and found it worked remarkably well. He was able to coach the full-court press, and get his players to buy into it, because he now believed deeply in it himself. He had had a transformational learning experience, and it enabled him to transform the culture of that basketball program (which had its first winning season in the school's history) and, to some extent, the lives of those players. But it never would have happened if he had not been open to new insights and constantly reflecting on his own past experiences and views.

As Jack Mezirow has defined it, transformative learning is "the process by which we transform our taken-for-granted frames of reference (meaning schemes, habits of mind, mindsets) to make them more inclusive, discriminating, open, emotionally capable of change, and reflective so that they may generate beliefs and opinions that will prove more true or justified to guide action." Its basic principles are 1) experience, the sum total of our life's learning; 2) critical reflection, our ongoing examination of our underlying beliefs and assumptions; and 3) development, which entails the perpetual growth of the individual or continuous learning fostered by experience and critical reflection.

Virtue-Based Leadership Models

A simple yet useful way of looking at leadership involves a triangle, as depicted in the diagram below. At the three points of the triangle are knowledge, attitudes, and skills, with competence in the middle. This implies that, in order to be a competent leader, one must possess the requisite attributes.

Knowledge

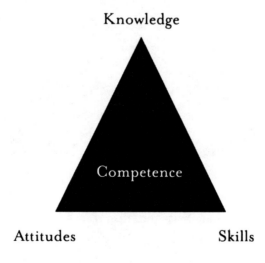

Competence

Attitudes   Skills

All of that is true—but perhaps it does not go far enough in explaining how virtuous leaders develop. As we noted above, virtue-based leadership is not merely a function of acquiring information or behaving in certain ways. It is not even necessarily about attitude, although having a good attitude is certainly important. After all, how can we *make* ourselves have a good attitude? Very often, we cannot. Our positive mental approach to situations and circumstances has to come from a deeper place.

A more comprehensive model of leadership emerges as we flesh out this pyramid, as shown below. In this case, the triangle has been divided into four smaller triangles, with the top one stacked on two others. In the middle is the leader, and the two triangles that form the base of the pyramid represent personal characteristics and context or situation. Resting on top of these is the triangle representing behaviors or skills.

This diagram implies that specific behaviors and skills are not merely coexistent with personal characteristics; they actually arise from those characteristics. It also acknowledges that no one operates in a vacuum and that context must always be taken into account. The two of us like the way this model depicts the developmental nature of leadership, suggesting that proper actions arise from positive character traits. This model is getting closer to what we are proposing in this book.

Yet we still find this model deficient, in that it places the leader at the center. For us, *virtue* must be at the center of any truly meaningful discussion of leadership. Thus, we can transform the triangle into a set of concentric circles. Personal characteristics, which include the Nine Virtues, occupy the center circle. In the next ring, we find behaviors or skills, implying that they revolve around, and arise from, the virtues at the very core. And in the outer circle is context, which is always an important consideration but never the most important.

In other words, who you are is more important than what you do. If you are the right kind of person and leader, your actions will reflect that, but all of us know from sad experience that leaders can say and do the right things without being fundamentally virtuous at the core. Both of those qualities—who you are and what you do—are more important than what is going on around you. As Rob used to tell his basketball players when they complained about poor officiating: "You can't control what happens to you; you can only control how you respond to it."

Even though we prefer the circle diagram to the triangle, it also leaves out something important: the role of lifelong learning. The model below incorporates everything we have been talking about in this chapter and shows how all of those elements relate to each other:

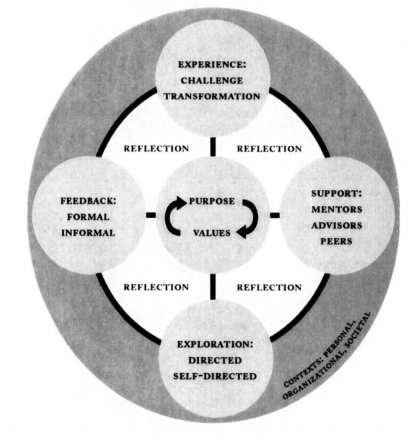

In this model, think of a person's character as being at the very center, divided into *values* (what one believes and regards as important) and *purpose* (how one puts those beliefs into action). Surrounding this core are the four pillars of leadership development: experience, support, exploration, and feedback—all connected by reflection.

Experience involves dealing with the challenges that you face every day and the inevitable transformations that result from those encounters. *Support* comes from the people you surround yourself with, including mentors, trusted advisors, even your peers. *Exploration* is a step beyond mere reflection and can be either directed by others—as when a supervisor assigns a research project—or taken upon yourself. *Feedback*, which can be formal (as in an annual performance review) or informal (as in conversation with a coworker or client), forms the last component of the cycle.

Please note that this is indeed a cycle. Developing leaders experience the world around them, reflect upon those experiences, and discuss them with a friend or mentor. This process leads to further exploration and, ultimately, feedback or some sense of whether or not they are on the right track. Then, the leaders take what they have learned into the next experience, and the cycle repeats itself. The model represents a continuous system of learning.

In this way, leaders become purposeful, lifelong learners, meeting the challenges that face them, transforming their experiences into knowledge and their knowledge into action. They are good leaders because they are constantly learning, and they are constantly learning because they are good leaders.

Learning to Lead, Leading to Learn

Up to now, this chapter has been about the way that leaders learn. In closing, we would like to discuss the way that good leaders help those around them learn to become better leaders. Virtuous leaders do not only learn to lead; they assist others along the same path by setting a good example, creating a learning-centered environment, and encouraging others both to learn and to lead.

Example. Both research and experience tell us that one of the most effective ways to teach is by example. Think of all the non-physical characteristics you got from your parents. Were they actually inherited, or were they learned? The answer is that they were nearly all learned, in many cases without your even being aware of it. You may have inherited their brown eyes or slender frame or even their intelligence, but you adopted their mannerisms, their ways of speaking, and their attitudes because you were around them all the time. You watched them, you listened to them, and ultimately you began to act like them.

The same holds true for adults in a professional setting. To some extent, people naturally adopt the behaviors and vocabulary of those they admire. And even if they are just mimicking at first, over time those adopted behaviors become part of their essential character.

This process has profound implications for leaders. It means they have an obligation to their followers to model the right kinds of behavior. And we do not just mean being moral or ethical, although of course they always should strive for that. We are talking specifically about behaviors that reflect and reinforce the nine leadership virtues, which we will address in detail in later chapters.

In keeping with the topic of this chapter, though, leaders also must model the behaviors of the lifelong learner: the constant search for knowledge and understanding, openness to new ideas and ways of looking at the world, ongoing study and reflection, desire for constructive feedback. Remember that, for the leader, lifelong learning is indispensable. If those you lead see that you constantly are learning and growing, they will come to regard that as a natural feature of leadership.

Environment. Merely setting a good example is not enough. As a leader intent on promoting lifelong learning, you must also create a work environment in which people are free to learn and grow.

Creating this environment means, first of all, that you must work to provide as many learning experiences as possible for the people in your organization, whether those experiences occur in a formal setting or not. Sometimes a training class or seminar is the best way to help people learn, but sometimes mentoring them one-on-one—or allowing them to mentor each other—works better. Sometimes the very best way to enable learning is to place people in situations (or allow them to get themselves into situations) in which they are bound to learn by experience.

And yes, that means they probably will fail from time to time. That's why micro-managers are so destructive to an organization. They insist that everything be done just so, exactly as they would do it, and rarely give others an opportunity to figure things out for themselves. As a result, no learning takes place. The leader who understands the importance of lifelong learning, of the growth and development of human beings, also has the ability to tolerate mistakes, because he or she recognizes that mistakes are an indispensable part of learning.

In a way, we are back to the topic of leading by example. Everyone screws up from time to time. One of the differences the two of us have noticed between effective and ineffective leaders is that the former are more likely to acknowledge when they have made a mistake, take ownership of it and responsibility for it, and then do whatever is necessary to rectify that mistake. What a powerful example this sets for other members of the organization. It is not only a lesson in humility but also a message that, as long as staff members are constantly learning and growing and moving forward, making mistakes occasionally is okay.

An organization in which everyone is terrified of making a mistake, for fear of how the leader will react, is an organization that is not moving forward. Nor are those people capitalizing on their leadership and learning potential.

Encouragement. Finally, in addition to setting a good example of lifelong learning and providing a nurturing environment in which people can learn and grow, the virtuous leader should engage in periodic, overt encouragement.

The pep talk has a long and glorious history in the world of sports and in the military. Banquet-circuit speakers often regale us with famous quotes from Bear Bryant or John Wooden or George Patton, inspiring us to be our best. And generally we are inspired, in part because the words themselves carry power and in part because of what we know about those individuals as authentically great leaders.

All organizational leaders find themselves at times needing to give some version of the pep talk. It may not always be an actual speech to the entire group (although sometimes it is). Sometimes it comes in the form of an e-mail, a pat on the back, or an encouraging word to an individual.

Not long ago, the institution where Rob now teaches was facing a difficult time financially. The president left, and an interim president was appointed to help the college navigate the crisis. One of the first things the new leader did was send an e-mail to all of the faculty and staff, essentially saying, "I'm not going to sugarcoat it: things are pretty tough. But I believe we have the team in place to fix the problems, and I believe that if we all pitch in and do our part, we'll come out the other side stronger than we were before." That, Rob recalls, was a turning point for many employees. They went from being fearful that the college would go under to resolving to make sure it survived. That is an example of leadership of the highest caliber.

Lifelong Learning and the Nine Virtues

The next chapter will provide an overview of the Nine Virtues of leadership. Later, we will delve into each of the nine in a chapter of its own. But before we start talking about the virtues, we want to close this chapter by pointing out the connection between them and lifelong learning.

Think back for a moment to Chapter 1. Remember that famous and oft-quoted statement by Aristotle? "We are what we repeatedly do. Virtue, then, is not an act, but a habit." In light of everything we have set forth in this chapter, we would like to modify that statement slightly in a way we think Aristotle would not mind: "We are what we repeatedly do—and we do what we have learned."

For virtue to become a habit, it must be learned by all of the means we have described: experience, mentoring, reading, reflection, exploration, feedback. It is true that for virtue to be virtue it must be practiced since it is about doing as well as being—but before it can be practiced, it must be discovered, understood, and internalized.

The process of becoming an active, lifelong learner is absolutely indispensable for anyone who wishes to develop the Nine Virtues described in this book. Because that is how long it takes—a lifetime. Do not be discouraged, though. Simply starting down that path will have an immediate impact on your life and on the lives of others.

Let's begin.

4. The Nine Virtues: An Overview

SO FAR, WE HAVE BEEN TALKING ABOUT THE CONCEPT OF VIRTUE, SIN-gular. However, our title refers to nine individual virtues. In this chapter, we will identify those Nine Virtues and provide a brief overview of each. Subsequent chapters will examine each of the virtues in detail, including concrete examples and specific behaviors related to it.

Our message is that these nine individual virtues combine to produce the quality known as virtue. Virtue is a condition or state of one's character; thus, we often think of virtues as characteristics. Of course, these Nine Virtues are not the only possible characteristics that could be regarded as defining virtuous leadership. As we worked on identifying the virtues to include in this book, we considered a number of attributes, all of which are good and worthwhile and all of which should be characteristics of good leaders. In the end, we settled on these nine, partly because we believe they are the most important ones for leaders to practice and partly because we believe that most other good qualities are contained within these nine. In short, we are convinced that if leaders embrace and practice these Nine Virtues, they will become the kind of people and the kind of leaders they should be.

It also is true—and worth emphasizing—that, in order to be truly virtuous, leaders must ultimately incorporate all of these virtues and not just the ones they like best or consider easiest to practice. Members of a society do not say that a thief is a good person just because he or she loves animals. By the same token, we cannot call someone virtuous who possesses personal courage but lacks humility or charity. For the virtuous leader, the goal is to acquire and practice *all* of these virtues, difficult as that may be. Just remember that it is a lifelong quest, an ongoing pursuit, and that success lies more in earnestly seeking than in checking items off a list.

Without further preamble, then, here is an overview of the Nine Virtues that characterize effective leaders.

Humility

In his *Autobiography*, Benjamin Franklin included humility last on the list of virtues he wished to acquire over his lifetime, which we take to mean that he saw it as the ultimate virtue, the highest virtue of all. (Either that or he hoped he would never get to it; your interpretation may depend on which stories about Franklin you happen to believe.) With apologies to Franklin, we are going to address humility first because we believe it is the most basic of all virtues. As Stephen Covey put it, "Humility is the mother of all virtues."

Philosophy and religion would seem to agree, as many of the world's great thinkers and spiritual leaders—from Socrates to Buddha to Jesus—have been noted both for their especial humility and for their teachings that humility is the paramount virtue. Socrates, for instance, said that "true wisdom comes to each of us when we realize how little we understand about life, ourselves, and the world around us." And Jesus famously taught his disciples that, in order to enter the Kingdom of Heaven, they had to humble themselves and become like little children.

Within the context of leadership, true humility means, first of all, being willing to listen to others. Many leaders seem to suffer from the misconception that their position of authority gives them the right to pontificate and bloviate, to dominate every conversation, even if they manifestly do not know what they are talking about. Think of the pointy-haired boss in the Dilbert comic strips, through whose character cartoonist Scott Adams lampoons the leader-as-bombastic-know-it-all. The best leaders understand, in Socratic fashion, that they do not know it all, and they are willing—eager, even—to provide a forum for and listen to those who can add to their knowledge.

Good leaders also are humble enough to be teachable, to learn from others and from their own experiences, and to take those lessons to heart. Some leaders in the academic world behave as if they think they are the smartest people in the room. Of course, that is very rarely the case, especially on a college campus or in another organization where knowledge and intelligence are primary forms of currency. Not only does this attitude indicate a lack of humility (dare we call it arrogance?) that other members of the organization find off-putting, to say the least; but it prevents the leader from learning and growing, as effective leaders must.

Likewise, effective leaders recognize both their own weaknesses and the strengths of others. What good is leading an organization brimming with intellectual capital if you do not avail yourself of it? Yet an amazing number of leaders are too proud to admit they do not know something or to ask for meaningful input. They either honestly think they have all the answers, or they are full of bluster, or both. But the truth is that, especially in large and complex organizations, it is impossible for one person to have all the answers. Admitting as much is not accepting defeat or confessing to ignorance; it is merely acknowledging the reality of one's own limitations, along with the expertise that others bring to the table. Otherwise, the organization falters, the initiative fails, all because of one leader's lack of humility.

As an aside, merely *pretending* to be open-minded and teachable usually backfires. Karl tells of an academic leader at an institution where he once consulted who made a major production of what he called "listening" to faculty and staff, holding open meetings to which all were invited, ostensibly to speak their minds. But what generally happened at those meetings, as Karl and many others observed, was that the leader did the majority of the talking. Very little listening took place. The leader was even known to become visibly angry during meetings and publicly embarrass people who expressed a point of view contrary to his. As a result, that leader earned a reputation on campus not for being inclusive or for seeking to gain consensus, but for being arrogant and narcissistic.

Remember what we said in the first chapter: the purpose of this book is not to offer a formula for becoming a virtuous leader—as in "Number 1: act like you're listening to people"—but rather to help readers internalize and practice these fundamental virtues of leadership.

Finally, we believe that the ultimate expression of humility is service. Much has been written in recent years on the topic of servant leaders, and while we will not rehash those views here, we also do not want to discount them. Our belief is that the desire to serve others, and the will to follow through on that desire, both stem from an attitude of true humility.

The Buddha taught that "a life of service and compassion are the things which renew humanity." They are also the things that inspire an organization, as happens when those in positions of authority—who have the power to insist that others cater to their wants and needs—instead selflessly put the wants and needs of other, lower-ranking organization members first. This service to others is seen in the lieutenant on combat patrol who takes the first watch so his exhausted men can sleep; the academic vice president who insists that faculty members' computers be upgraded before hers; the CEO who takes a pay cut in order to help fund a day-care center for employees. Such expressions of true humility create better leaders, better organizations, and a better society.

Honesty

There are a lot of terms we could have used to describe what we mean by this virtue: truthfulness, transparency, integrity, honor, trustworthiness. Any and all of those would have sufficed. But we decided that the simple, old-fashioned term "honesty" covers all of those characteristics and more.

Being honest is, first, a matter of telling the truth, even when it is painful or has negative consequences for you personally. This includes being truthful in the things you say and even in the impressions you give, as well as not leaving things out (sometimes referred to as "lies of omission"). Followers have a right to expect their leaders to tell them the truth and not to leave out important details that could impact their own situation or decision-making processes.

At the same time, as Franklin notes in his discussion of virtue, leaders should not use the truth to harm people. An example would be telling people things they do not really need to know or hear just to make them feel bad or to make the bearer of the news feel superior. There are times, to be sure, when people need to hear the truth regardless of the consequences, but as a leader you must be certain that your motives are pure: that you are being brutally honest in order to help that person and not as a means of lashing out. Knowing the difference sometimes requires a great deal of wisdom, another of the Nine Virtues, which shows how interconnected they can be.

Another term we hear a lot is "transparency," frequently used in the context of politics. In fact, one thing we all have learned (to our sorrow, perhaps) is that, often when politicians go out of their way to promise to be transparent, they almost certainly will not be. The failings of elected officials aside, transparency is vitally important for leaders, meaning that the people they lead know and understand what they are doing, why they are doing it, and what impact the action will have on them. In this sense, transparency is a form of truthfulness, because it requires leaders not to hide information or conveniently leave it out of the discussion.

Perhaps the leading candidate for the name of this virtue, besides "honesty," was "integrity," which is in fact often used synonymously with honesty. But we decided that integrity is a subheading under honesty, because it involves being honest not only with others but with yourself. We like the way engineers and builders use the term, as in "structural integrity," meaning that a structure will continue to be what it was designed to be. However much stress is placed upon it, a bridge will remain a bridge, providing egress across a span. Integrity, then, is about being true to oneself as a prerequisite for being truthful with others.

Honor, for many, is an antiquated concept, but we associate it with honesty because it involves doing the right thing—including telling the truth—for the right reason. Of course, as you will see, honor also is closely associated with other virtues, such as courage, perseverance, and justice. Once again, you cannot truly have one without the others.

Finally, honesty includes trustworthiness, which itself has two components. First, being trustworthy means simply that people can trust you: that you keep your word, that you follow through, that you do what you say you are going to do, that you tell people the truth, that you do not betray confidences. In recent years, an entire branch of leadership studies has developed around the concept of trust. (Could that be because people these days have such a difficult time trusting their leaders?) While we believe this focus may be a case of emphasizing one virtue over the others as a type of silver bullet—a kind of personality ethic or formula-based approach—we do recognize how important it is for leaders to have people trust them.

The other side of the trustworthiness coin is that the best leaders tend to have a lot of trust in the people they lead. This trust is neither blind to human weakness nor ignorant of reality. But good leaders understand that most people, and especially most professionals, do their best work when given trust and autonomy in the way they perform their duties. The two of us are big believers in the old saying, "Hire the best people, then get out of their way and let them do their jobs." The opposite of this approach is micromanaging, and in our experience, micromanagers not only do not trust people, but they tend not to be trusted and therefore do not make effective leaders in the long run.

Courage

If, as Covey says, humility is the mother of all virtues, then courage is their father: "We need great courage to live our lives by correct principles and to have integrity in the moment of choice," he wrote. Most of us understand quite well, from long experience, that doing the right thing often requires a great deal of personal courage because the consequences of doing the right thing are not always immediately positive. When we were children, we embraced a simplistic view of the world that said if we do good, people will like us. As adults, we may have learned the hard truth that some people will hate us and wish to do us harm specifically because we do good.

This ill intention tends to be true even if concepts of right and wrong or good and bad are stripped of their moral component—that is, if we merely are talking about decisions made in a professional context, decisions that may have little to do with ethics but everything to do with organizational growth and success, such as whom to hire or which software platform to utilize.

Too many leaders seem petrified by indecision, so afraid of making the wrong choice that they do not make any choice at all—which, in the long run, may be even worse than making the wrong one. Clearly, when your head is on the chopping block, you need a great deal of courage to step up and make the call, partly because you know that to some extent you are "damned if you do and damned if you don't." Making the wrong decision can certainly get you fired, but even making the right one, and especially making the right one consistently, can unintentionally make enemies of colleagues who resent your success. Making decisions is the responsibility of leadership, and that is why courage is such a key virtue in good leaders.

You also need courage to make decisions that are different from the ones everyone else is making. The easiest thing for any leader to do is check which way the wind is blowing and simply go along with the crowd, making essentially the same decisions as other leaders in the organization or industry. But no great leader ever thought that way. From Abraham Lincoln to Martin Luther King, from Susan B. Anthony to Mother Teresa, great leaders have always had the courage to take chances, to buck trends, to do the unexpected. Make no mistake: being that kind of leader does require great courage, because the more you defy conventional wisdom, the greater your chances of making mistakes—or, at least, the greater the chances that you will be *perceived* as making mistakes. And yet, where would the world be without leaders who, because they were not handcuffed by fear of failure, succeeded beyond everyone else's wildest dreams?

At the same time, for great leaders, courage always is tempered by humility. Often the area where we require the most courage is in our daily interactions with those closest to us, and that is no less true in a professional setting than in our personal lives. Sometimes you need a great deal of courage to confront people within the organization whom you believe are not moving the enterprise forward—especially if they are people you like or even your superiors. And you must have even more courage to go into such a confrontation with the humility of spirit that will allow you to be successful, seeking to listen, understand, and persuade, rather than simply trying to bend people to your will.

Ultimately, the scariest thing of all can be admitting you are wrong. Few things a leader does require more courage, yet few things have as much potential for having a positive impact on the organization.

Ultimately, leadership itself requires the greatest courage, especially in difficult times. Everybody, it seems, wants to be in charge; most people would love the opportunity to tell others what to do, at least for a day or two. But when the bullets are flying, who is prepared to step to the forefront, rally the troops, and lead the charge? Answer: the courageous leader.

Perseverance

We all understand intuitively, and perhaps based on personal experience, that success in any endeavor sometimes is simply a matter of plugging away at it, day after day, year after year. There are stories of the "10-year overnight success," like the author whose book gets picked up by a major publisher and hits the bestseller list—after it languished in a drawer for a decade after being rejected by 30 other publishers. While such perseverance by itself may not guarantee success, without some degree of perseverance success in most endeavors is highly unlikely. The major league baseball player who hits a grand slam his very first time at bat is noteworthy precisely because he is such a rarity.

However, not every person possesses that kind of iron-willed determination, which is why it is one of the virtues we admire and value so much in leaders. Great leaders are known not only for refusing to give in, but for inspiring others to stay the course despite whatever hardships and obstacles they encounter. One of the most enduring sound bites from World War II is Winston Churchill's famous rallying cry, in the speech he delivered at Harrow School on October 9, 1941, following months of German bombing attacks on London: "Never give in. Never give in. Never, never, never, never—in nothing, great or small, large or petty—never give in, except to convictions of honor or good sense."

Perseverance, then, involves a certain amount of what we may call stubbornness—a trait usually regarded as negative. But stubbornness can be a good thing, in the service of virtue. Virtuous leaders stubbornly insist on doing what they believe is right, even when everyone else is taking a different path, even when they are ridiculed and criticized for not going along with the crowd or following conventional wisdom. Virtuous leaders stubbornly refuse to give in to doubt, to naysayers, to seemingly insurmountable obstacles, and in doing so inspire others to adopt the same single-mindedness of purpose.

Obviously, stubbornness can be a bad thing as well. History is rife with examples of leaders who marched their followers straight into catastrophe because they refused to be dissuaded from some disastrous course of action. That is where humility comes into play: a perfect example of how the virtues work together in harmony. A leader who has a strong will but lacks humility will usually end up failing, often in spectacular fashion, while taking the rest of the organization down as well. But the humble leader—always listening, forever learning, constantly seeking knowledge and truth—is more likely to choose a wise course, and a stubborn insistence on maintaining such a course is undoubtedly a good thing.

Perseverance, however, is about more than just stubbornness or lock-jawed refusal to quit. In the virtuous leader, it also entails that rarest of traits in professional life (and perhaps personal life as well): a willingness to see a task through to the end. We have become so accustomed, in all areas of our lives, to people who fail to follow through—from remodelers who never show up to finish a project to servers who do not stop by to refill our glasses to subordinates who cannot be counted on to meet a deadline—that we hardly register more than mild annoyance at such unprofessionalism.

At the same time, people who do follow through, who actually finish what they start, tend to stand out. And if that is a trait that we value in the people who work for us, how much more important is it in leaders? A subordinate who misses a deadline can cripple a project, but a leader who consistently fails to follow through can destroy an entire organization One of the highest compliments that can be paid to leaders is that "they do what they say they're going to do."

Perseverance is a matter of patience, of taking the long view. The reason great leaders are unlikely to be deterred from what they regard as the right path is that they have a vision; they see the destination in their mind's eye. They recognize the stakes involved and understand that if they but stay the course, the positive outcome they have foreseen ultimately will come to pass. Perhaps the greatest example of this in history is Abraham Lincoln, who steadfastly refused to acknowledge secession, refused to give in to those on both sides who thought he should allow the South to go its own way and be done with fighting. He envisioned a reunified nation, stronger than ever, and believed that, with enough time and determination, it could be accomplished. Millions of Americans have his courage and perseverance to thank for the freedoms they enjoy.

Hope

Perhaps another way of explaining Lincoln's stolid determination, through four years of bitter and bloody civil war, is to say that he had hope—hope in the future of this country, hope in the nation he believed could emerge from the smoke of battle, hope in its people. No doubt the same could be said of Churchill and every other great leader who has stayed a difficult course in the face of enormous obstacles and great personal risk.

The word "hope," in this case, does not refer to pipe dreams or starry-eyed longings. Rather, it is an unshakeable belief in what can happen, what inevitably *will* happen, if you set out and continue on the right path. It is related to perseverance, but if perseverance is the difficult upward climb, hope is the rope that tethers you to reality and provides a means of moving forward. Perseverance places you firmly on the path and prevents you from going back or turning aside; but hope is why you continue putting one foot in front of the other.

One attribute of great leaders that often is addressed in the modern-day leadership literature is vision. Indeed, one of the best things you can say about leaders is that they are visionary. When a highly regarded CEO or university president retires, that term often is applied as a tribute.

Vision was, in fact, one of the attributes we discussed in writing this book. But when we asked ourselves, "what makes a person a visionary?" we ultimately decided that what people call "vision" is but the outward manifestation of a deeper virtue: hope. Visionaries are people who see what an organization has the capability to become because they know what its people are capable of and have great faith that, with the right decisions, they can and will realize their potential.

Hope, then, involves faith—faith in oneself, faith in other people, and faith that doing the right things will lead to a positive outcome. It does not mean you merely *think* that if you do certain things (work hard, treat people well, stay the course), you will get certain results (success, satisfaction, progress); it means you *know* you will. You expect those results, and that is what motivates you to keep moving forward.

Hope also involves patience. No doubt you have heard the old saying "Patience is a virtue." We agree, but would argue that patience ultimately stems from hope—from a firm belief in what things can be, what they *will* be, in time. Impatient people are constantly (and usually unsuccessfully) trying to mold the world to conform to their expectations. Leaders who practice the virtue of hope not only are patient but long-suffering, willing to endure any hardship, overcome any obstacle, because in a sense they already know the outcome.

Obviously, this is an incredibly optimistic way of looking at the world. But in our view, very few things can transform an organization like optimism at the top. Ronald Reagan was an incorrigible optimist when it came to what he saw as the potential of the United States; that sunny outlook led to two landslide elections as most voters embraced his ebullient vision.

Rob recently ran into a friend who teaches at a local high school that had gone through a change in leadership. The former principal had a rather dour personality—not a pessimist, exactly, but certainly a battle-weary pragmatist. The new principal, in contrast, came in visibly excited about what he saw as the school's great potential, and his optimism quickly became infectious. As a result, Rob's friend told him, the climate at the school had been completely transformed. For the first time in years, he said, he actually looked forward to going to work each day.

Ultimately, that is the power of hope: to inspire others to see their world, their job, their role, not as it is, but as it could be ...as it *will* be. The virtuous leader is one who understands what others are capable of and has the ability to help them see themselves through his or her eyes.

Charity

The word "charity," in the modern vernacular, usually refers to a worthy cause or the act of contributing to that cause. Sometimes it can even take on negative connotations, as in "charity case" or "I don't want your charity." However, the Latin word that we usually translate as "charity" is *caritas*, which literally means love. Obviously the idea of giving to worthy causes in order to help our fellow human beings is contained in the word, but that is not all it means.

The Bible and many other religious texts suggest that charity is the paramount virtue. Jesus taught that the greatest commandment of all is to "love thy neighbor as thyself." This famous admonition has two components, one of which is often overlooked: if we are to love others as we love ourselves, this implies that we must first of all love ourselves.

Self-love, in this sense, means neither arrogance nor narcissism but rather a healthy appreciation of one's own human potential. It is the opposite of self-loathing. Another piece of ancient wisdom with which most of us are familiar is that "misery loves company." A corollary could well be that people who hate themselves tend to hate others too. Perhaps many of us have witnessed this firsthand: the leader who, attempting to compensate for his or her own perceived inadequacies, nitpicks and exaggerates the failures of others—especially when those others are more capable and successful, and their failures correspondingly minor in comparison.

Leaders who have a healthy self-regard, on the other hand, who are comfortable in their own skin, tend to be more forgiving of others' weaknesses and more appreciative of their strengths. Confident in their own abilities, they have no need to make themselves look better by dragging others down. Perhaps this self-confidence is why so many great religious leaders have taught that loving others begins with loving yourself.

Loving others also entails accepting them as they are. That does not mean you should not help people improve themselves by consolidating their strengths and overcoming their weaknesses. It just means that, if you love someone, you will not expect them to be something they fundamentally are not. Lasting marriages offer the perfect example of this kind of love. Of course, neither partner ever lives up to a spouse's ideal. But in a marriage built on true love, each comes to accept that the other will never be perfect and learns to appreciate that person for what he or she brings to the relationship. Productive relationships between colleagues, or between supervisors and employees, are no different.

Love and appreciation of others means that forgiveness is an indispensable component of charity. When we truly love people, we forgive their inadequacies, just as we expect them to forgive ours—often without a word being said on either side. Finger-pointing, remonstration, and blame-shifting are acts not of selfless love but of ultimate selfishness. An effective leader eschews such unproductive activities as a matter of course.

Being patient with and forgiving of others constitutes what we may call generosity of spirit. But charity connotes another kind of generosity, as well—the kind that involves putting your money where your mouth is. In an organizational context, that may mean forgoing a raise or a bonus when other, lower-ranking members of the organization are not getting raises due to budget cuts or a difficult economy. It may mean making a personal donation to a worthy cause, such as a daycare center for employees, not for show but out of a genuine desire to help. Leaders cannot buy loyalty—not in the long run, at least—but a little well-placed financial generosity certainly can serve as an outward indication of true love for others, which will ultimately be repaid many times over.

Of course, we all know that being generous with money often is easier than being generous with one's attention. As much as possible, great leaders are generous with their time. Sometimes what members of an organization need and want most is "face time" with the leader: to see and be seen, and above all to be heard. Carving out time for those kinds of personal interactions can be a challenge, but we intuitively understand that the leader who takes such a hands-on approach—the general who walks up and down the battle line, clapping individual soldiers on the shoulder, rather than the one who stays at headquarters—is more likely to garner the respect and loyalty of his or her followers. People feel loved when they feel valued, and they feel most valued when they know that you are listening to them. This, in a sense, is what servant leadership is all about: putting yourself out there for the people you expect to follow you, doing things not only for them but with them, so that you become part of a shared enterprise.

Another element of charity is simple kindness—basically, treating people well. When was the last time you had a supervisor you would describe as kind-hearted? How did you feel about that person? Too often in our society, we mistake kindness for weakness. But the two of us are willing to bet that, if you think back on a leader who consistently treated you kindly, you will realize that you would do just about anything for that person. Such kindness is hardly weakness; rather, it is an incredible form of power: the power to command people's loyalty by a simple kind word or gesture.

Finally, one of the greatest attributes of the best leaders is that they love the organization, love the mission, and love the work. The greatest teachers have two things in common: they love their students, and they love their subject matter. Teachers who clearly despise students—and, sadly, there are too many of those—or who do not take their field seriously will never be successful. So it is with leaders. Love is infectious, and once people know that you love what you are doing, and love them too, they will become more enthusiastic about their jobs and about the organization. Love begets love. It is as simple as that.

Balance

Balance is, first and foremost, the opposite of fanaticism or obsession. Consider the stories about the NFL head coach who puts in 20-hour days, sleeping on a cot in the film room, or the fiercely driven CEO and her 100-hour work weeks. Often such leaders are held up to us as models of success. Yet what the stories do not say, but what most of us know from experience, is that those people usually end up burned out, fired, miserable, or divorced—or all of the above. We may admire their financial success, but we rarely admire them as human beings, which is another way of saying that we do not consider that kind of obsessive behavior to be a virtue.

True virtue lies in the opposite of such behavior: what we call balance. That means giving each area of your life—personal and professional, physical and spiritual—the amount of attention it deserves at exactly the right time. Of course, that is difficult to do; even if we strive for balance, we frequently find ourselves out of kilter, struggling to bring the various elements of our lives back into harmony. Just remember that balance, like all the other virtues, is a lifelong pursuit. Simply recognizing the need for balance, and then striving to achieve it, constitutes more than half the battle.

The key to finding balance lies in setting priorities. Those for whom family relationships are truly the most important thing in the world are unlikely to spend so much time at work that they damage those relationships. At the same time, truly balanced people understand that, on occasion, work—or exercise, or study—must take precedence if they are to achieve their goals, not only for themselves but for their families.

Being organized helps, because it allows you to schedule your various activities, allotting time as needed based on importance and urgency. Finishing that report may be more important, in a given week, than attending your daughter's soccer game; then again, it may not. The level of importance depends on the situation. That is why you have to set priorities and why the setting of priorities is such an ongoing struggle. In some cases, if you are extremely organized, you may be able to finish the report *and* go to the game.

At the same time, in addition to being organized, you should be flexible. A friend of ours, who is extremely organized by nature, told us about his recent family vacation to Disney World. He had everything planned out, practically to the minute. He had even researched the best times of the day to get in line for each ride, and he dragged his wife and three kids back and forth across the park accordingly. At one point, the kids begged to go back to the hotel and swim, but he looked at his written schedule and did not see any time for swimming allotted. "We were so busy following the schedule," he lamented, "that we forgot to have fun."

That is a perfect illustration of the truism that, while organization can enhance balance, it also can impede it if organization for its own sake becomes an obsession. To find balance, you must set priorities; having (and mostly sticking to) a schedule certainly can help. But you also must have the flexibility to decide, on the spur of the moment, that something else is more important and turn your attention to that instead of what is on the schedule.

When we think of balance in our professional lives, we usually think immediately of what is often called "work-life balance": that is, balancing our work lives with our personal and home lives. Most of us would agree that such a balance is essential to happiness and feelings of well-being, even though most of us struggle, in varying degrees, to balance the demands of our professions—not to mention our need to earn a living—with the demands of home and family.

Another type of balance that may be just as important, however, is what we call "work-work balance." All of us, in our professional lives, find that there are tasks we enjoy and tasks that we do not enjoy nearly as much. For most of us, the early stage of a career entails more of the latter and less of the former. But as we grow professionally and move up the ladder within an organization, one of the keys to happiness and fulfillment is to organize our worklives to include more of what we enjoy and less of what we do not enjoy. Sometimes this approach means pursuing other interests outside of regular working hours, in what sometimes is known as "leisure work"—the accountant who gets up early to work on her novel or the corporate CEO who spends evenings in his woodworking shop.

For leaders, embracing balance means not only finding it personally but also allowing and encouraging it in others. Perhaps no leaders are despised more than the hard-driving fanatics for whom the office is their whole life—and who therefore expect everyone else to feel the same way. Virtuous leaders understand that people need time away from work to reflect, relax, and recharge. They need time with their families. They need time for themselves. They need opportunities to improve themselves personally and professionally. Virtuous leaders not only model this kind of balance and allow for it in others; they also do everything in their power to create a work environment that actively fosters it.

Wisdom

Wisdom often is thought of as the appropriate application of knowledge. While we believe that is not a bad definition, it certainly is more than that. Wisdom involves knowledge, but it also relates to understanding; it entails application, but it also has a moral component. Ultimately, wisdom amounts to making the right choices consistently for the right reasons, in such a way that others perceive, and are inspired by, the rightness of those choices.

Obviously, the basis of wisdom is knowledge—and the most important kind of knowledge, as Socrates, Franklin, and other great thinkers have pointed out, is knowing that we do not know. This self-awareness ties in with humility, as we discussed earlier in this chapter. But let us go back a step further, to Chapter 3, where we talked about the leader as lifelong learner. Simply having a great deal of knowledge does not in itself make a person wise, as we all understand intuitively. Few clichés are more common in professional life than the "stupid smart" person. At the same time, in order to be wise, leaders must seek to acquire as much knowledge as possible—by reading, by studying, by listening—and continue seeking throughout their lives.

But beyond collecting bits of information, one who would be wise must seek to understand. Understanding involves grasping how a particular piece of knowledge may be relevant in a certain situation: how it could apply, for instance, to a specific dilemma. That sort of understanding is gained over time through reflection and often through trial and error.

With understanding comes the proper application of knowledge in the decision-making process, and for leaders that is the crux of the matter. Another well-known cliché is the wise man as recluse, the hermitical guru dwelling alone in his cave atop the mountain. That individual may well have gained wisdom, but it is of no practical use to anyone except himself—and maybe the occasional intrepid mountain-climbing truth-seeker. Wisdom, as one of the Nine Virtues of exceptional leaders, is a virtue only when it is used to benefit all.

Wisdom, as it applies to leadership, has a moral component because it entails making good choices. Such choices must be informed, in that they are based on sufficient and relevant knowledge and on a sound understanding. But true wisdom involves more than just an ethical calculation of right and wrong in a given circumstance. The wise leader recognizes not only what is right but what is best, often from among many possible choices that all seem, on the surface, equally good.

Recognizing what is best is not easy, and it is why no one will ever appear wise all the time. But the virtuous leader is one whom people trust to make good decisions consistently. That is because, as with all the other virtues, wisdom can be acquired over time through the constant pursuit of knowledge and understanding, along with frequent reflection, self-evaluation, and introspection. The virtuous leader has expended the time and effort necessary to acquire it. And again, few things boost an organization or imbue followers with confidence more than a belief that the leader will consistently make the best decisions for all concerned.

Justice

Justice is in many ways the culmination of the Nine Virtues, arising from the confluence of the others and bringing all of them into harmony. To be just, leaders must have humility, to not demand that "it's my way or the highway"; courage, to act justly even in the face of pressure to do otherwise; perseverance, to always seek the path of justice; hope, that what is right ultimately will prevail; love for others and a desire to act in their best interests; balance, in order to always see different sides of an issue; and, of course, wisdom, to be able to make good choices based on an understanding of what is right.

We often think of justice in terms of fairness, which means essentially that people get what they deserve. Of course, the hard part is figuring out exactly what the people around us—the people who work for us, the people who count on us—deserve. We need wisdom. Everyone loves to quote the Bible passage that reads "Thou shalt not judge," and no doubt they usually have a point. Often we are not in a position to judge and have no right to do so.

But sometimes we forget that one of a leader's primary tasks is to make judgments—not only about issues but about people as well. As a practical matter, leaders frequently are called upon to hire, fire, and evaluate employees. They mediate disputes between subordinates, or between subordinates and supervisors, or between employees and clients. Leaders make judgment calls all the time, sometimes dozens of them in a single work day, and those who are most successful in the long run will be the ones who earn a reputation for being fair and reasonable.

Another element of justice that is closely related to fairness is objectivity. In order to judge justly, a leader must be able to separate personal feelings from the matter at hand and look at the issue dispassionately. Doing so does not come naturally to most people; it requires a fair amount of wisdom, especially in the sense of self-knowledge: you must recognize and understand your emotions before you can divorce them from the decision-making process. That kind of objectivity also requires humility, because you are essentially acknowledging that there are more important factors involved than how you personally happen to feel. Some people, as we all know from experience, rarely recognize any force more potent than their own emotional responses; as a result, when in positions of leadership, they are unable to judge justly.

Justice is the virtue of being able to make the right decision consistently at the right time for the right reason, and in this regard it is also closely related to wisdom. If wisdom is knowing what to do, then justice is having the courage to do it. Of course, like all the other virtues, justice can be elusive; often we believe we have made the right choice, only to find out later that we made exactly the *wrong* one and further muddied the waters. As you embark on this journey of self-discovery, as you earnestly seek to act with humility, to face the world with courage, to persevere in the face of overwhelming obstacles, to move forward with hope, to love others as you love yourself, to find balance in your life, and above all, to pursue wisdom, then you will find that acting justly has become part of your nature—an integral part of what makes you a virtuous leader.

Developing the Nine Virtues

At the end of each chapter, we offer a number of suggestions for developing each of the Nine Virtues. You can think of these as homework if you like. Our basic premise is that, while much of this discussion is theoretical or conceptual, there are in fact concrete actions you should take on a daily basis that will allow you to put these concepts into practice while at the same time internalizing the virtues they represent.

As we have stated before (and no doubt will remind you again), acting as if you are humble or courageous or wise is not the same as actually *being* those things; but if you continue to behave that way over time, what is the practical difference? If you consistently show courage, for example, in what way are you not courageous?

More important, perhaps, we believe that by *practicing* these virtues—literally, by putting them into practice—you will make them intrinsic to you, in time. Remember that becoming virtuous is a lifelong pursuit; there may never come a time when you can rest on your laurels and say, "Okay, I'm courageous (or wise or humble or whatever) now. What's next?" The trick is to be in the game, to be striving constantly to develop these virtues and make them an integral part of who you are. Then one day, without really knowing it, you will have become a virtuous leader.

With all of that in mind, then, let us examine each of the Nine Virtues in more detail, exploring their various aspects and learning what you must do to acquire them.

5. Humility

IN THE SPRING OF 1963, DR. MARTIN LUTHER KING JR. TRAVELED TO Birmingham, Alabama, to help organize the marches and sit-ins that eventually brought an end to that city's Jim Crow laws. He was arrested almost immediately, accused of being an "outside agitator." While imprisoned, King penned the now-famous "Letter from a Birmingham Jail," calling upon white Christian ministers to acknowledge the justice of his cause.

That letter has since come to be regarded not only as one of the seminal documents of the Civil Rights movement, but also as one of the greatest rhetorical feats of all time—especially when we judge such feats by their effectiveness. Many of the societal changes that King championed came to pass in relatively short order, and the moral impact of his arguments continue to be felt to this day. A poll conducted recently by CBS News found that, 50 years after the events in Birmingham, four out of five Americans believe that King made things better for both blacks and whites in this country.

But what was it that made his rhetoric so powerful—so effective?

For one thing, he immediately identified a persuadable audience, comprised of people who may have been inclined to listen: the white ministers whom he addressed directly in his salutation as "My Dear Fellow Clergymen." Note that he was not writing primarily to black Southerners; that would have been preaching to the choir. Nor was he writing to the majority of white Southerners, most of whom probably would have paid little attention or dismissed him as a radical and a troublemaker. He aimed his arguments directly at clergy. Why? Because he himself was a minister by training. He spoke their language, and he hoped that, given what they professed to believe, those white clergy would be predisposed to take him and his ideas seriously and begin to exert influence to bring about positive societal changes.

And then—and this is the key point—having identified his target audience, he approached them with humility. Not hat in hand, as if from a position of servitude or weakness; nor with condescension, looking down as from the moral high ground. But as an equal, one person of good will speaking confidently to other people of good will. Look at the way King closes his famous missive:

> If I have said anything in this letter that overstates the truth and indicates an unreasonable impatience, I beg you to forgive me. If I have said anything that understates the truth and indicates my having a patience that allows me to settle for anything less than brotherhood, I beg God to forgive me. I hope this letter finds you strong in the faith. I also hope that circumstances will soon make it possible for me to meet each of you, not as an integrationist or a civil-rights leader but as a fellow clergyman and a Christian brother. Let us all hope that the dark clouds of racial prejudice will soon pass away and the deep fog of misunderstanding will be lifted from our fear-drenched communities, and in some not too distant tomorrow the radiant stars of love and brotherhood will shine over our great nation with all their scintillating beauty.

Viewed as a rhetorical tour de force, "Letter from a Birmingham Jail" is striking in the way that it maintains this delicate balance between meekness and forcefulness. Although King is in fact, for all practical purposes, instructing those white clergy on their moral responsibilities, he never sounds as if he is lecturing them—and more important, he never sounds as if he thinks he is better than they are. That is a remarkable accomplishment, given the times and what he himself was going through at the moment, locked away in a Birmingham jail cell.

King's example teaches us something vitally important about humility: that, far from the popular conception of "meekness" as a synonym for "weakness," it actually is a form of strength. Or perhaps we should say, rather, that humility is a *source* of strength, a reservoir of great power. Leaders who embrace and seek to internalize the virtue of humility do not simply fade into the background, as some may imagine. They do not become weak and thus prey for the strong in some Darwinian struggle for survival. In the end, they *are* the fittest, the strongest, the most capable of leading. That is the power of humility for the virtuous leader. And that power is manifested in a number of very practical ways.

Listening

One characteristic of the truly humble leader is being willing to listen to others. Listening is no small thing. Most people in positions of authority are accustomed to command—to having others listen to them. In fact, as we all know from experience, many people seek leadership positions specifically so they can tell others what to do, or perhaps because they are tired of having others tell them what to do. This view of leadership is so common that it has become a major component of the popular understanding of leadership: a leader is someone who tells others what to do, and they do it.

Of course there are times when a leader has to issue orders and expect to be obeyed, especially in a life-or-death situation. But, for most of us, our professional lives do not contain any life-or-death situations. Leaders who envision themselves as field generals, barking orders, may be effective in battle or in some team sports, but they typically are not very effective in a professional setting. (Which is why, when we are talking about leadership, sports metaphors can go only so far.) Intelligent, accomplished professionals tend to resent that kind of authoritarian approach and ultimately end up rebelling against it—if not openly, then at least in passive-aggressive ways that nevertheless undermine the leader's authority and effectiveness.

Karl and Rob have certainly known leaders like that in the academic world, such as the one who reveled in constantly referring to himself as "the Dean." He was known to say, on occasion, by way of explaining some controversial decision, that he was doing such-and-such "because I'm the Dean"—a terse pronouncement intended to stifle any opposition. In truth, in a supposedly collegial environment, he should have been little more than first among equals. Constantly lording his title over those he was supposed to be leading did little to endear himself to them. In the long run, they did not respect him, and they ended up subverting his authority at every opportunity. He did not last long in that position. Even if those "underlings" have not risen yet to the leader's exalted status, they still have a great deal to offer, by virtue of their intellect, education, and experience. Any leader who does not take time to listen to such people is foolish and ultimately doomed to failure.

By listening, we are not talking about window dressing—or just pretending to listen so that you can call yourself "inclusive" or a "consensus builder" on your resumé. Here we must go back to one of the main concepts discussed in Chapter 1: leading by virtue is not a mere fad, nor is it the latest leadership strategy. It may take time—it *will* take time—for a leader to develop these virtues, but if those efforts are not genuine, then they are essentially meaningless. Our experience has been that almost every new leader comes into the job promising to listen, but too few take time to sit down with people, pay attention to what they are saying, and then adjust their own point of view based on the legitimate perspectives of others.

The reason most leaders do not listen empathically to others is because of pride. They have not thought it important to practice and develop the virtue of humility. They are convinced that they are smarter than everyone else, that their ideas are better than everyone else's—the fact they are the leaders proves it, right?—and they are afraid that listening to others, not to mention actually taking their advice, might be perceived as weakness.

In this regard, leaders who are humble enough to listen have a tremendous advantage. Consider the example of George Washington, who, as the iconic leader of the American Revolution, was persuaded to attend the First Constitutional Convention held in 1787. At that time, the new nation was languishing (many thought) under the Articles of Confederation, which left many states at odds with each other and provided for no strong centralized leadership. Washington, along with James Madison, Alexander Hamilton, and others, believed that a new constitution was needed, one that would invest more authority in the federal government. And yet, when he was elected Chair of the Convention, he set aside those personal beliefs in favor of hearing both sides. As one historian puts it, "Presiding impartially over the Convention, Washington took no active part in its debates, nor in the subsequent ratification debates in the several states. But it is a mark of the power of Washington's character, and of the depth of his countrymen's recognition of his moral stature, that despite this official silence he played a critical role throughout."

Like King, Washington understood that power does not always derive from being the loudest or the most insistent. Sometimes it is simply a matter of sitting and listening.

Being Teachable

Another key aspect of humility is being teachable. This quality of course is closely related to listening—and especially to *really* listening, as opposed to pretending to listen—but it goes beyond that. Humble leaders recognize that they do not know everything; that, on the contrary, they know very little and have much to learn. In this regard, they have grasped the Socratic dictum that the first step toward true wisdom is understanding just how little we know.

Physicist and philosopher Marcelo Gleiser uses the analogy of the sum total of our accumulated knowledge as constituting an "Island of Knowledge," surrounded by a vast ocean of what we do not know. It is an imperfect metaphor, but imagine the island growing and the ocean receding as we discover more about the world and ourselves. The growth takes an uncertain path: sometimes the coastline is a jagged boundary; at other times the coastline erodes and recedes as we jettison what we thought we knew. We may expect that, the more our knowledge grows, the closer we come to some sort of finality: a Theory of Everything.

However, for a variety of reasons, including the inherent limitations of our scientific instruments and the cosmic speed limit set by light, there will be no Theory of Everything—ever. As our island of knowledge grows, so do the shores of our ignorance: the boundary between the known and the unknown. As Socrates noted centuries before, the more we know, the more we are exposed to our ignorance, and the more we know to ask.

Being teachable manifests itself, in part, through the kind of lifelong hunger for knowledge we described in Chapter 2. Humble leaders are constantly seeking, constantly reading and studying, constantly reflecting on what they have learned and trying to make sense of it in a larger context, precisely because they are so fully conscious of the limits of their own Islands of Knowledge.

Too many leaders, by contrast, are not interested in that sort of lifelong learning because they believe they already know what they need to know. Indeed, some of them clearly are convinced that they know everything, at least within their supposed area of expertise. They are not interested in the words of the great thinkers or the findings of modern researchers or even the data the IT department has accumulated, especially if it contradicts their preconceived notions. They know what they know, and please do not confuse them with facts.

Humble leaders, by contrast, are willing to learn from others, including people who are below them on the organizational chart or the social scale. In fact, they tend to be so conscious of their own limitations, and so enamored with acquiring knowledge, that they are willing to learn from anyone. A truly humble leader is one who can sit down with a child and come away with some startling new insight.

Mostly, though, in a professional context, being teachable means being willing and able to learn from those around you, those who may know various aspects of your job better than you. The humility in that approach comes from recognizing that there *are* people who know more than you and that there is no shame in admitting it. That humility manifests itself in the behaviors of listening, internalizing, and then modifying your behavior—in other words, what we call *learning*.

Consider the example of an academic administrator Rob knows who was brought in from outside the institution to create stability for a fractious department. However, he did not know the department was fractious when he took the job. He knew only that internal candidates had been considered but he had gotten the job—on his own merit, he assumed. He had no idea that he was walking, as he later told Rob, "into a hornets' nest."

Those first few months on the job were uncomfortable. A sizeable faction of the faculty did not want him or anyone they considered an outsider; they had supported an internal candidate who had not gotten the job, and they felt slighted and ill-used. For weeks, the new leader had a constant stream of those faculty members, as well as some who had backed other candidates and even a few who had remained neutral, come by his office to speak with him. What nearly all of them really wanted was to "give him the score," as they saw it, and to tell him how he ought to run things, in their opinion.

Fortunately, that new leader was humble enough simply to listen to all those people. He realized that he had not really known what he was getting into, and he understood the only way to rectify that was to listen to people who did know the situation on the ground—even if they had their own agendas and misconceptions. So he listened carefully and politely to everyone, even if they were rude, and after a few weeks he was able to start putting together a fairly accurate picture of the department's strengths and weaknesses, its problems and opportunities. Not only was the information he gained vital as he began to move, slowly, to make necessary changes, but the fact that he listened had a profound effect on the department, engendering a certain amount of trust and camaraderie where none had existed before. As he told Rob later, he was profoundly grateful that he had not simply ridden into town, proclaimed himself the new sheriff, and started making changes. That approach would have been disastrous.

In the end, leaders who think they know everything are kidding themselves and setting themselves up for failure. Successful leaders recognize just how little they know and actively seek to address that deficiency by listening and learning as much as they can. They are humble enough not to care where or from whom they learn, because they understand intuitively that, if knowledge is power, then ignorance is weakness. And no one is weaker or more ineffective in the long run than the proud fools who think they already know it all.

Let us return to Gleiser for a moment. When it comes to the mysteries of the universe, science has given us tremendous insight, but if Gleiser is right—and the two of us think he is—there are limitations on our scientific knowledge that will never be overcome. Likewise, effective leaders know *they* have limitations they will never overcome. But this message need not be a depressing one, nor should it contribute to any self-doubt. On the contrary, this level of humility requires a great deal of confidence. As you work to gain the virtues of a humble leader, you may eventually learn to see your imbalances, your fallibilities, as gifts. After all, they are what keep you striving to achieve what sometimes may seem impossible.

Empathy

Empathy has gotten a great deal of good press as one of the "emotional intelligences" that psychologist Daniel Goleman writes about in his widely read book of that name. Goleman defines empathy as "intuiting another's feelings ...from non-verbal clues" and suggests that people who are more adept at this are "better adjusted emotionally, more popular, more outgoing, and—perhaps not surprisingly—more sensitive." He also points out that "empathy builds on self-awareness; the more open we are to our own emotions, the more skilled we will be at reading feelings."

True empathy, as Goleman acknowledges, goes far deeper than simply reading feelings. The word comes from the Greek *empatheia*, which means literally "feeling into," and was originally used, as Goleman explains, "by theoreticians of aesthetics for the ability to perceive the subjective experiences of another person." Goleman also cites the work of an earlier American psychologist, E.B. Titchener, whose "theory was that empathy stemmed from a sort of physical imitation of the distress of another, which then evoked the same feelings in oneself." Empathy, Titchener said, is distinct from sympathy in that it involves not just understanding someone else's plight but actually, to some extent, sharing in it.

So what does empathy have to do with humility? Well, first of all, to be empathic, as Goleman notes, means that you have a high degree of self-awareness. You know who and what you are and what you are *not*, recognizing not only your strengths but your weaknesses. Seeing yourself clearly requires a great deal of objectivity, but it also requires a great deal of humility. Simply put, people who are not humble tend to see only their strengths and either do not recognize or else refuse to acknowledge their weaknesses. As a result, such people are virtually incapable of understanding others' weaknesses—that is, of feeling empathy.

Second, being empathetic means recognizing that you are not at the center of the universe but instead are surrounded by people just as unique as yourself, with needs and desires just as important as yours.

There is an episode of the popular television series *Downton Abbey*, about the British aristocracy and their household in the early part of the 20th century, in which the lord of the manor slowly comes to see one of his servants, for the first time, as a human being, with his own set of hopes, dreams, and problems. The look on Lord Grantham's face is priceless: he obviously had never before thought of this servant as a distinct individual, and doing so is not only a revelation to him but opens up whole new worlds of possibilities.

Organizational leaders are not English lords and ladies—but sometimes they act as if they *think* they are. Humility requires that we stop dwelling on our own problems long enough to see the plights of others. To be an effective leader, you must be able to set aside your ego, or "self," and understand what other people are feeling—and feel it with them. Such is the theme of a poem, the author known only as Robi, that is titled "The Other Side of the Desk":

Have you ever thought just a wee little bit
of how it would seem to be a misfit,
And how you would feel if you had to sit
on the other side of the desk?

Have you ever looked at the man who seemed a bum,
as he sat before you, nervous, dumb,
And thought of the courage it took him to come
to the other side of the desk?

Have you thought of his dreams that went astray,
of the hard, real facts of his every day,
Of the things in his life that make him stay
on the other side of the desk?

Did you make him feel that he was full of greed,
make him ashamed of his race or his creed,
Or did you reach out to him in his need
to the other side of the desk?

May God give us wisdom and lots of it,
and much compassion and plenty of grit,

So that we may be kinder to those who sit
on the other side of the desk.

Selflessness

Setting your "self" aside is easier said than done; but perhaps that is because too few leaders understand the powerful impact such selflessness can have on an organization. In fact, one of the most difficult concepts for leaders to grasp is that, when the group does well, they also have succeeded—even if others get more credit. To illustrate that point, we are going to revert to a sports metaphor.

John Wooden received a great deal of credit for UCLA's 11 national championships in men's basketball while he served as head coach. As a result of all those titles, he is probably one on the most famous and revered coaches in the history of the game. Yet it would be fair to say that Wooden did not *take* a great deal of credit for that unprecedented and unmatched string of success. Indeed, has there ever been a more self-effacing yet phenomenally successful person than John Wooden? He became a household name because of what he—or rather, because of what his teams—accomplished. But, considering the way he lived his life both during and after his coaching career, he does not appear to care about fame. He just wanted to win basketball games, and he understood early on that if he was going to be successful, than meant his players had to be successful. He was more than happy to give them the lion's share of the credit (and he did so, regularly) because they were taking him where he wanted to go.

We say "he just wanted to win basketball games," but that is not entirely true. He also took very seriously his responsibility to the young men on the teams to help them reach their full potential as human beings. When any of his famous players, such as Bill Walton or Kareem Abdul Jabbar, talk about Coach Wooden, they always mention that first: not his greatness as a recruiter or a tactician, but how he helped them grow and develop as individuals. Wooden not only put his own ego on the back burner; he also made nurturing and developing others a priority. That is what we mean by selflessness.

Compare John Wooden with another famous college basketball coach: Bobby Knight. Knight, whose Indiana University teams won three national championships, often has been criticized for being bombastic, dictatorial, and arrogant. Critics have noted that Indiana, during Knight's tenure, produced very few players who went on to greatness at the next level—unlike UCLA under Wooden. Indeed, some have even suggested that Knight intentionally recruited second-tier players because, when his teams won, he wanted the majority of the credit to go to his coaching ability; he did not want people to think he won just because he had great players. As a result, Knight was not as successful as Wooden; nor is he as revered today.

Selflessness seems to be a concept that few leaders grasp, and even fewer embrace. Becoming a leader at all without having a healthy ego is hard. You have to believe that you have something to offer, that you have worthwhile ideas, and in most cases you have to put yourself out there as a candidate. Unfortunately, the act of constantly putting yourself out there can easily translate into egocentrism—or at least be interpreted that way by others. To put it another way, leaders sometimes get so used to tooting their own horns in order to acquire those leadership positions that they keep right on tooting after reaching their goal. Achieving a balance between strength and meekness—between ego and humility—seems quite beyond them.

Once again, this is a virtue that effective leaders constantly work to develop. For all but a very few of those who have a strong enough will and sense of self to rise to leadership, self-effacement probably does not come naturally. But in the end it comes down to a set of behaviors. Remember the philosophy of William James that we discussed back in Chapter 1: if you behave as if you are something for long enough, eventually you will become that thing. Being humble or self-effacing is not a gimmick or an act. You have to earnestly try to develop and internalize this virtue. But to do that, you have to train yourself to act in certain ways.

First, as we mentioned above, you must be willing to listen emphatically to people and learn from them. Furthermore, they have to observe you learning and changing your perspective and your patterns of behavior based on what you have heard. Hand in hand with listening, you must come to see other people's strengths (along with their weaknesses, to be sure, but too many leaders focus primarily on the weaknesses of the people they lead; we are suggesting you focus on strengths instead). Then look for every opportunity to praise and reward good work, whether by a few kind words of acknowledgement or something more formal.

Do be careful about creating reward systems that are essentially meaningless and may tempt staff members to try to game the system. Those tend to do more harm than good. In a professional setting, of course, the most common rewards are raises and promotions. But when those are not possible or appropriate—and everyone usually knows when that is the case—then simply recognizing someone for a job well done can go a long way toward building trust and loyalty.

Finally, and most important, you have to be willing sometimes to take a back seat to others, even to your subordinates, putting them front and center and letting them receive the accolades instead of you. This sort of behavior may not necessarily come naturally to the kind of people who have the strength of personality to become leaders; but remember that it does not always have to be about you. When the people you lead look good, you look good, too.

Putting Others First

Being selfless means putting other people before yourself—that is, coming to regard their needs, wants, hopes, and desires as being more important than your own.

Once again, this idea has profound implications for leaders. Remember that organizational leaders tend to be people who are used to getting their way; some of them, in fact, gravitate toward management or administration specifically because they *want* to get their way. Once such people get into positions of authority, they quickly make it clear to everyone under them that *their* agenda is the only agenda; that their way of doing things is the only way of doing things; and that everyone else's focus should be on making them happy.

But what if leadership is not about you, or even about the organization? What if it really is about the people you lead? What if the long-term success of the organization relies not on your well-being but the well-being of others?

Such thinking would represent a major paradigm shift for many leaders. "But somebody has to be in charge," they may protest. "Somebody has to tell everybody else what to do. There has to be a clear chain of command. We can't just let the inmates run the asylum."

The "asylum" comment may reflect the attitude of that kind of leader; but in an industry where the "inmates" are at least as smart and as well educated as the leaders (and often more so), such as higher education or professional services, how important is it, really, for one person's vision to dominate? For one person, with perhaps a few "helpers," to determine the direction of the organization? Look at some of the most successful corporations of our day, such as Apple, Google, and Facebook, and you will see organizations that are not hierarchical. These are organizations in which individual employees—in some cases, even very low-ranking employees—have a great deal of say in the way the company is run. They are listened to by management, and their ideas are taken seriously and, very often, put into effect. These organizations have highly recognizable and influential leaders, but they are leaders who appreciate the contributions of others.

In contrast, Rob has a good friend who recently retired as an executive at a large multinational corporation, a recognized leader in its industry and a well-known brand. This executive started out loading trucks and worked his way up through the organization, partly because he had ability and a strong work ethic, but also because of the extremely employee-centered nature of the company. By the time he retired, however, that ethos had given way to a more top-down management style, as a new group of managers brought in their bottom-line-oriented approach. Rob's friend regards it as no coincidence that, at the time he left, the company had lost significant market share, and its stock price had fallen precipitously.

Being "other-centered" requires leaders to direct the focus away from themselves to those they lead. This does not come naturally, as most human beings are wired to seek praise and recognition, not to deflect it onto others. By putting others first, however, leaders build stronger organizations over time—something that benefits themselves as much as everyone else. You should not put others first just because it is to your advantage to do so; that would be wholly cynical, the antithesis of true humility. But there is no question that it is to your advantage to become less self-centered and more other-centered.

Service

Of course the ultimate manifestation of selflessness and other-centeredness is service, and no doubt that is why the concept of "servant leadership" has gained traction in recent years, stemming from Ken Blanchard's book *The Servant Leader*. Our intention is not, in this section, to review Blanchard's book, although we do highly recommend it. Instead, we would like to focus on service as an expression of humility.

Despite the best efforts of Blanchard and others, the word "servant" in our culture has retained its negative connotations. In current parlance, a servant is barely above a slave—someone who is beneath all others in social stature, who performs menial tasks for minimal pay. This makes being described as a "servant" a bitter pill to swallow for most leaders, who are more accustomed to deference and respect. For them, adopting the persona of a servant definitely requires a great deal of humility because they view it as a major step down in status.

Words like "service" and "serve," meanwhile, have fared somewhat better in our culture as organizations openly compete to see who can best serve clients or offer the best customer service. Yet, as we all know from sad experience, too often what masquerades as customer service actually is more like what personal finance guru Clark Howard refers to as "customer no-service." But even in organizations that do serve their customers relatively well, the idea remains that service is something provided by lower-level, hourly employees. Rarely is there the thought that the higher-ups—the organizational leaders—should also provide service, much less serve the people who work for them.

As a practical matter, what does it mean for leaders to serve the people below them in the organizational structure? And is there a point at which such service can become detrimental to the organization rather than beneficial? After all, those of us who are parents understand full well that, however we may be inclined to serve our children, if we serve them too much we rob them of initiative and of the opportunity to learn and grown from adversity. Not that we should carry that analogy too far: subordinates are not children, and to think of them that way is the very definition of patronizing. But there clearly are certain parallels, the most obvious being that, if we do too much for the people we lead, they will be less inclined to do things for themselves.

For leaders, serving others means, first of all, doing the things we have discussed so far in this chapter: listening to them, learning from them, giving them as much credit as possible, putting their needs before yours. But beyond that, it means doing everything in your power to make their jobs as easy as possible, short of doing their jobs for them. A campus CEO whom Karl greatly admires once said his job was "to make sure there's enough chalk on the chalkboard trays." In other words, even though he was ostensibly the person in charge, the one to whom everyone else deferred, he saw his role as supporting faculty—making sure they could do their jobs without having to worry about mundane things like chalk. That's service leadership.

Serving the people you lead also means providing opportunities for them to learn and grow professionally and move up in the organization. A college basketball coach that Rob knew always told his staff that he hoped they all wanted his job. Of course, he did not mean he wanted them to undercut him and literally try to take his job away. He meant he wanted assistants who all were striving to become head coaches one day, and he was signaling to them that, if they were willing to work at it, he was going to do what he could to help them gain the necessary experience and skills. He could best serve them by helping them attain their career goals—and in return, they would serve him by helping to put together an excellent basketball program.

To take that kind of approach requires tremendous personal confidence as well as a great deal of humility.

Actually, It Is NOT About You

The antithesis of the humble leader is the narcissistic tyrant who surrounds himself or herself with sycophants—"yes-men" and "yes-women," as we sometimes call them. Unfortunately, this authoritarian style of leadership is so prevalent in higher education that Rob has written about it on several occasions, most notably for *Academe Magazine* ("How to Climb Down from Top-Down Leadership") and, more recently, for *The Chronicle of Higher Education* ("A Song of Vice and Mire"). In the latter piece, he noted that the two most common governance models in higher education are what he calls the "feudal model" and the "soviet model." Both, he says, "feature relatively small groups who place themselves in orbit around the leader, jockeying for position and seeking to consolidate their own power through flattery and zealous support of the official agenda. Neither model is particularly kind to dissidents or independent thinkers."

Of course, that leadership style is also found in the corporate world. In his classic management text, *Good to Great*, Jim Collins identifies what he calls the "genius with a thousand helpers" model:

The most classic case comes from a man known as the Sphinx, Henry Singleton of Teledyne.... Through acquisitions, Singleton built the company from a small enterprise to number 293 on the Fortune 500 list in six years. Within ten years, he'd completed more than 100 acquisitions, eventually creating a far-flung empire with 130 profit centers in everything from exotic metals to insurance. Amazingly, the whole thing worked, with Singleton himself acting as the glue that connected all the moving parts together....[However] once Singleton stepped away from day-to-day management ...the far-flung empire began to crumble.

Collins goes on to cite a 1978 feature story in *Forbes* magazine that stated, "Singleton will win no awards for humility, but who can avoid standing in awe of his impressive record?"

The story of Teledyne, in Collins's book, is contrasted with that of Wells Fargo during the 1970s and '80s, when the bank began making a committed effort to hire the best people possible and give them the freedom and authority to make decisions independently. Dick Cooley, Wells Fargo's visionary CEO at the time, was quoted as saying in an interview, "That's how you build the future. If I'm not smart enough to see the changes that are coming, [these people we're hiring] will. And they'll be flexible enough to deal with them." That is exactly what happened, as Wells Fargo embarked on a period of unprecedented growth that lasted more than 25 years, even as the banking industry was undergoing seismic changes.

Think about that for a moment. Here is a leader, Dick Cooley, who was humble enough to admit that he did not know everything, that he was not the smartest person in the room. And look how his organization profited from that mindset, not only during his tenure as CEO but for many years after he retired. Now compare that to Singleton's approach at Teledyne. There is no question that Singleton was brilliant; probably, most of the time, he actually *was* the smartest person in the room. But how did that help his organization once he was gone?

Together, these two stories illustrate one of the most important reasons for leaders to cultivate humility: because they will not always be the leaders. Because their responsibility is to the organization, and to the stakeholders, not to themselves. Leaders who listen, who are teachable, who put others first, who set an example of service—those leaders create a sustainable climate of leadership growth and development within the organization. They encourage others to learn and grow from their mistakes as well as their successes; to contribute freely to the decision-making process because they know they will be listened to, their opinions valued; and ultimately to develop their own decision-making abilities, independently of the leader.

Prideful, narcissistic, opinionated, self-centered leaders, on the other hand, not only breed distrust and disloyalty—who would be loyal to someone who behaves that way, except perhaps someone else who behaves that way? They also end up destroying the very thing they are charged with safeguarding. They become leadership vampires, sucking all initiative and independence from the organization.

Those sorts of practical considerations are not the only reason, or even the main reason, for leaders to seek humility. Virtue, as always, is its own reward. But if your natural tendency as a leader is to take an authoritarian, "my way or the highway" approach, you may want to reconsider that in light of what we have talked about in this chapter. We invite you to engage in the following exercises and see if they improve your relationships with the people you lead and, ultimately, improve the efficiency and effectiveness of your organization.

Practicing Humility

Humility is often said to be the most elusive of virtues because the moment you think you have acquired it, you have lost it. While there is a lot of truth to that statement, it also is true that humility, like any other virtue, can be developed over time through practice and attention. What follows is a list of exercises, for lack of a better term, that you can practice in your own leadership situations in order to become more humble.

Bear in mind, once again, the idea we outlined in Chapter 1: although acting humble may not be the same thing as actually *being* humble, over time the two become the same. If you behave with humility often enough, and for long enough, you eventually will in fact become humble.

Embark on a "listening tour." Set aside a significant amount of time, scheduling it as necessary, specifically for the purpose of listening to people within your organization, especially the people whom you lead. You can do this in group meetings, but in that case you must be extremely careful to listen to what others are saying and not give in to the temptation to do the talking (which may be exactly what you are accustomed to doing as group leader). You also can arrange to visit with people individually in their work spaces; these meetings should not be in your office unless people come to you of their own volition. We have found that people tend to be much more at ease, and therefore more talkative, when they are in familiar territory and do not feel that they have been "called on the carpet." Most of them also will appreciate your taking time out of your busy schedule to come and see them.

Either way, your task is to ask leading, open-ended questions—such as "What do you think about the direction of the organization right now?" or "What can we do better? How?"—while also inviting questions from them. Then sit back and let them talk while you *listen*. Do not allow yourself to become judgmental or defensive, and do not let what people say in these sessions influence your attitude toward them or your relationship with them. Once they see you are really listening and not holding anything they say against them, they will be much more likely to talk, to tell you things. You may be amazed at what you learn.

Learn someone else's job. Resolve, over the next few months, to learn the job of one person in your organization, preferably a job with which you are not already familiar. At first the person whose job you are learning probably will be extremely uncomfortable, but as you explain what you are doing and why and demonstrate your earnest desire to learn—making it clear that you regard your colleague as the expert—two things will happen. First, you will learn how important that particular job or function is, perhaps more important than you ever imagined, and how it fits into the overall scheme of the organization. Second, the individual who is teaching you will become more confident and competent in his or her job, which also benefits the organization.

Read up on a topic of interest. Over the next year, commit to increasing your knowledge of some topic not directly related to your job or profession: history, art, literature, music. You could choose a historical period or event that interests you but you do not know much about, such as the French Revolution or Manifest Destiny, and read as many books and articles about it as you can find. Or read the collected works of Shakespeare, William Faulkner, or Maya Angelou.

Practice empathy. The next time a subordinate comes to you with a problem, instead of just dismissing it (politely or otherwise) or showing impatience or frustration at the interruption, try a different approach. Listen carefully as the person describes the problem, attempting to hear what is *not* being said as well as what is said. Pay close attention to the person's tone and body language in order to determine his or her frame of mind. Is the person nervous? Anxious? Frustrated? Angry? Afraid? Given the problem being discussed, why would he or she feel that way? Try placing yourself in that person's position—on the other side of the desk.

Deflect praise. The next time someone (especially someone above you in the organization) praises you for an accomplishment, immediately think of all the other people who were involved in that success. Then, give them credit for their contributions, mentioning them by name and outlining the specific roles they played. For example: "Thank you, but I couldn't have done it if Greg hadn't done such terrific research and if Marsha hadn't created such a sophisticated spreadsheet. Eric and Wanda also contributed by taking care of the day-to-day chores while we worked on this project." Remember that you can do this without being utterly self-effacing. The point is not to play down your own role, in an "aw, shucks" kind of way; rather, you are giving credit where credit is due—and recognizing that you are not the only hard-working employee in the organization.

Nominate someone. If your organization has a mechanism for recognizing people for their good work, by handing out awards or other perks, be sure to nominate the people you lead as often as possible—which is to say, when the opportunity presents itself and when their work merits it. Remember that when they look good, you also look good.

Lead a service project. Identify a project that would benefit a large number of people in the organization, such as updating the lunch area or repainting the lines in the parking lot. Organize a group of volunteers among the staff to carry out that project during their off hours, and solicit donations of money and materials as needed. Be sure to make very clear that participation is purely voluntary and will not reflect on anyone's evaluation. Of course, you should participate in the project yourself, visibly contributing as much and working as hard as anyone. You may even want to ask someone else to serve as group leader, so that while working on the project, you are just one of the gang and not the boss.

Alternatively, you could identify a worthwhile service project in your community and organize a group to address it, following the same steps outlined. When choosing a project, you may want to solicit suggestions from others in the organization or allow the group to vote on it. Again, be very careful how you approach the project: the idea is for the people you lead to see you in a different light, working hard to serve others.

By enacting some of these suggestions, or taking other similar actions that you identify for yourself, over time you will not only develop a reputation as a humble leader; you will begin to acquire humility. When that starts to happen, be careful not to brag about it. If you did, you would have to start all over again.

6. Honesty

MOST OF US ARE TAUGHT, PRACTICALLY FROM INFANCY, THAT "HONesty is the best policy." Yet as we grow older, we are not always convinced that is true. All around us we see people who are lying while seeming to prosper, even as incentives to lie for personal gain, to make ourselves look good, or to get out of trouble are ever-present. But occasionally, events take place in our lives that demonstrate the power of honesty. Karl experienced one such event several years ago, and it helped shape his attitudes and behavior ever since.

He was leading a strategic planning retreat for a large, academically minded, government organization—a lot of smart, opinionated, busy people who were not especially thrilled to be attending a strategic planning retreat. Prior to the retreat, he surveyed all those smart, opinionated, busy people to get some idea of the organization's cultural values in preparation for a workshop on the way values shape planning. The results that emerged, as his staff sorted through the survey responses, were quite definite concerning what members of the organization valued most.

However, as Karl shared those results with attendees at the workshop, many of them balked. Several, in fact, became visibly incensed, insisting that the items said to be at the top of the list were *not* their organization's chief values, and that in fact the opposite was true: those were the things they valued *least*. Flummoxed, Karl called the project manager who had compiled the results of the survey and discovered, as he questioned her, that she had inadvertently transposed the list— that, indeed, the angry attendees were correct: the very things they had reported valuing least somehow appeared at the top.

The news, of course, left Karl with an ethical dilemma. He could have just continued with the charade, deflecting their anger by falling back on the numbers. No doubt he could have endured their grumbling for another day or two, taken their money, gone on to his next job, and forgotten the whole mess.

Instead, he decided to come clean. As difficult as it was under the circumstances, with such a hostile group, he admitted the mistake, apologized, and produced the revised (and more accurate) survey results. And then a strange thing happened: instead of becoming even angrier because he had initially presented them with bogus numbers, created a great deal of unnecessary consternation, and wasted their time, they suddenly were not as angry. Their hostility toward the whole process subsided, and they were able to accomplish their task of developing a viable strategic plan.

No doubt Karl's decision to be honest benefitted him and his firm in the long run, as word got out that here was a man who could be trusted. And that, of course, is one of the great benefits of being honest: a reputation for honesty is perhaps the single most valuable asset any professional, and especially any leader, can possess. Such a reputation is extremely difficult to acquire—indeed, it can be acquired only by passing through the crucible of situations such as the one described above—and, as many others before us have noted, it is quite easy to lose. One lie, one act of dishonesty, and a lifetime of behaving honorably can be destroyed.

So there are very practical reasons to be scrupulously honest in all your dealings. But this book is not primarily about practical reasons for behaving virtuously; rather, it is about embracing virtue for virtue's sake. Honesty is indeed the best policy—but not just because it is in your best interests. Honesty is in the best interests of *everyone*, especially those you lead.

Truthfulness

When we think about honesty, we most often think about simply truth-telling. How many of the morality tales we were told growing up were based on this fundamental principle?

Telling the truth is indeed at the very heart of honesty: "the truth, the whole truth, and nothing but the truth," as the legal profession puts it. Note that this includes a) speaking the truth—that is, not lying; b) telling the entire truth rather than leaving out parts and thereby lying by omission; and c) not saying anything that is not entirely true. Because the fact is that there are many forms of lying and many ways in which people rationalize not being truthful. For example: "I didn't exactly lie; I just didn't tell the whole truth." "It may not be entirely true, but it's close enough." "That was the truth, as far as it goes."

But acquiring and practicing the virtue of honesty means developing the personal habit of telling the truth, regardless of the outcome. As a practical matter, in a professional situation, when we tell people the truth, we give them all the information they need in order to make informed decisions. If we twist the facts or leave out important points, for whatever reason, we are doing them a disservice because they cannot reach a correct conclusion.

Perhaps the most common reason people lie is to make themselves look better—not necessarily on any large scale, but within the context of everyday life. While big lies usually will be found out (remember Enron, Watergate, etc.), small lies often are considered to be almost a kind of social lubricant, reducing the friction of our daily interactions. We even have a name for these lies, which reflects our attitude toward them: "white lies," we call them. They are not deep and dark. They are light and fluffy, harming no one.

When we are late for a meeting, we say we were stuck in traffic. When we fail to return a call or e-mail, we say we never got it. When we do not want to go somewhere, we say we have another commitment.

There is just one problem with these types of lies: they *do* harm someone, and that someone is you. You may not be doing any real damage to the people around you—what does it matter to them whether you actually were stuck in traffic?—but over time you can easily acquire a reputation as someone who always has an excuse, always has a glib answer, never takes responsibility. In other words, someone who is untrustworthy. And our general assumption is that people who cannot be trusted in small things definitely are not to be trusted when the stakes are much higher. To have a reputation as someone who owns up to failures, even minor failures, and takes responsibility for his or her own actions is far better. This is, of course, especially true for leaders.

Besides, learning to tell the truth about relatively minor failings can help make you a better person. Other than lying about being stuck in traffic, how else can you keep from making yourself look bad as you walk into that meeting 15 minutes late? Obviously, by not walking into the meeting 15 minutes late. By being on time. If you have determined not to lie, then your only alternative is to behave in such a way that you do not feel any need to lie. Lying about small mistakes can easily become a kind of crutch that enables you to make more and more of those mistakes. Eventually, white lies become a kind of leprosy: white spots eating away at your reputation until only the bones remain.

In addition, lying can easily become habitual, until your default response in any difficult situation is to lie until you feel the pressure is off. Even though all organizations have their fair share of liars, becoming known as the guy who never tells the truth can be a career-killer. At the very least, that reputation will make people reluctant to follow you because they cannot trust you, can never know where you stand on any issue, can never accept any information from you at face value.

The good news is that telling the truth also can become habitual. There is no question that, under certain circumstances, telling the truth can be extremely difficult because you will end up looking bad. You may have to acknowledge some failure on your part or admit to being less than perfect. But being known as the person who always tells the truth, regardless of the personal cost, can cement your reputation as a person of integrity and character—unless, of course, you are having to admit to too many failures or gaffes, in which case your problem is not lack of honesty but lack of competence.

Of course, another reason people lie in social or professional settings is to keep from hurting others. We say that we forgot to call when the fact is we cannot stand speaking to that person, fudging the truth not because we are embarrassed by our actions but because we do not want to hurt that person's feelings. That is understandable: we should not use the truth to injure. Being truthful does not mean speaking out loud every truth that comes to mind, particularly when our primary goal is to point out other people's failings and make ourselves look better by comparison. Sometimes the best thing we can do is simply say nothing at all, at least for the time being. Saying nothing is not being dishonest; it is being charitable and perhaps wise as well.

Generally speaking, though, your policy as a virtuous leader should be to tell the truth in every situation, unless you are doing it specifically to hurt someone. Truth-telling may mean saying things to people they will not like but need to hear. It may mean owning up to your own mistakes, as uncomfortable as that may be. It certainly will involve acknowledging things to yourself that you would just as soon ignore or deny.

Ultimately, the most important person to whom you must tell the truth is yourself. Self-delusion and self-deception are probably responsible for more ills in this world than all the spoken and written lies combined. Avoiding this most fundamental type of dishonesty can be an ongoing battle since most of us do not really know ourselves as well as we like to think. However, the battle begins with humility, as we discussed in the previous chapter, and continues with wisdom, which we will examine in Chapter 12.

Transparency

A note to those who may be reading this book straight through: one of the challenges we discovered in writing the subsections within each chapter is that all are related to each other, some very closely. Thus, we confess that we constantly run the risk of repeating ourselves, seeming to cover the same ground, or sounding as if we are splitting hairs. But as experienced conference presenters, we have learned that a little repetition is useful—especially if the points being repeated are, well, worth repeating.

Transparency, then, obviously flows directly from the concept of truthfulness as described above—especially the idea of telling "the whole truth." What it means specifically is that someone in a position of authority or leadership behaves in a manner that is open and forthright, so that everyone below on the organizational chart can see clearly what is happening. There are no dark secrets, no hidden agendas, no political deals hatched in back rooms. Everything is done in the open, so that the leader is accountable to those being led because they can see what is happening and how it is happening and judge for themselves whether it is good or not.

Sometimes it seems that every time a leader of a large organization takes office, from the President of the United States on down, he or she pledges to be transparent, to the point at which "transparency" has become a popular buzzword. And yet, to those in the trenches, very little seems to change. Whether in the board room or the Oval Office, it is always "politics as usual," by which we mean decisions are made over which none of us has any control and about which few of us even have a clue.

Basically, people do not like that sort of behavior in their leaders. It makes people feel as if they are not important and that, perhaps, they are being ill-used. Why would leaders hatch backroom deals if not to advance their own agendas by doing things of which the people they lead may not approve?

Of course, leaders cannot always just throw everything they know out on the table for public consumption. Some information is confidential and for good reason. Obviously, information that could compromise the security of the organization falls under this heading, which is why our nation's leaders do sometimes have to operate in secret, as do college presidents and corporate CEOs. Giving out such information, whether negligently or out of malice, could do great harm and therefore violates the constraint against using the truth to injure. It can also get you sued, or worse.

There are times, in fact, when withholding information is a type of honesty. A few years ago, Karl's company, AAL, had submitted a proposal to conduct a feasibility study on a new college for a large university. The university delayed acting on the proposal; in the meantime, another university in the same region approached AAL about conducting a similar study and was ready to sign a contract immediately. Karl contacted the president at the first university and informed him that AAL had a conflict of interest and was withdrawing its proposal. When the president pressured Karl to reveal the conflict, he politely declined. And even when another member of the administration at that institution offered to keep Karl "in the loop" regarding their expansion plans, Karl had to say, "No, thanks." In that case, the flow of information in either direction—too much transparency—would have been a form of dishonesty.

Perhaps a good rule of thumb would be the following: if you are withholding information to protect someone else's privacy, assuming that person has a reasonable expectation of privacy under the circumstances, then that is not dishonest, especially if you are straightforward about the fact that you are withholding information and why. You may even be able to justify withholding certain information about yourself to protect your own and your family's privacy. But if the only reason you are keeping people in the dark is that they may not like what you are doing and that could reflect badly on you or interfere with some self-serving agenda or perhaps cost you your job (think Nixon and Watergate), then that is dishonest.

And, by the way, it is dishonest even if you believe you are acting for what you consider "the right reasons." As long as no one (except possibly you) is being harmed by the revelation, then the people you lead have a right to know what is going on and decide for themselves whether it is in their best interests. Virtuous leaders understand this concept and do everything in their power to behave as openly and transparently as possible.

One of the best ways to achieve transparency is through inclusiveness, consensus-building, and group decision-making. Some college faculty members have an old joke about the way that top-level administrators typically approach the notion of shared governance—the ideal that running the institution should be an enterprise shared among administration, faculty, and staff. When campus leaders appear to make all the important decisions without input from any of the constituency groups, faculty members say to each other, "Yep, that's 'shared governance,' all right. They governed, and then they 'shared' it with us."

True shared governance is a model that works well not only on college campuses but for other organizations as well. It involves bringing to the table everyone who will be impacted by a particular decision or at least representatives of each major group. Then, decisions can be made collectively, with some sort of general consensus if not 100 percent agreement. Of course, the various groups may not always agree, or they may occasionally want to do something that is not in the best interests of the organization. As we were writing this chapter, a West Coast university had lost its accreditation because, apparently, faculty groups had attempted to usurp the authority of the board and administration. In situations like that, the decision falls back on the leadership, who despite all attempts to build consensus may end up having to do something very unpopular.

But there are several advantages to that degree of inclusiveness. First of all, there is a good chance of reaching a decision with which most people are comfortable. And secondly, even if people do not like the decision, they understand how it was made and why, and they feel that they had a voice. It was not made behind closed doors or simply decreed and handed down from on high. That is a level of transparency few leaders achieve but to which all should aspire.

Integrity

As we were deciding on the chapters of this book, there was some debate over whether to title this chapter "Honesty" or "Integrity." Obviously, the two are closely related. The real question, it seemed to us, was whether honesty is an aspect of integrity or integrity is an aspect of honesty. In the end, we decided that what we most wanted to talk about in this chapter is being honest—and we define that, in part, as having personal integrity.

Often, the terms "integrity" and "honesty" are used interchangeably. But we believe that there is a lot more to integrity than simply telling the truth, as important as that is. We like to think of the word "integrity" as it is often used in engineering, in reference to a structure such as a bridge or an airplane. "Structural integrity" refers to the ability of a structure to manage the load placed upon it and resist the failure that occurs through fatigue, fracture, or deformation. *The Oxford English Dictionary*, in addition to defining "integrity" as "the quality of being honest and having strong moral principles," also offers the following definition: "the condition of being unified, unimpaired, or sound in construction; internal consistency or lack of corruption."

In other words, integrity in an object is the state of being what that object essentially *is*. The flying machine actually flies, and it remains aloft as its wings continue to function according to design. The bridge holds firm, spanning the gulf as it was meant to do, perpetually facilitating passage from one side to the other.

If we apply that same definition to a person, then integrity means being what you essentially are at your core, being true to yourself—or rather, to your *self*, that being who is really you, stripped of all pretense and social camouflage. We are convinced that you (like everyone else) have the seeds of virtue within you. Integrity, then, in its purest sense, means nurturing those seeds and allowing them to grow, as over time you become the person you were meant to be—the person that, in a sense, you already are.

Let us return to those engineering terms. Note that structural integrity involves withstanding external pressures. Likewise, being true to yourself means having the ability to resist any onslaught against your essential character.

Here we need to go back to our discussion in Chapter 1 about values, those deep-seated beliefs about what is right, what is wrong, and what is most important. One of your values, for example, may be the very thing we have just been talking about: the belief that you should tell the truth. Such values are an integral part of the essential you. Yet you will constantly, in both your professional and your personal lives, face situations that cause you to question those values—or even worse, tempt you to abandon them. You also will encounter individuals who want you to compromise or sacrifice your values, usually so they can gain something for themselves, although they may very well offer you something in return.

Integrity, as we are defining it in this section, means that you have the inner strength—the structural integrity—to withstand such attacks without breaking down and becoming something less than what you really are. Just as the bridge stands fast against tide and wind, you remain true to yourself, regardless of the forces operating upon you.

Another word we may not always think of as connected with integrity, but which is included in the *OED* definition, is "sound." That is instructive, because the word is commonly applied to people as well as structures: we often speak of someone as a "sound" individual. But what does that mean? It means that the person is level-headed and clear-thinking. That he or she has good judgment. That this person can be trusted to give good advice or complete some important task efficiently and effectively. No doubt we would all like for our coworkers, not to mention our superiors, to describe us as "sound" individuals. But perhaps we can best understand what it means to be sound by examining its opposite.

This point brings us to the final element of the *OED* definition: "internal consistency or lack of corruption." The analogy that springs to mind immediately involves computer files. When a virus attacks a hard drive, it corrupts the files, so they are no longer what they were. We cannot trust the corrupted files, either to reflect the original material or not to damage other files.

We intend to discuss more about external consistency—being perceived by others as being who you say you are and doing what you say you are going to do—a little later in this chapter. Here, however, the emphasis is on *internal* consistency; that is, on remaining true within yourself to what you most deeply believe, on being who you really are, at your core. Corruption, in this sense, is what happens when that core is eaten away: when your words and your actions do not conform to your most cherished values. That kind of corruption may not be visible to others because they may not even be aware of your values. They may not know what you believe or what you tell yourself you believe, which is why corruption is so insidious. Abandoning your core principles when no one else even knows those principles exist or what they are is easy to rationalize.

But *you* know. That is why integrity is such an important aspect of honesty. It also is the reason integrity is a subheading under honesty and not the other way around: because it relies on telling the truth—consistently, even brutally, if necessary—to the person who needs to hear it most: yourself. As Lord Polonius says to Laertes in *Hamlet*, "This above all: to thine own self be true/ And it must follow, as the night the day/ Thou canst not then be false to any man."

Honor

Another concept associated with honesty, one that may seem rather old-fashioned these days, is honor. This concept is related to integrity because honor involves doing the right thing just because it is the right thing to do. But honor also includes an element of selflessness, of setting aside one's own desires and personal agenda in order to act for the greater good.

Modern society tends to celebrate those most adept at navigating the political waters. If there is one thing that successful adults learn very quickly, it is that every aspect of life has a political component; this especially is true of professional life. How often, for instance, do we speak of office politics? However, we seldom use that phrase in a positive context; usually, we are complaining about or otherwise commenting on what most of us regard as a fairly negative feature of everyday life.

Politics too often is the art of advancing one's self-interests. It is all about power. Many politicians will give you what you want, but only because they calculate that doing so will enable them, in the long run, to get what *they* want. If you cannot help them reach their personal goals, they are not interested in you. And if they perceive that you are somehow in their way, watch out. Self-interest is just as real in the department meeting or conference room as it is in the halls of the nation's Capitol.

Honor, in many ways, is the complete antithesis of egocentric politics. Honorable people refuse to play the political game for its own sake or to advance selfish agendas. They put the needs of the organization, and even of other people within the organization, ahead of their own, making decisions based not on self-interest but rather on the greater good. In politics, the honorable leader has the good of the state, organization, department, or unit as his or her goal. As a mid-level academic administrator, Rob witnessed many examples of both political maneuvering and honorable behavior, especially in the arena of resource allocation. Once a year, division heads would meet to divvy up the resources allocated by the central administration, which included faculty positions as well as certain budgetary funds. Every year, there were those administrators who could be counted on to put their unit's needs or, more likely, mere preferences ahead of everyone else's—falsifying information, conniving, and gleefully throwing colleagues under the bus, all to get what they wanted. They appeared to care nothing for the institution as a whole, as long as they "got theirs."

Yet there also were those—and quite a few of them, Rob is pleased to note—who consistently put the greater good ahead of their own agendas. They made their pitch for a fair share of the resources, but did so honestly and forthrightly. To whatever extent they advocated for their unit, they did so in good faith, without rancor, flattery, or demagoguery. In the end, they were often willing to give up something they had won by virtue of their arguments because they saw that some other unit had an even greater need and that the college as a whole would be better served by filling that need first.

A large part of what behaving with honor means is being honest enough with yourself and with others to acknowledge what is right—as opposed to merely what you want—and then having the courage to do it. Behaving honorably also means that you value your reputation more than you value financial rewards or advancement or winning an allocation. You would rather do the right thing and lose (a promotion, a raise, a share of resources) than do the wrong thing and win.

Before we conclude this subsection, there is one more aspect of honor that we would like to discuss: honoring others. This aspect entails showing respect for others as people, but it is more than that. In particular, honoring others means that you do not merely pretend to be interested in what they have to say, but you genuinely value their opinions. You believe those you lead are important enough to listen to and take seriously, wherever they happen to fall on the organizational chart. There is an old maxim, apt in this context, that you can tell a great deal about people by the way they treat those ranked below them on the social or economic scale. When you have a sense of honor, it tends to be reflected in the way you view and interact with others.

Trustworthiness

One of the most recognizable characteristics of honest people is that they are trustworthy—which, as we are using the term here, literally means "worthy of trust." Trustworthy people can be counted on to keep confidences. They are reliable, in that they are where they are supposed to be, when they are supposed to be there, doing what they are supposed to do. They are consistent, meaning not given to wild mood swings or variations in judgment, either due to their own personal vagaries or the frequent testing of political winds. You know where they stand, because their principles are constant; therefore, you can predict how they will react in a given situation.

As a leader, you constantly will be in possession of privileged information. Some of it will be official in nature, such as your employees' social security numbers and other personal information, and no doubt your organization will have policies for dealing with those kinds of data. But if you have any sort of relationship with the people in your organization, you also will constantly have people coming to you and telling you things they do not want you to divulge. Such confidences may be personal or professional in nature, but what they have in common is that they are secret and the person is entrusting you with that secret.

In the experience of the two of us, secrets come in two types: those you should keep, and those you have no business keeping. A common example of the former would be if someone in your unit confides about having marital difficulties. Obviously, that is not the sort of thing you should tell the rest of the unit; if you do, that person will never trust you again—nor will anyone else in the unit, however delighted they may have been to hear the juicy gossip in the first place. They would be right not to trust you. You violated a confidence.

On the other hand, you may occasionally have people tell you things you definitely need to share with the right people. Those might be about drug problems or other self-destructive behaviors, instances of abuse, or illegal or unethical behavior involving themselves or other members of the organization. As a leader, your first obligation is to the organization as a whole and to the other people involved, not to that one individual. If what that person is telling you could cause problems for the organization or for others, then you need to pass it on to the appropriate people, even if the teller asks you not to. The same holds true if the information could hurt that individual—thoughts of suicide, for example, or violent fantasies.

When someone comes into your office, closes the door, and says, "Can you keep a secret?" the best answer is usually, "It depends." In some cases, that person is just coming to gossip or spread malicious rumors about colleagues, in which case you probably do not want to hear it. Even if the person has serious information to share, you cannot commit to keeping it secret until you know what it is and how it will affect that individual and the rest of the organization. It is best to make it clear, early on in the conversation, that you will keep the information confidential if you can. As long as that is stated up front, others cannot rationally accuse you of breaking confidences.

Another aspect of trustworthiness is reliability, meaning that people can count on you to do what you are supposed to do and what you say you are going to do. This sounds simple, but it is no small thing. Is there anything more common these days—or anything we dislike more—than people who do not follow through? The parent in your carpool who neglects to pick up your kids after swim practice and does not even bother to call. The home remodeler who says he will finish the job next Tuesday then disappears for a month. The colleague who promises to have that report on your desk by the end of business, but allows two days to go by without so much as an apology e-mail. These are the tiny sharp rocks in the shoe of life, robbing us of enjoyment, contentment, and peace.

Conversely, how disproportionately overjoyed are we when the neighbor actually drops off the kids, the contractor finishes the project on time, or the colleague comes through with the report? Sadly, mere competence seems to have become the new excellence. As Woody Allen famously put it, "80 percent of success is just showing up."

A nephew of Rob's, a gifted woodworker, was considering opening his own cabinet-making business and asked Rob for advice. Here is what Rob told him: "If you give people reasonable estimates; do not charge them more than those estimates without a clear reason; show up to begin the job when you say you are going to show up; make good-looking, functional cabinets; and finish the job within a day or two of when you say you'll be finished, you'll have more work than you can handle. You'll be turning it away. You don't even have to make the very best custom cabinets. Just do what you say you're going to do. Follow through. Nobody does that anymore." His nephew took the advice and prospered.

Of course, the virtuous leader must do more than just "show up" and do acceptable work. For someone who truly is self-motivated, excellence is its own reward. But showing up and doing what you say you are going to do is not a bad place to start. That is how you develop a reputation for reliability—really an active form of honesty—that will serve you well all your life.

Lastly, the trustworthy person is distinguished by consistency. This attribute involves having a guiding set of bedrock principles that remain unchanged because they are part of your core being. A simple example in an organizational context is the college dean who used her institution's strategic plan as a guide to decision-making and resource allocation. Department chairs and faculty could count on the dean consistently assessing existing and proposed initiatives based on how well they promoted the vision, mission, values, and goals of the institution. This leader's consistent application of principles and guidelines built trust for her in her followers.

Some leaders are prone to violent mood swings, so that subordinates and colleagues never know what to expect when approaching them. How can you take a problem to someone if you cannot predict, with some reasonable degree of accuracy, how he or she will react? Whether the leader is going to offer you a drink, embrace you and cry, or start screaming in purple-faced rage? Such behavior is a form of self-centeredness and self-indulgence on the part of the leader, one whose emotions override professionalism. It also can be a form of dishonesty, to the extent that such behavior is often an affectation.

As a virtuous leader, understand that you cannot afford to act that way. Instead, you must strive to remain affable and unruffled day after day, regardless of your personal circumstances or what is happening at any particular moment. That may be difficult to do, depending on what is going on in your personal life or in the life of the organization. But think of the calm and confidence a military officer must exhibit before leading troops into battle. The people who work for you, and with you, deserve no less.

Consistency also transcends politics. Too many leaders can be counted on to do only one thing: spout the party line in any situation, like an old Soviet commissar. Such leaders have no core values, except their own aggrandizement and advancement. There can be no honesty because there is no truth to begin with. They only say what others tell them to say, and since that can change from one week to the next, subordinates never know what to expect.

Virtuous leaders are honest in that they are consistent. They have core values, and they remain true to those values, regardless of the circumstance. Those who work with those leaders always know what to expect: they know that core values exist, they know what the values are, and they trust their leaders to follow those values, no matter what.

A good way to develop this kind of consistency is to think of a leader you admire, someone with a great deal of personal integrity, whose core values are well known and who can always be counted on to behave ethically in any situation. Then, when you are faced with a situation in which you do not quite know how to respond, ask yourself, "What would so-and-so do in this situation?" Looking to role models and paragons of virtue for inspiration is an excellent way for leaders to reflect on what action they should take.

This model may be someone at a distance, whom you have read about or observed from afar. Or you may choose someone you know personally whose honesty and integrity has had an impact on your life or career. Karl's role model is an old friend of his, now deceased, whom he greatly admired for the habit of giving candid feedback and holding himself and others to a high ethical standard. When Karl is in a quandary, he often thinks about his friend and asks himself what that friend would do.

By being consistent in your responses and decision-making, reliable in fulfilling your duties, and trustworthy in keeping confidences, you can have a tremendously positive impact on your organization and the people you work with. And maybe someday, some of them, when faced with an ethical dilemma, will be asking themselves what *you* would do in that situation.

Practicing Honesty

There are steps you can take to catch yourself when you are not being honest to make the necessary correction, as well as habits you can develop that will enable you to make honesty a defining characteristic in your life. Developing those habits is the focus of this chapter's practical section.

Review your performance. Reflect on your recent interactions with colleagues, subordinates, managers, clients, and others. Were the statements you made to them always truthful? Or did you occasionally fudge the truth; if so, why? Were you trying to make yourself or your unit look better? Were you covering up for some mistake, either your own or someone else's? Were you exaggerating your competence or accomplishments (or those of your team)? Or were you just trying to blow them off politely?

As you identify the things you have said that were not entirely true—and, if you are like most people, you probably will identify a lot of them—ask yourself what you could have said or done differently. How would the outcome of your interaction have been different if you had told the truth? If the answer is that it would have been less favorable for you, then what could you have done differently beforehand—what *should* you have done differently beforehand—so that you would not have felt the need to lie?

This sort of reflection should enable you to see yourself in a different light: even if you consider yourself to be a relatively honest person, chances are that is not always the case. Resolve to be more meticulous about telling the truth in the future.

Check your e-mail. If simple reflection is not enough, go back and read through your e-mail exchanges with various people, keeping an eye out for white lies especially. Try this little exercise: go through a week's worth of e-mail exchanges—in particular, your responses to others—and make a list of every type of lie you find, no matter how minor. This can give you a startlingly (and unsettlingly) accurate picture of just how much you deceive others on a daily basis. Again, as you identify each instance, ask yourself, "Why did I lie? What was I trying to accomplish? Was the potential damage to my character and reputation worth it?"

You may not be able to do much about these white lies at this point. But what you *can* do, once you recognize this pattern of dishonesty in your everyday correspondence, is resolve to be more truthful in the future.

Offer an apology. If, upon reflection, you identify a recent instance in which you lied to an individual or group of people, go to that individual or group and come clean. Confess your lie, without making excuses for your behavior; then tell the truth and commit to being more truthful in the future.

Have no illusions: this experience will likely be very painful, and it may hurt your reputation in the short term. That is one reason apologies are effective deterrents to bad behavior: they are so embarrassing and difficult to make that most people would rather just do the right thing than have to offer one.

Besides motivating you to tell the truth next time, an apology will go a long way toward repairing the damage caused by your dishonesty—whether you or the other person even realize that damage occurred. You may initially have to deal with some loss of trust, but the fact that you apologized will work in your favor. If you resolve to be more truthful in the future, over time that trust can be rebuilt.

You can hardly hope to develop the virtue of honesty while you still have major, unresolved issues with dishonesty hanging over your head. Remember the old religious maxim: "Confession is good for the soul."

Embrace inclusion. As we discussed earlier in this chapter, one of the best ways to increase transparency and build trust within your organization is to become more inclusive in your decision-making.

If you do not have them already, consider forming advisory groups made up of various constituencies within your organization. For example, if your organization is large, you may have a group made up of salespeople, another consisting of clerical workers, and one for mid-level managers. If your organization is small, you could have one advisory committee made up of representatives from each group. (You may want to allow staff members to elect their own representatives, rather than appointing those people yourself, to avoid the appearance of favoritism or cronyism.) Then, schedule regular meetings with those groups to discuss various policy issues, decisions, and so forth. You can use these meetings to put forward your agenda and try to get some buy-in, but you also should (as we discussed in Chapter 4) spend a great deal of time listening to the groups' ideas and suggestions.

Write a personal "mission statement." Begin by making a list of your core values as the things you believe in most deeply. Then use that list to construct a personal mission statement: a brief document that outlines the things you value most and describes your purpose in life based on those values. There is no single way to develop a mission statement, but consider completing this sentence: "My mission in life is ____." This statement is not something you need to publish or hang up for others to see although you may do so if you wish. (If you do, be prepared to strictly live up to it, every minute of every day.) But you *do* need to put this statement in writing, and make sure to place it where you will see it frequently—in the front of your planner, for instance, or taped to the inside of your top desk drawer. This will force you to review it constantly, assessing the extent to which you behave as the person you claim to be or at least aspire to be.

Review your promise-keeping performance. Make a written list of all the promises you have made to people, or at least all the ones you can remember, and when you made them. Does it comply with the test of external consistency? Include on this list both professional and personal promises. Then, to the side of each, note whether or not you have kept that promise. If the answer is no, indicate the reason. Perhaps you forgot or got distracted. Perhaps you just have not gotten to it yet. (How long has it been?) Or maybe you overpromised to begin with, as so often happens.

Next, over the next few weeks or months, take each broken or unfulfilled promise in turn, and do what you have to do in order to keep it. Keeping the promise may require—probably *will* require—a great deal of effort on your part and perhaps no small degree of embarrassment. Some people may even think you are a little crazy. But that is okay. You are not necessarily keeping the promise for their sake; you are doing it for *your* sake, because as long as a promise remains broken or unfulfilled, you cannot claim to have embraced the virtue of honesty.

If you cannot fulfill a promise yet but intend to do so, communicate to the person or people involved that you have not forgotten your promise and that you still intend to keep it. Include, as appropriate, an explanation of the reasons you have not kept it yet. You can avoid excuse-making simply by being honest and not trying to present yourself in an undeservedly positive light. If the problem is you—you just have not yet done what you said you were going to do—then say so. And if you find that fulfilling a particular promise is simply impossible, then you must go to the person or people to whom that promise was made, explain to them why you cannot keep your promise, apologize, and commit to doing your best to keep future promises. Doing so may well entail not overpromising in the first place.

We have defined honesty through the lenses of truthfulness, transparency, integrity, and honor. As you consider practicing honesty, look at yourself through these lenses to see where you need to grow as a leader. Practice honesty not only in relation to others, but also in your self-assessment.

7. Courage

COURAGE TAKES MANY FORMS. THERE IS THE KIND OF COURAGE THAT compels a soldier to jump off the back of an amphibious vehicle into the teeth of enemy machine gun fire; and then there is the kind of courage needed just to roll out of bed some days. Most of us assume that the former is far nobler than the latter. And yet, as even battle-hardened veterans can attest, sometimes nothing requires greater courage than getting up in the morning and facing the day ahead.

In this chapter, we want to talk about the different types of courage the virtuous leader must have, along with some of the leadership situations that require courage. We also will present examples, both from history and from our own experience. Our purpose is not merely to inspire you with profiles in courage. Rather, we want to help you understand what courage is, what it is not, how it is acquired, and how you can practice it on a daily basis. We recognize that you, just like the two of us, probably do not feel particularly courageous much of the time. No doubt you have wondered how you would respond if you were next in line to jump off the back of that amphibious vehicle. We all have.

Just remember: courage, like all the other virtues in this book, is not something some people naturally have while others never will. Like the other virtues, courage is a habit that can be practiced and acquired over time. You begin to develop courage when you acknowledge you may not be especially brave but make a conscious decision to behave courageously nevertheless. Remember our earlier quote from William James: "If you want a trait, act as if you already have the trait." What, after all, is the practical difference between *being* brave and *act-*

ing bravely? You do the same thing in either case. And in the long run, if you continue to behave courageously—especially when you do not want to—you will develop the virtue of courage.

Courage does not mean you are not afraid; it means you do what you believe is right and necessary *despite* being afraid. As Nelson Mandela put it, "Courage is not the absence of fear but the triumph over it." In a very real sense, without fear there can be no courage. The soldier who has passed the point of caring whether he lives or dies does not exhibit courage in stepping onto the battlefield. The study in courage is the recruit so afraid that she wants to run away—but does not.

Paradoxically perhaps, courage cannot exist without fear. But what does the average organizational leader have to fear? Not death, surely. (Unless your organization is a much less pleasant place to work than ours.) But there are plenty of other things to fear besides death: looking incompetent in front of your supervisor or coworkers or (worst of all) clients; being shunned by colleagues for violating organizational culture; making a big mistake that costs your client or organization a lot of money; losing a coveted promotion, raise, or bonus; getting demoted, laid off, or fired. Those are all realistic fears in that they happen to people on a regular basis, and there is some likelihood they could happen to you. Knowing your own vulnerabilities is what requires courage on your part: the courage to do what you know needs to be done even though it might lead to one of those consequences. So how do people find the courage they need?

Models of Courage

By models, we do not mean examples of courage, although we will be citing several of those. For our purposes here, the term refers to models in the rational sense: ways of thinking about and examining courage analytically.

One way of looking at courage is to suggest that there are four types: personal, physical, political, and societal. Personal courage has to do with threats to the individual's self-esteem, as opposed to his or her physical body: that person's reputation, happiness, mental well-being, and so on. Physical courage involves facing up to bodily injury and perhaps even death. Political courage is required when an individual faces the potential loss of position, influence, career, or ambitions. (Note that it is not just politicians who need political courage. Politics is present in every organization and thus something we all have to deal with.) What we call societal courage involves standing up for others and for the greater good despite opposition.

We can also look at courage as a three-level hierarchy, with standing up for yourself at the bottom, standing up for others above that, and standing up for principle at the top:

STANDING UP FOR PRINCIPLE

STANDING UP FOR OTHERS

STANDING UP FOR SELF

Although we placed standing up for yourself at the bottom of this scheme, there is nothing wrong with doing that when the situation warrants. If you are being attacked despite being in the right, you are justified in standing up for yourself—as long as you exercise proper restraint and humility, as discussed in Chapter 5. Sadly, in too many cases, nobody else is going to stand up for you. You have to do it yourself, and that requires courage. Sometimes it is easier to simply accept an injustice because the prospect and potential consequences of fighting back seem worse than the original attacks. But good leaders, if they want to retain their moral authority, cannot allow injustice to stand.

One of the virtuous leader's primary obligations is to stand up for those whom he or she leads. It may be true that all too often no one will stand up for you; but as a leader, you cannot afford to perpetuate that destructive cycle. You have to be the one who stands up for others when they are in the right or being treated unjustly, even if doing so means great cost to yourself and your career. If there is one consistently detestable quality in leaders, it is a readiness to throw others under the bus—as the alarmingly evocative metaphor puts it—in order to save their own skins or make themselves look better. Frederick Douglass, the former slave who became the conscience of the nation in the years following the Civil War, put it this way in speaking of an overseer he once had: "[He] acted fully up to the maxim laid down by slaveholders: 'It is better that a dozen slaves suffer under the lash than that the overseer should be convicted, in the presence of the slaves, of having been at fault.'"

The days of legalized slavery in this country are thankfully far behind us, but sadly the mentality Douglass described is alive and well. There are still those leaders among us—many of us work with them every day—whose sole objective in life is to advance their own careers and make themselves look good, regardless of the cost to others. That attitude is not only unjust, it also is cowardly.

Courage means just the opposite. Courageous leaders use whatever power or authority they have to protect those who have less power, even if it costs them personally. A dean for whom Rob once worked came to his defense when he was accused unjustly of failing in his responsibilities and then quickly came under fire herself. The fact that she had documented Rob's accomplishments, and that her own were prodigious, certainly helped, and the situation was resolved; but what impressed Rob most was her willingness to put her own neck on the line for him. She did so solely because she was convinced he was in the right. What a wonderful example of courageous leadership.

Please note that we are advocating support of people when they clearly are in the right or at least when you believe they are. We do not advocate blind loyalty nor covering for people who have been caught in misdeeds. There is no quicker way to lose the trust of the people you lead than by being perceived as supporting those who are clearly in the wrong. Unfortunately, there often is no such thing as clearly right or clearly wrong. Making that determination will require your best judgment, as well as probably a certain amount of communication with constituents and colleagues so they understand what you are doing and why. Nothing can build trust like being perceived as having other people's backs.

The greatest expression of courage, however, lies in standing up not for people but for principle—for what we believe is right. Defending others and even yourself may at times be a matter of principle; what we are addressing in this case, though, is holding fast to deep-seated beliefs, regardless of how your stance affects you and others. History is replete with examples of people such as this, although many of them are controversial: whether you consider them heroes or villains may depend on whether you share their beliefs. Farm worker advocate César Chávez and President Ronald Reagan probably both fall into this category. Perhaps one example we all can agree on, however, is one with which we are all familiar because of an iconic photograph: the lone Chinese man facing down a column of tanks in Tiananmen Square in 1989. He was standing up for himself, but not just for himself; he was standing up for all oppressed Chinese, but not just for them, either. Ultimately, he was standing for the principles of freedom and democracy, and the courage it took for him to do so is almost unimaginable for those of us who take those ideals for granted.

Finally, we can look at courage by placing it on a continuum. It certainly takes courage to charge a machine gun nest or face down a line of tanks, but it also takes courage to be a good parent or a good boss. And even though those last two examples may be at the opposite end of the spectrum from the first two, they are honorable and difficult in their own way. We all face situations daily that require us to take a deep breath, square our shoulders, and keep moving forward, even though we may prefer to stop where we are or even turn back. The virtuous leader is the person who continues putting one foot in front of the other, in spite of adversity—and in doing so sets an example for others.

Courage to Do What Is Right

A type of courage the virtuous leader must display is the courage to do what is right, regardless of circumstances. Too often leaders reduce right and wrong to mere political calculations, based on convenience or what most benefits them. Henry David Thoreau addressed this issue a century and a half ago, in his marvelous essay "Resistance to Civil Government." He was responding to William Paley, an influential philosopher, who had defined matters of morality in terms of expediency:

> *So long as the interest of the whole society requires it, that is, so long as the established government cannot be resisted or changed without public inconveniency, it is the will of God that the established government be obeyed, and no longer.... This principle being admitted, the justice of every particular case of resistance is reduced to a computation of the quantity of the danger and the grievance on the one side, and the probability and expense of redressing it on the other.*

Not so, said Thoreau, who offered his own perspective: "If I have unjustly wrested a plank from a drowning man, I must restore it to him though I drown myself. This, according to Paley, would be inconvenient." Thoreau then went on to apply that same moral logic to the key political issues of his day: "This nation must cease to hold slaves, and to make war on Mexico, though it cost them their existence as a people."

Some may disagree with Thoreau's conclusions—especially as they apply to the political issues of our time—but we cannot help but recognize the moral authority inherent in his argument. Although he was not a CEO or a college president, we believe there are lessons in his words for organizational leaders everywhere. What is your organization doing, or what are you doing personally, that gives you a little bit of moral discomfort—that you believe, in your heart of hearts, may be unjust? According to Paley, you should weigh the severity of that injustice against the "inconvenience" of addressing it. If you speak out or refuse to go along, you could get smacked down, be demoted, or even lose your job, and that certainly would be inconvenient. But as Thoreau argues, once you understand what is right, you must do it at any cost.

Let us look at a hypothetical situation: over time, you notice your organization has a distinctly "old boy" flavor, that almost all the people in positions of responsibility are men, and that nearly every time there is an opening for a promotion, a man gets the job, even though there are a number of well-qualified women. You become increasingly uncomfortable with this situation, as it violates one of your core beliefs and your sense of right and wrong. What do you do?

By the way, this strikes us as the perfect hypothetical for everyone to consider, because the dilemma is the same whether you are a man or a woman. Any man in a leadership position in that organization has benefitted from its unwritten policy of sexual discrimination. However well-qualified he may be and however well he has performed, there can be no doubt one of his chief qualifications was being male. As for the few women who have somehow been promoted despite the systemic sexism, why would they want to make waves? They got theirs, and to speak out now would be to risk losing everything.

If we reduce this moral dilemma to some sort of Paleyan calculation, the answer may be that you should not speak out. The inconvenience of losing your job might outweigh the perceived injustice of others' lacking an equal opportunity to hold the same job. But if you accept Thoreau's moral absolutism, you *must* speak out, regardless of the potential consequences to yourself.

Obviously, that would take courage—perhaps a great deal of courage, depending on your circumstances. Your fears are well founded: you could lose your position, your job, your livelihood. That would frighten anybody, particularly any responsible adult with bills to pay and a family to support. Remember our definition from the beginning of this chapter: having courage means acting as you believe you must act, despite your legitimate fears.

We wish we could say that, if you show courage in a situation like this, nothing bad will actually happen. Unfortunately, that is not true; if it *were* true, then it would not require courage. Sometimes really bad things do happen to people who demonstrate great courage. Just ask Joan of Arc.

Even so, we see at least two positive consequences that could result from a decision to stand on principle. The first is that you will become a better and more effective leader—if not for your current organization, then for another. People will recognize you and look up to you as a person of integrity, and as we noted in Chapter 6, few things in professional life are more valuable than such a reputation. People also will trust you and want to follow you because they perceive you are more interested in doing the right thing than in advancing your career. Conversely, by consistently refusing to speak out against what you know to be an injustice, you will, over time, become the kind of mealy-mouthed, wishy-washy leader that nobody (including you) really trusts—and certainly does not trust enough to follow.

The other potentially positive outcome is that, if your decision to speak out has any impact—if the people above you in the organization actually listen—then the organization itself will be stronger and better. What they were doing, in our hypothetical situation, was not only wrong it was also stupid (to put it plainly). No doubt some of the organization's best leaders would be women, and the fact that they were not being given the opportunity to put their abilities to good use meant that the organization itself was not operating at its fullest potential. Or think of the matter another way: if you do not speak out, and no one else does either, how long before the organization falters because it is not using its human capital wisely?

To be successful in the long run, an organization must have leaders who are willing to stand on principle, just as individuals must do if they are to succeed as leaders. Of course, standing up for what is right entails actually knowing what is right, and that requires both a great deal of humility (as we discussed in Chapter 5) and a great deal of wisdom (which we will get to in Chapter 12). But once you understand what is right, as a virtuous leader you must have the courage to embrace it and advocate for it, regardless of the consequences.

Courage to Take Risks

Another type of courage that virtuous leaders must have is the courage to take risks—on ideas, on others, and sometimes on themselves. Although some people are less risk-averse than others, we are the product of thousands of years of human evolution that has taught us to place personal safety above all other considerations. Obviously, there was a time when this sort of survival mentality was necessary to the perpetuation of the species, and it became a dominant trait because those who took fewer risks were more likely to live long enough to reproduce.

Now, in the 21st century, most of us have the good fortune to not have to be as concerned about physical survival—the possibility of being eaten by wild animals or dying from exposure. But there are lesser types of survival as well as other types of risk that we face each day: risks to our careers, to our livelihoods, to our family's future. Just like our long-ago ancestors, most of us are inclined to play it safe, both personally and professionally.

There are still plenty of times when safety is a wise course of action. We are certainly not advocating recklessness, either in personal behavior or in professional decision-making. Moreover, not all risks are worth taking; in fact, most probably are not. The leader who takes too many risks eventually ends up with loss and failure. It also is true that those who thrive on risk, who find it exhilarating, are not really displaying courage.

But leaders who refuse to take risks, who always play it safe, cannot be successful in the long run. The environments in which we operate are constantly changing, and organizations often have to change accordingly or risk obsolescence. Playing it safe is sometimes the greatest risk of all. Yet embracing new ideas also incurs risk and therefore requires courage because we cannot always know which changes are for the better and which are for the worse or what those changes will mean for us or our organizations in the future. As leaders, we must be lifelong learners (see Chapter 3), constantly gathering new information to inform our decisions; we have to be teachable and open to advice from the best minds both inside and outside our organizations; and we have to cultivate wisdom in order to know what changes are good and necessary. Even so, there always will be risks.

We incur risk, too, when we put our trust in others. The simplest example of this for organizational leaders involves hiring. Because you count on the people who work for you to perform certain necessary functions and to hold up their end professionally and because their performance will reflect on you, you take a calculated risk every time you bring a new employee on board. Obviously, hiring is necessary for an organization to grow and prosper, yet one bad hire could have the opposite effect, setting the organization back for years or even bringing it tumbling down.

Assuming that sort of debacle happens rarely, a better example may involve what we sometimes refer to as "letting go." Although nobody likes leaders who constantly pass the buck, refusing to take on their fair share of the work or accept their share of the responsibility, we tend to be even less enamored of leaders who have the attitude "if you want something done right, you have to do it yourself," and those micromanagers may in the long run be more detrimental to an organization. No doubt we do this as leaders because we do not trust people to do the job as well as we would, either because they genuinely do not deserve our trust—in which case, there is a problem with the recruiting process—or because we have not learned to delegate and let go. Either way, trusting others to do their jobs and do them well can involve tremendous risk and thus requires a great deal of courage.

And yet we have to trust others. No organization of any size can survive with just one person doing the work. No one person can do that much and do it well. Moreover, when we refuse to let others do their jobs, we not only are hurting ourselves; we are hurting those people, who will suffer from not being allowed to grow. They also, no doubt, will sense our lack of trust and, if they are motivated, look to go someplace where they will be trusted and valued—which means we are hurting the organization, too. Turning over tasks to others that we would prefer to do ourselves may be risky; but to be effective, leaders must have the courage to do so.

Finally, leaders must have the courage to take chances on themselves. As human beings, we are beset occasionally by self-doubt and feelings of inadequacy. Sometimes, taking on a new role or a new project feels a little like stepping out onto a high wire, without a net or even a balancing pole. We can tell you from experience that writing this book felt exactly that way for the two of us. All we had was a basic belief in the ideas we wanted to get across and our ability to communicate them. It was a risk taking on a project like this because our reputations were at stake. At the very least, we could spend the years required for this project and end up with something that did not accomplish what we intended: to help leaders grow and develop the Nine Virtues. That precious commodity of time would therefore have been wasted.

Ultimately, we decided writing the book was worth the risk and that our fundamental belief in ourselves warranted stepping out onto the tight rope. We also realized that, if we did not take the risk now, we might never do it. To us, the risk of looking back on our lives, wishing we had taken the time to write this book, was far greater in the long run than any short-term discomfort we experienced from actually writing it.

Virtuous leaders, both in their personal lives and in their roles as leaders, must make these kinds of decisions all the time. You have to decide whether to take that new job, accept that assignment, go forward with that proposal, embark on the reorganization. Risks are always involved, to be sure, and sometimes great risk. Just remember that sometimes playing it safe is the greatest risk of all—and the greatest source of regret.

Courage to Buck Trends

Speaking of taking risks, we often hear people talk today about "thinking outside the box." In an attempt to escape this hackneyed phrase, leaders like to toss around terms like "innovation" and "creativity" as if the words themselves have magical properties and simply spouting them will make average organizations appear excellent and unique. But mostly what leaders mean by "being innovative" is incremental, safe, and highly predictable change. The fact is, in professional life, original thinkers are about as rare as teetotalers at a beer festival.

Why is that? Because everyone is afraid, not just of failing, but of looking irresponsible or incompetent in the process. They are afraid that if they deviate from the same tried and true methods that everyone else is using and things go wrong, then that failure will be blamed on their unorthodoxy—which is to say, on them personally. Conversely, they reason that if they do what everyone else is doing, they are likely to get the same results as everyone else or at least not too different. In other words, they might fail, but they will fail small and in a way that people are unlikely to notice. And of course they can always express befuddlement at their failure because, after all, they did things in the accepted way.

In every industry and organization, there are tried and true methods of doing various things—"best practices" we sometimes call them. People may have been using those methods for years, if not decades, because they work. Leaders are wise to be familiar with those methods or, if they are new to an organization or industry, to become familiar with them. Making changes simply for the sake of making changes, or just to show that you can, is never a good strategy.

But much of what we consider tried and true is really just tradition. People tend to do something a certain way because "it's always been done that way" and not for any other logical reason. Perhaps those methods produce acceptable results, but that is not to say other methods would not produce even better results if people but had the foresight and the courage to experiment.

Rob's wife, a middle school teacher, has often experienced this traditionalist mind-set first-hand. As a new teacher at one school, for example, she was confused by the mid-day schedule. Students had a long period interrupted by lunch and, to top things off, had to change classrooms after lunch. Nothing could be done about the lunch schedule without interfering with other classes and other grades, but she did suggest to her colleagues that students stay in the same classroom so they would not have to carry their book bags with them to lunch. At first her suggestion was met with resistance because the other teachers had always done it that way. But when they looked her idea objectively, they saw it could be achieved with just a few minor adjustments to the schedule and that the advantages outweighed any minor inconvenience—so they made the change.

The trick for leaders is knowing which practices need to be changed and which should be kept. That requires a certain amount of wisdom, but a little humility also helps. Listen to the people who have been there for a while, get a variety of opinions, then think the situation through and decide. And always be prepared, if you make a change that turns out to be problematic, to go back to the old way.

Perhaps even more stifling than tradition are the new leadership and management fads that seem to crop up on a regular basis. People may not have been doing something for years, but suddenly everyone in the industry is doing it *this* way and, if you do not do it *this* way, then you are not current. You are outdated, a curmudgeon, and the times have passed you by. You are behind the times even if the way you have been doing things has produced excellent results and even if you are trying new and innovative things that do not happen to follow the popular zeitgeist.

Nowhere is this type of thinking more apparent perhaps than in higher education's rush to offer as many online classes as possible to as many students as possible. Many failed to consider that not all subjects can be taught well in an online format and that not all students perform well in the virtual classroom. What are the implications of lower completion rates in online classes compared to traditional, face-to-face classes? What do employers prefer? Too many institutions failed to answer these questions and moved forward to follow others in a rush to provide online courses.

Bucking this sort of trend and making wise choices about change and innovation requires courage. If you do not go along with the crowd, you risk failing and looking bad. Courage is certainly required to change things that need changing, but also *not* to make changes you believe could be harmful just because everyone else is making them. Above all, courage is necessary to follow your own vision or the shared vision of your organization, regardless of yesterday's traditions or today's fads.

Courage to Lead

Many people say they would like to be in a leadership position; but what they really mean is that they find the idea of being a leader attractive. They envy the adulation leaders often receive, along with the subservience of others. They crave the personal recognition and credit. They want to be able to tell people what to do instead of always being on the receiving end. They covet the perks that often go along with leadership: the salary increase, the corner office, the company car, the seat at the table of power.

Of course, those of us who have been in leadership positions, and especially high-profile positions, understand that leadership is not always what it appears. Along with the recognition comes responsibility and, in many cases, blame. Even if you are in a position to tell people what to do—and many leaders, especially in academia, often are not—obedience is spotty and subservience rare, except perhaps from a handful of annoying sycophants. Even the perks, when they exist, are not necessarily worth the hassle. Much of the time, in many organizations, leadership merely involves extra work for not much more pay and added responsibility with very little additional authority.

So why would anybody want to be a leader?

Let us answer that question by first acknowledging that those who seek leadership positions for the superficial reasons noted above usually do not make the best leaders. That is not to say there is anything inappropriate about wanting to be recognized for your accomplishments or that it is wrong to wish you made more money. Those are natural desires, and to the extent they motivate us to work hard and do a good job, they can certainly be beneficial. But if those are your primary reasons for getting into management or administration, then you are probably doing it for the wrong reasons.

In our experience, the best leaders are often those who are somewhat reluctant to take on the role. Such individuals tend not to be self-aggrandizing, focusing on the best interests of the organization as a whole rather than on their narrow self-interests. They pursue leadership assignments or accept them when offered because they believe they have skills and abilities that can help the organization and they feel an obligation to use those abilities for the greater good—even if they do not really want to.

That sense of duty is one reason we say that leading requires courage. Remember our definition of courage at the beginning of this chapter: it involves doing something that challenges you, maybe something that you do not really want to do, something that may well have negative personal consequences. To people who are not single-mindedly pursuing their careers to the exclusion of everything and everyone else, the idea of taking on a leadership role is sometimes a scary thought.

You may gain some of the advantages, such as a higher salary and various perks, but you also stand to lose a great deal: time with family, personal time, a degree of anonymity, your relatively stress-free life. If the things you risk losing are more important to you than what you will gain as a leader, then you should reconsider your ambition to lead.

Being in a leadership role also makes you extremely vulnerable, professionally speaking, which is another reason we say that leadership requires courage. As a rank-and-file employee, you are responsible for yourself and your one work area; but as a manager or positional leader, you are responsible not only for a much broader area but also for a number of other people. When things go wrong, you doubtless will be held responsible to some degree, whether or not you actually had much control over the outcome. If the error is bad enough, you even could lose your job. That is the risk people in leadership positions take.

Despite what you may have heard in recent years about the concept of leading from behind, true leadership involves being out front. The obvious analogy here again involves the military. While the very top leaders, the key generals, are too important to lose in battle and thus stay to the rear, the vast majority of mid-level leaders—lieutenants and captains—find themselves right in the thick of the fighting. Invariably, those who prove to be the best leaders, who inspire the most confidence from those they lead and therefore who are most likely to be followed, are the ones who willingly place themselves in harm's way before asking their soldiers to do the same. Obviously, that kind of "out-front" leadership requires tremendous courage.

Fortunately, for most of us as organizational leaders, the term "enemy fire" is just an analogy. But the shots we take are real in their own way and definitely can be fatal to our careers. One of the defining characteristics of virtuous leaders is that they accept their role, even if they would personally prefer just to be one of the gang. They do what needs to be done in order to help move the organization forward, for the good of all, even if it means losing friends, putting personal priorities on hold, or risking their careers.

Courage to Get Results

Taking the lead is one thing; actually achieving the desired objective is something else altogether. The first obviously requires courage, but the second may require even *more* courage or at least a different kind of courage. It also requires wisdom and perseverance—virtues we will discuss in later chapters—because there are so many different ways to get results and none of them involves quitting or giving up.

Think again of the military unit commander, those young lieutenants in charge of their first platoon. They need a great deal of courage to lead their soldiers into battle, especially if they are leading from in front as they should. But seeing their mission through and achieving its objective—taking the hill, holding the high ground—requires something more. One of many truisms about courage is this: if at any point you cease behaving courageously, whatever courage you may have shown up to that point becomes mostly moot.

One way leaders get results is by inspiring the people they lead. Sometimes merely demonstrating courage provides inspiration enough. The leader who takes up the standard and wades into the fray may well inspire others to follow: because of the leader's example; because others, seeing that leader, are reminded of *their* duty; because they are ashamed to hang back while another moves forward; or because of some combination of all those complicated motives. Setting this type of example usually is what we mean when we talk about inspiration, and there is no doubt it is a real and powerful force.

But sometimes leaders have to work a little harder at inspiring. Most of us who have been in leadership positions for any length of time have had the experience of taking up the standard, wading into the fray—and looking back to see no one following. At that point, we have to ask ourselves why: Is the objective not clear? Is it simply not compelling enough to motivate people to action? If the answer to either of those questions is no, then the next question must be "why not?" Have we failed to communicate the importance or perhaps the urgency of the situation? Or is the objective itself flawed, perhaps in some way the followers can see and we cannot? After all, you might be about to carry that standard right off a cliff, and everybody knows it but you. Seeing the situation clearly requires not only wisdom but a certain amount of humility. No one will follow a leader for long, even one who shows great personal courage, if that courage is spent in pursuit of suspect or unattainable goals.

Rob once worked for a college president who wished to expand the mission of the college. He demonstrated personal courage and perseverance in pursuing that objective because doing so meant openly opposing his bosses, the system leaders, who did not agree that the college's mission needed to expand. Unfortunately for that president, he failed to get strong buy-in from faculty and lower-level administrators, most of whom were also satisfied with the institution's current niche and were suspicious of the president's motives. While some of them may have admired his guts for going out on a limb, they also thought he was a little crazy, or at least misguided. They were not inspired to go out on the limb beside him because the objective did not seem worthwhile to them.

Assuming, though, the objective is worthwhile and enough stakeholders agree, the leader's job is to inspire people to go out on that limb. If example is not enough, then the leader must resort to persuasion—cajoling, appealing to followers' better natures, and, if nothing else, their own self-interest. A good analogy could be to a coach in the locker room, with the team down at halftime. All in the room agree the objective is to win the game, and none would dispute that is a worthwhile objective. But, assuming the players have the talent to win if they just put forth a little extra effort, how does the coach inspire them to make that commitment? There is no right answer to that question, but some strategies good coaches employ include painting the objective in the best possible light, appealing to the players' pride, and pointing out the consequences of failure. Obviously, the coaches who do this best are the most successful and go on to become legends, such as John Wooden.

We should note that the potential strategies for motivating follow-ers should *not* include threats. First of all, threats, while they at times can be motivational, hardly qualify as inspirational. Moreover, we have found that threats are rarely effective in the long run; sometimes, they even have the opposite effect of what was intended. Simply put, smart, talented, independent-minded people—the kind of people you most want in your organization—generally do not respond well to threats. If subjected to that sort of abuse for any length of time, they are likely to rebel and either leave or rise up against a leader they perceive as overbearing.

In addition to inspiring, another way leaders accomplish their ob-jectives is to correct. This method also requires a great deal of courage, and for some personality types, it may require more courage than al-most any other aspect of leadership. Even those who willingly charge into battle may find their courage wavers when confronting a colleague about his or her failure. Often the best leaders are those who have a stubbornly positive outlook regarding both the situation and the peo-ple around them. They do not like to dwell on the negative, and they do not like being perceived as authoritarian. Yet there are times when, as a leader, you simply have to gird your loins and make corrections as necessary, regardless of what people think of you.

Keep in mind two things about correcting people. The first is that correction is not necessarily a negative, confrontational experience. Good leaders are able to point out people's deficiencies and suggest remedies in ways that are non-threatening and lead, in the long run, to improvement and appreciation from the one receiving correction. Think of the way an exceptional professor deals with a graduate stu-dent's work. The point of correcting is not to embarrass or to belittle but to help that person succeed, while at the same time enabling the entire educational enterprise to achieve its goals.

The other principle to remember is that correction is an absolutely indispensable part of leadership. If, as a leader, you are not constantly making minor corrections as necessary—or major ones when called for—then the entire organization can veer quickly off course, with disastrous results for all, from the one who needed correction but did not receive it to those who saw correction was needed and were waiting for you to make it. Everyone goes down with the ship, all because you did not have the courage to address poor performance when you needed to.

The key to correcting in a constructive way is the virtue we covered in Chapter 5: humility. Too often leaders who are not humble may correct others to show their own superiority or to establish their authority, to "put people in their place." Any followers worth their salt will not tolerate that sort of behavior indefinitely. Humble leaders, on the other hand, correct people for their own benefit as well as for the benefit of the unit or organization, and they do so in ways that are as nonthreatening and nonjudgmental as possible. People generally respond well to correction when they perceive the leader is truly humble and has their best interests at heart.

Besides, humility may be important for another reason: because *you* are the one who needs correcting. All things being equal, leaders are just as likely as anyone else to make mistakes, as any truly humble leader will quickly acknowledge; but they may not have someone looking over their shoulder all the time. True, even leaders usually have bosses, but often those who have risen to positions of authority have a great deal of autonomy. That autonomy is why it is incumbent on them—on you, if you find yourself in that situation—to self-correct as necessary. Self-correction requires humility because it entails recognizing you may be the real problem. It requires courage because all leaders fear admitting failure and looking bad in front of those they lead. (Recall the earlier quote from Frederick Douglass.)

The truth is that people tend to respect leaders who have the insight, the humility, and the courage to admit when they are wrong and make changes in their own behavior for the good of all. They will accept correction more quickly from leaders who do not spare themselves the rod, so to speak. And they are more likely to be inspired when they see the objective as a common goal for which all—both leaders and followers—share responsibility.

A Final Note on Courage

One of the themes of this book is that the Nine Virtues work together in concert; in order to become virtuous, a leader must work throughout his or her lifetime to acquire and display all of them. Someone who has personal courage but is not humble or charitable, for example, cannot rightly be called a virtuous person.

Consider the 9/11 hijackers. There is no question what they did—intentionally flying airplanes into buildings, willingly giving up their lives for a cause—required a trait that looks like courage. Some might argue they were such fanatics, and in the grip of religious fervor, they did not really experience any fear as those aircraft hurtled towards their targets. However, we would argue that the trait they exhibited was cowardice, not courage. Their actions against innocent and defenseless people constituted a terrible crime against humanity.

Brazenness, defiance, and zealotry are not virtuous habits, and they do not translate into courage, which can be defined only in relation to the other virtues. Courage, like the other virtues, must be understood in relation to others. Virtue is a state of character that promotes the well-being of others and self. Courage remains one of the most visible, the most readily apparent, of the Nine Virtues, and it is without question a quality almost everyone admires. You cannot be truly virtuous—or become an effective leader—without consistently displaying courage.

Practicing Courage

As with all of the other virtues, but perhaps more so than most, being courageous requires a constant act of will. You have to recognize your fears, confront them, decide to act in spite of them, and then actually act. Here are some suggestions for practicing those behaviors on a daily basis.

Take a stand. Make a list of some of the moral dilemmas currently facing your organization or ones you are facing personally. Then choose an item from that list, perhaps the one you believe is most significant or bothers you most. Chances are, you already know the right answer intuitively; but if not, do whatever you need to do to resolve the dilemma. Do some reading or research on the topic. Consult with others within or outside your organization who may have special knowledge or at least learned opinions. Then, spend some time in deep personal reflection until you have decided what constitutes the right move in that instance.

Once you have identified the right thing, do it, even if it puts your position or reputation or career at risk. If doing the right thing is not something you can accomplish on your own—if the decision will have to be made by a group, for instance, or at a level above yours—then seek out opportunities to advocate for that course of action. Speak out at a meeting. Write a memo to the CEO. Organize like-minded colleagues to mount a campaign. If you truly are humble, you can carry out these steps respectfully and in good faith. However, you must do everything in your power to persuade the organization to make the right decision once you recognize what that is.

Stand up for others. Identify an individual or group within your organization who is being treated unjustly. Determine what, in your opinion, would constitute fair treatment. Then do two things: first, take whatever actions you personally can take to rectify the situation. Second, advocate in whatever forums are appropriate for the necessary changes to take place.

For example, if you are a unit supervisor, you may decide that part-time employees are not paid fairly or treated as valued members of the business. The first thing you can do is begin treating them as colleagues and as equals, as much as it is within your power. Speak to them civilly. Seek out their input into decisions that impact them. Hold meetings at times when most of them can attend. Invite them to serve on teams. Advocate for better pay and working conditions for part-time employees. If you have the courage to take such steps, over time conditions for these employees may improve.

Take a risk. What steps does your organization need to take to achieve its goals? What steps do *you* need to take in order to achieve *your* personal goals? Chances are, the answer to either one of those questions involves risk, perhaps to a significant degree.

Again, spend some time in contemplation and consultation to determine the answers to these questions. Research what other organizations or individuals are doing and what seems to be working for them. Decide what you personally need to do and what you can do, even if it involves risk. Then resolve to carry out those actions, despite the risk, and not to be deterred.

Take the lead. Identify a worthwhile project or activity within your organization that is suffering from lack of leadership (not that the existing leadership is poor—that is another issue—but just that no one has stepped forward to take the lead). Then, resolve to step into that gap.

If the project already has a nominal leader, perhaps you could approach that person with an offer to assist. Unless that person is highly territorial—and sometimes people are, even with assignments they did not want in the first place—your offer probably will be welcomed. You may find yourself acting as *de facto* leader, if not in an official capacity, as the nominal but unenthusiastic leader allows you to take on more and more responsibility.

If there is no leader for that project or activity, then you can approach the person in charge and volunteer. We pretty much guarantee your offer will be accepted, probably with much relief.

There is one other possibility here: if you cannot think of a project that needs a leader, you always can create one. This project does not, by the way, necessarily have to be a professional project. It could be organizing a group to "Walk for the Cure" or perform a community service project. Whatever you do will require you to set aside your reservations, step up to the plate, and lead.

Make a course correction. Finally, identify a situation under your direct control, involving someone you lead, that requires a course correction. You probably are thinking of such a situation even as you read this; you know, that awkward confrontation you have been putting off for weeks or months. At the same time, you know that situation is hurting the organization. So act courageously and deal with it.

Just bear in mind: the exchange, as we noted above, does not have to be confrontational. Good leaders usually can correct in ways that genuinely help the individual or, at the very least, minimize resentment. A little humility on your part goes a long way. Even if the individual gets upset—if he or she causes a scene and the entire episode turns out to be just as bad as you imagined—that is why courage is required.

Remember: where there is no fear, there can be no courage—and no real leadership.

8. Perseverance

THE OPPOSITE OF A VIRTUE IS ITS CORRESPONDING VICE. FOR EXAMPLE, the opposite of humility is pride, and the opposite of honesty is dishonesty. Vice can sometimes also be found in the extreme. Take courage, for instance. Its opposite is cowardice, which is a vice, but so is its extreme, foolhardiness. Aristotle taught that virtue is a mean between two extremes; thus, courage is the mean between cowardice and foolhardiness.

Whether a character trait is a virtue or vice often depends upon context: how one acts, when one acts, and the degree to which the trait is expressed. Think of perseverance. We could say that those who stick stubbornly to a foolish or unjust ideal are persistent or dogged, but we would not consider them virtuous leaders any more than those who embrace the other extreme: indifference.

Abraham Lincoln is a great example of perseverance in a leader. After the Southern states seceded from the Union and throughout the entire Civil War, Lincoln refused to acknowledge there was any such entity as the Confederate States of America. He consistently referred to the South with terms such as "those states currently in rebellion against the United States." He even went so far as to refuse to meet with ambassadors from the Confederacy because, as he saw it, a nation that did not exist could not have ambassadors.

Obviously, Southerners did not appreciate his attitude. They, and many in the North, viewed Lincoln as a pig-headed old fool. But history has been good to him and his vision. From the perspective of time, we see how Lincoln's refusal to admit the country had ever split made it easier for him, in the end, to talk about "binding up the *nation's* wounds"—not just the North's wounds but the entire nation's. Sadly, that healing agenda was cut short by his assassination, and we all know about the decades of chaos that followed. We acknowledge Lincoln was right to be adamant about that particular ideal, and we admire his perseverance in the face of great hardship and opposition.

A modern example of this dynamic is found in the American Civil Rights Movement of the 1960s. Consider the case of James Meredith, the first African-American to be admitted to the University of Mississippi. In *The Battle of Ole Miss*, Frank Lambert details Meredith's determination and his struggles not only to be accepted to the University of Mississippi, but to complete his degree there despite great adversity. Although the U.S. Supreme Court had ruled in *Brown v. Board of Education of Topeka* in 1954 that state laws creating separate public schools for black and white students were unconstitutional, Meredith, in 1961, still had to file suit (which *also* eventually ended up in front of the Supreme Court) in order to be admitted to a state college. The state of Mississippi tried everything in its power to deny him admission, including turning him away at the door.

Meredith ultimately did enroll, but things did not get much better. Many white students went out of their way to make his life miserable, shunning him on campus and even dribbling basketballs at night in the dorm room above his. The fact that he graduated with a degree in political science and went on to an influential career in politics is a tribute to his indomitable spirit—in other words, his perseverance.

In this example, the vice of stubbornness is equally apparent in those opposing him. Think of all the trouble the state of Mississippi, and particularly its governor, Ross Barnett, went to trying to keep Meredith out of Ole Miss: fighting multiple, expensive legal battles, physically barring him entrance. No doubt that seemed to Barnett at the time the correct course of action, and in his own way he displayed just as much determination as Meredith; they were locked, it seems, in a proverbial battle of wills. Looking back, however, we see (and many saw at the time) that Barnett was on the wrong side of that issue; thus, his perseverance becomes not admirable but reprehensible—stubbornness that is not a virtue but a vice.

Perseverance, as much as any of the Nine Virtues we examine in this book, must be embraced with the other virtues. These include courage, because persevering often involves overcoming fear; humility, because the combination of stubbornness and pride can be as destructive as any force on earth; justice, because the highest manifestation of perseverance is in pursuit of the common good; and wisdom, because we have to understand which is the correct side of any issue. Otherwise, what in common parlance we may call perseverance really is a vice that corrupts one's character and harms others.

Determination

Many of you have probably heard of *The Help*, Kathryn Stockett's 2009 bestselling novel about African-American maids working in white households in Jackson, Mississippi, during the Civil Rights era. But did you know that Stockett's manuscript was rejected 60 times before it finally was picked up by an agent then sold to a publisher? We all have heard of famous novels that were turned down multiple times before finally being published—ranging from *Moby-Dick* to *Harry Potter and the Sorcerer's Stone*—but 60 rejections? Can you imagine asking people out on dates 60 times and being told no every time—and still asking a 61st time? Or striking out 60 straight times, then going back up to the plate for at-bat number 61, still hoping to hit a home run?

Most of us would give up after a few attempts. There can be little doubt that one of the qualities that most clearly distinguishes those who succeed spectacularly from those who fail—or at least fail to live up to their full potential—is simple determination. When *Inc.* magazine asked Sam Altman and Alok Deshpande, creators of the innovative mobile banking service GoBank, how they managed to break into such a crowded industry, they had a simple response: "We refused to take no for an answer."

Obviously, an attitude like that presupposes people are sometimes, and perhaps often, going to say no. In other words, it accepts the possibility of failure, which is why courage is such an important element of perseverance. Business guru Jim Collins, author of *Good to Great*, observed this dynamic while working with cadets at West Point. Noting that failure is such a daily occurrence in the rigorous physical and academic environment of the nation's premier military academy, Collins marveled at the way cadets nevertheless displayed such an overall positive attitude. Why was that, he wanted to know?

"Failure is part of life here," explained one cadet. Another added, "It's better to fail here and have others help you get it right than to fail in Afghanistan, where the consequences would be catastrophic." A third cadet expanded on that idea by saying, "Here, everybody knows it's a learning experience."

Those responses reminded Collins of a conversation he had a few years earlier with Tommy Caldwell, widely considered one of the greatest rock climbers of all time. At that point, Caldwell had attempted to free-climb El Capitan's Dawn Wall three times, each attempt ending in failure. As he prepared to try a fourth time, Collins asked him, "Why do you keep throwing yourself at this? All it does is give you failure upon failure." Caldwell replied, "Because success is not the primary point. I go back because the climb is making me better. It is making me stronger. I am not failing. I am growing."

Similarly, Stockett's persistence in getting her novel published is instructive not merely because she persevered but because of the way she handled her repeated failures and turned them to her advantage. In a first-person account she wrote for *More* magazine in 2011, she described her reaction to the very first rejection letter—after she had polished the manuscript and considered it finished: "Six weeks later, I received a rejection letter from the agent, stating, 'Story did not sustain my interest.' I was thrilled! I called my friends and told them I'd gotten my first rejection! Right away, I went back to editing. I was sure I could make the story tenser, more riveting, better."

Did you get that? She went *right back to editing*. Rather than give up or conclude that her novel would never be good enough to be published, she took that first failure as an opportunity to go back to work and make the story better—even though she was convinced that it was already pretty good. Just like rock climber Tommy Caldwell, failure did not make her quit; it made her stronger.

Of course, Stockett's story does not end there. She received 59 more rejections, often in batches of a dozen or more at a time. She admits there were days when she "sloth[ed] around that racetrack of self-pity—you know the one, from sofa to chair to bed to refrigerator, starting over again on the sofa." But, she says, "I just couldn't let go." Each time, she would pull herself out of depression, go back to work on the manuscript, making it better, tighter, and more readable, and then resubmit it. And lest we forget, the novel that we have today as *The Help*—the one that sold more than five million copies and was made into a blockbuster film—is not the original manuscript she submitted to that first literary agent. It is the final version, the product of all those changes. Without the 60 rejections, we would not have the book we have today; and no doubt that is a large part of what Caldwell meant when he talked about failure making us better.

Perseverance also contains an element of humility: true perseverance, that is, as opposed to obstinacy, which often is the product of pride. To demonstrate the determination of a Caldwell or a Stockett or those West Point cadets, we have to accept that we are not going to be perfect, or even at our best, the first time—and maybe not the second or the third or the sixtieth. Ultimately, to succeed in the face of failure, we have to be imminently teachable, able not only to embrace our failures but to learn from them, grow, and then move on. In that direction lies true success.

This is what virtuous leaders understand: as long as they are striving, as long as they are moving forward, failure is not an end but merely a means. As Michael Jordan once put it, "I've failed over and over and over again in my life, and that's why I succeed." Failure can be a great motivator, as well as one of the best teachers, as long as we do not give in to it.

The best leaders apply this philosophy not only to themselves but to those they lead. Countless studies have shown the most productive work environments are those in which employees feel empowered to fail as long as they are working constantly toward success. Fear of failure, or of the consequences of failure, causes people to play it safe, to avoid trying something new or innovative that might just revolutionize an industry—or it might not. But you will never know if you are afraid to try or if you are afraid to let your employees embrace the possibility of failure. As Thomas Edison said, "I have not failed. I've just found 10,000 ways that won't work."

Tenacity

In the introduction to this chapter, we noted that the flip side of perseverance is stubbornness. But that does not mean stubbornness is necessarily bad. In her article for *More*, Stockett offers the following insight into her personality: "If you ask my husband my best trait, he'll smile and say, 'She never gives up.' But if you ask him my worst trait, he'll get a funny tic in his cheek, narrow his eyes and hiss, 'She. Never. Gives. Up.'" Perseverance exists in a family of virtues: most notably, courage, humility, and wisdom. Leaders—and anyone else, for that matter—must have courage to believe in themselves and their ideas, even if no one else does. They also have to be teachable, to recognize that failures come for a reason. And finally, they have to be wise enough to know which hill to die on, so to speak: which ideas to hold onto, to go to the mat for, and which to let go. Letting go of a bad idea because you recognize it as a bad idea is another kind of determination: the kind to get it right and ultimately succeed.

At the same time, failure to go to the mat for a just cause can hardly be described as virtuous. Once you have determined an idea or principle is worth fighting for, then you have a moral obligation to fight for it, come what may. This willingness to fight can require a level of determination some would call tenacity.

History provides a wonderful example of this concept in the form of Leonidas and his 300 Spartan warriors. Most people are familiar with the story, not least because it was made into a big-budget Hollywood film. To briefly recap, Leonidas was King of Sparta, a city-state that was part of the Greek confederacy. When the Persian King Xerxes invaded Greece in 480 B.C.E., Leonidas was put in command of a relatively small force of about 14,000 men, including 300 Spartans, charged with holding back the invading force at a mountain pass near Thermopylae long enough for the Greek army to mount a more organized resistance. This they managed to do for several days, despite being outnumbered more than ten to one. (Legend says that Xerxes had two million men, but modern scholars believe that number is an exaggeration.)

On the seventh day, no doubt perceiving they were finally about to be overwhelmed, Leonidas ordered the bulk of his army to withdraw, while he and his 300 Spartans (along with 1,500 soldiers from other Greek city-states) remained behind to cover their retreat. Although some of the other remaining troops ultimately laid down their arms in the face of the advancing Persian hordes, Leonidas and his Spartans refused to surrender, fighting and dying to the last man. Many historians credit Leonidas with preserving the majority of his fighting men and buying time for the Greeks to regroup and ultimately drive out the invaders, which they did at the Battle of Plataea the following year.

The question is: what can we learn about perseverance from Leonidas? Taken at face value, he hardly can be said to have persevered, in the traditional sense of overcoming obstacles and eventually coming out on top. His greatest obstacle was the Persian army, which he did not in fact overcome. Nor did he come out on top. He died, and all of his men with him. Technically, they were defeated.

There is a question as to whether Leonidas actually expected to be defeated. He was a warrior, after all, from a warrior society, so he may have been confident enough in Spartan prowess to believe he and his little band could defeat the entire Persian army. But that seems doubtful. Whatever he may have thought going in, as the battle progressed, the impossibility of their winning must have become obvious, as evidenced by his sending away the bulk of his army. Yet he remained behind with his tiny force, surely knowing they faced certain defeat. Was that perseverance? Determination? Or sheer tenacity? Was it courage or just stupidity?

The answer probably is all of the above. But there are two salient points here, as far as leadership is concerned. The first is that Leonidas chose to do what he did because he believed deeply in the cause. As King of Sparta, he had agreed to join with other Greek forces and fight against invaders—and he was committed to keeping his word and following through, regardless of the cost. The pass at Thermopylae was, to him, a hill worth dying on. It is easy for us, as armchair generals, to second-guess that decision, to conclude that Leonidas and his men died in vain, or that they should have lived to fight another day. But in their minds, at least, they were merely doing what had to be done.

Shifting from history to fiction, there is a marvelous passage in J.R.R. Tolkien's epic fantasy trilogy, *The Lord of the Rings*, that illustrates this point perfectly. After the hobbit Frodo Baggins discovers he is to play a critical role in the battle against growing evil, he initially shrinks from the task. He says to the wizard Gandalf, his friend and advisor, "I wish it need not have happened in my time." And Gandalf replies, "So do I. And so do all who live to see such times. But that is not for them to decide. All we have to decide is what to do with the time that is given us." It is worth noting that, as the story progresses, Frodo carries out his all-important task with a dogged determination that borders on sheer stubbornness—refusal to quit, long beyond the point when practically anyone else probably would have. Like Leonidas and Kathryn Stockett, he simply would not give up. That is tenacity.

Is that the way virtuous leaders are expected to behave? The answer is yes, when such behavior is called for. Sometimes that behavior is simply part of being a leader—not to mention a person of courage and integrity.

The second lesson we can learn from Leonidas's story raises a point we intend to explore further later in this chapter, and that is how the Spartan king inspired others to follow him even into certain death. Either his comrades felt just as strongly about their commitment to fight for Greece as their leader did, or else they felt strongly enough about him as a leader to lay down their lives beside his—or both.

Endurance

Most of the virtues we are discussing in this book are both active and passive in nature. Perseverance can involve either striving toward a goal or simply bearing up under stress—what we would call enduring. Let us examine the latter for a moment.

In Chapter 2, we discussed the Judeo-Christian basis of much of our modern, Western notions of virtue, and perseverance serves as a good example. In the New Testament book of Hebrews, King James Version, Paul says, "Let us run with patience the race set before us" (12:1). Other versions translate the word "patience" as "endurance": holding out until the end of (metaphorically speaking) our lives here on Earth. The Greek word usually translated as "patience" or "endurance" is *hupomone* (hoop-oh-mow-nay), which can be also translated as "perseverance." Note too that the Greek word for race is *agon*—the root for our word "agony."

Anyone who has run a distance race understands exactly what Paul is talking about. To be sure, there is an element in such a race of striving toward a goal, trying to win. For most runners, though, a long-distance race is a matter of gutting it out, of continuing to put one foot in front of the other despite the bodily pain and the voices screeching in your head that if you had any sense, you would stop and walk or sit down.

There is another common and necessary, yet often overlooked, element of enduring or persevering. Pain is not always physical; sometimes it is emotional or psychological. In *Culture and Value* (1948), the philosopher Ludwig Wittgenstein wrote the following about the great classical composer Johann Sebastian Bach: "Bach said that all his achievements were simply the fruit of industry. But industry like that requires humility and an enormous capacity for suffering, hence strength. And someone who, with all this, can also express himself perfectly simply speaks to us in the language of a great man." Note that Wittgenstein acknowledges the importance of humility, one of the virtues we already covered, but he also cites a "capacity for suffering" that itself is a type of strength and thus leads to greatness.

Of course, no one wants to suffer, whether physically or emotionally, and leaders are no different. The agony of striving for excellence, with all the pressure and stress it brings—both external pressure and the pressure we put on ourselves as achievers—is not for the faint of heart. Just as every runner, at some point in a long race, wants to quit, so too are leaders often tempted to "sit this one out" or pass the responsibility for a particular function or project to someone else.

The old aphorism states "Good things come to those who wait"; but we doubt that refers to simply sitting around doing nothing—and it certainly does not involve giving up, quitting, or passing the buck. Rather, it is about the virtue of endurance. Virtuous leaders understand that no one can win the race, or even finish, who lacks the fortitude to enter the race to begin with. No doubt there will be suffering, perhaps great mental anguish. Lincoln suffered horribly throughout all those years of terrible war, when the country was being torn apart and men were dying by the hundreds of thousands. The responsibility for all of that fell squarely on his shoulders, as he understood too well. Yet he bore it because he believed all of the suffering, both his and the nation's, would in the long run be for the greater good. And he was right. Virtuous leaders know that most races are marathons, not 60-meter sprints.

Let us go back to Wittgenstein for a moment. As parents, teachers, and leadership facilitators, we found what he said next fascinating:

I think the way people are educated nowadays tends to diminish their capacity for suffering. At present a school is reckoned good "if the children have a good time." And that used not to be the criterion. Parents, moreover, want their children to grow up like themselves (only more so), but nevertheless subject them to an education quite different from their own....Endurance of suffering isn't rated highly because there is supposed not to be any suffering—really, it's out of date.

Wittegenstein wrote this in 1948. We can look around us now, at all the institutions in our society that cry out for strong leadership, and see just how right Wittgenstein was. Plenty of people long to take on the trappings of leadership—the perks, the deference, the perceived power—but precious few have the capacity for suffering that true leadership requires.

That observation suggests both an opportunity and a challenge. Those who *do* possess the internal fortitude certainly can benefit from the leadership vacuum. But the challenge is that no matter how much we may want to do things on our own, in the end we simply cannot. We need others, especially from the generations coming behind us, to develop that same fortitude and become willing to take on the responsibilities of leadership instead of merely coveting the salary and corner office.

Perhaps, as parents, we should re-examine the way we respond when our kids are struggling with a difficult school assignment or dealing with a harsh teacher or coach. As leaders, we need to reconsider the way we develop other leaders in our organization. Do we simply take anything off their plates that may be too difficult? Hesitate to give them challenging assignments? Or do we allow them to take on those challenges and endure those hardships?

Seeing Tasks Through

An important definition of determination, according to leadership guru John C. Maxwell, "is the ability to see a task through to completion. Many people start; few people finish; many people have a dream; few people achieve their dreams."

Why is that? Those people lack, or have not yet developed, the virtue of perseverance—and perhaps one or two other virtues as well, such as courage and wisdom. Courage is often necessary because, no matter how glorious and hopeful dreams seem at the beginning, most worthwhile endeavors are fraught with hardship, opposition, and even danger. Courage to face those obstacles is as important as a stolid determination to get past them.

Moreover, wisdom is required, in many cases, to know which tasks we ought to begin in the first place and which we should leave alone. Remember the old adage "his eyes were bigger than his stomach," referring to someone who took too much food on his plate and could not finish it all? Well, some leaders constantly take on more than they can handle and thus rarely finish anything. Most of us know people like this in our personal lives, whose homes, yards, and garages are filled with half-completed projects, many started years ago. Leaders who do not persevere can find themselves in an analogous place within organizations.

Such habits are magnified in the workplace, where large numbers can be affected by one individual's lack of "stick-to-it-iveness." Those who work with someone like this can find their daily work life incredibly frustrating, as they constantly have to make adjustments to their own schedule due to others' half-finished projects. Also, in many cases, the responsibility for finishing those projects falls to people who are lower on the organizational chart and who usually have more than enough on their plates already. Such cascading responsibilities are why few leaders are more unpopular than those who constantly jump at new initiatives that everybody else in the organization believes will become more unfinished projects, getting in the way of those who are attempting to carry out the important work of the organization.

Rob once worked for a leader who frequently volunteered her unit to lead the way on some new task or initiative. Her cheerful volunteerism never failed to elicit silent groans from her staff members, who often questioned the worth of those initiatives and also saw clearly that the bulk of the work (if not all of it) would fall to them, along with the lion's share of the responsibility for making it happen. Moreover, based on their experiences with this leader, the staff members understood that she probably was not volunteering because she believed deeply in the project or in her group's ability to pull it off; rather, her motive almost always was to make herself look good in front of her boss and to one-up the other unit leaders, whom she viewed as her competition for the next rung on the ladder. Her staff knew that, long before they could make any headway on the new project, their leader would have moved on to some other, newer initiative and expect them to pile *that* on their plate, too. No wonder she was unpopular.

A similar and related behavior that leaders sometimes exhibit involves behaving like a toddler with a new toy. If you have ever observed a two-year-old in a room with a bunch of new toys, you will understand this analogy. She will toddle over to the first toy that captures her attention and play with it for a minute, until some other toy across the room catches her eye, whereupon she throws down the first toy and heads straight for the new one—and so on, from toy to toy, around the room.

Many of us have worked with leaders just like that, for whom new tasks, projects, or initiatives are like toys—played with for a while, then quickly discarded in favor of something newer and shinier. Such leaders may well have the best of intentions, but there are few behaviors in which they may engage, short of outright dishonesty, that have the

145

capacity to create more chaos in an organization or do more damage to morale.

Please do not misunderstand our intent here. We are not suggesting that leaders should not take on new tasks, both for themselves and for their units. Of course, they should. Many new initiatives are just that—initiatives, demonstrating new ideas and approaches—and thus well worth the effort. Moreover, as human beings, we must continue exposing ourselves to new concepts, learning new methods and technologies, accepting new challenges, even taking risks (which brings us back to courage). That direction, and that direction only, offers progress.

However, we must use wisdom in deciding which new tasks are worth our efforts and which are not. We also need to have a little humility in determining whether we are beginning some new initiative for the right reasons: will it benefit the organization, or just ourselves? Once we decide that a project is worthwhile for all concerned and we take it on, we have to have the courage and sheer determination to see it through, regardless of the obstacles. Follow-through may be the most important application of the virtue of perseverance in a leadership situation.

A couple of final points before we leave this section. First, although we have focused on long-term projects, the same principles can apply to shorter tasks. Archie Bland, writing for *The Independent*, cites best-selling psychologist Daniel Goleman's observation that people nowadays—and especially young people—are having more trouble than ever focusing on tasks and seeing them through. Goleman and others believe that technology is to blame: that with their smartphones and tablets, their Facebook accounts and Twitter feeds, people are constantly being distracted and pulled away from more important pursuits. He quotes a young college professor who confessed, "I can't read more than two pages at a stretch. I get this overwhelming urge to go online and see if I have a new email. I think I'm losing my ability to sustain concentration on anything serious."

Admittedly, this is different from failure to carry out a lengthy and laborious project. But we should know what we are up against; this may be especially important for older leaders—those who are not digital natives—to understand about their younger subordinates. Technology overload is a significant challenge many of them must overcome in order to be successful and, one day, assume the mantle of leadership. It may be a different kind of challenge, but the way to overcome it is the same: by developing and internalizing the virtue of perseverance.

Finally, a word about quitting. The essence of perseverance is often summed up in the words cited earlier with which Churchill used to encourage a shaken British citizenry: "Never give up." Parents, teachers, and coaches echo that phrase, encouraging their charges to never quit. Rob, for example, recalls that, when he was growing up, his father would not allow him to quit anything: "There were times I wanted to quit piano lessons because they were hard or quit the ball team because I wasn't playing enough, but my dad would never let me. He taught me not to be a quitter, and I'm grateful to him for that. I've tried to teach my own kids the same thing."

On the other hand, as the great American troubadour Kenny Rogers put it, "You gotta know when to hold 'em, know when to fold 'em." There are times in life when "folding" is the only reasonable course of action. A person cannot stay in an abusive relationship, for instance. Nor can people stay forever in a job that continues to exploit them or consistently fails to reward their contributions. Sometimes, as a leader, you have to know when to let a project go, perhaps in favor of something better, or when to retreat so you and your organization can live to fight another day. Yes, that is quitting, and it certainly is not a habit you want to form. But you need a great deal of wisdom, humility, and even courage to recognize that, however much you may wish to persevere, sometimes you just cannot.

Inspiring Others to Persevere

History records that the winter of 1777-78, which the young Continental Army spent hunkered down at Valley Forge, Pennsylvania, served as a turning point in the American Revolution. Conditions were harsh, rations short, the weather brutal. An estimated 2,500 men died that winter of exposure, disease, and hunger, and many deserted. But thousands more did not desert, and those who held on emerged in the spring of 1778 a stronger, more determined fighting force, winning an important victory over the British at the Battle of Monmouth and driving the Redcoats out of Pennsylvania. According to historian Russell Freedman, author of *Washington at Valley Forge,* Washington later expressed his belief that the perseverance those soldiers learned at Valley Forge is what bound the Continental Army together and enabled them later to win the war, in the face of long odds.

We may ask ourselves: what would motivate a soldier to stay at Valley Forge—away from his family, under terrible conditions—when he could easily have deserted as so many of his comrades did? Obviously, he would have to believe deeply in the cause, and no doubt that was the case for many of those men. But there can be no question that Washington's leadership, his force of personality, also played a major role. Those soldiers at Valley Forge persevered, in large part, because their leader persevered and inspired them to do the same.

Most of us, as leaders, will never face a situation that dire. Yet we *are* bound to encounter many significant challenges, both personal and organizational. In the case of the latter, persevering individually is not enough; we also have to persuade those we lead to stay the course, even when they want to quit, drop out, or turn back. What sorts of behaviors do leaders exhibit that inspire others to follow them even through hardships?

The first is that leaders must show wisdom in motivating others toward a common goal. The men at Valley Forge not only believed in their leader; they believed in the cause he embodied. Those who thought he was championing a lost cause or leading them to certain defeat no doubt went home. Why would they endure such hardships for a cause they did not believe in or a fight they thought they could not win?

Likewise, leaders today have to be very selective about the causes they elect to champion, the battles they choose to fight. Most people will work long hours and endure a great deal in order to complete a project they believe has an excellent chance of succeeding and benefitting the organization as well as themselves. Those same people are much more likely to drag their heels if they believe the project is senseless or has little chance of success. A series of poorly chosen projects will send many good employees to the want ads, looking for a job where they will not feel they are banging their heads against the wall. If you want people to follow you as your unit takes on some difficult task that probably will require a great deal of perseverance, you must make sure they understand the potential outcome and see that outcome as desirable—in other words, that they believe their efforts will make a positive difference. Nothing kills morale like perceived make-work projects that have no clear benefit.

Nothing, that is, except maybe projects that are seen as benefitting only the leader or those higher up. Most people will sacrifice much for the greater good, as long as they feel they are included in the greater good—that is, as long as they believe their careers will somehow be enhanced in the long run. Asking them to sacrifice and endure hardships just to enhance *your* career is insulting as well as demoralizing. If it is all about you, they will catch on quickly, regardless of fancy rhetoric or other spin.

To inspire people to endure with them through hardships, leaders must be willing to endure those hardships themselves. They have to lead by example. One of the reasons so many of Washington's men stayed through that difficult winter is that Washington himself was there with them, enduring all they endured. He was not 20 miles away in Philadelphia, enjoying the relative comfort and plenty of city life. They saw him every day as he moved among them, giving them encouragement, hope, and a sense of what was at stake; undoubtedly, they thought to themselves, "If he can do this, so can we."

Finally, a leader who wishes to inspire people to persevere must be willing to support them. Few things motivate people more than leaders who consistently go to the mat for them—just as few things are more demoralizing than leaders who constantly throw others under the bus in an attempt to protect and promote themselves.

When several members of Congress complained to Washington that his army was failing to do its job while taking what meager shelter it could during the harsh winter, he replied:

"I can assure those Gentlemen that it is a much easier and less distressing thing to draw remonstrances in a comfortable room by a good fireside than to occupy a cold bleak hill and sleep under frost and snow without cloaths or blankets; however, although they seem to have little feeling for the naked and distressed soldier, I feel superabundantly for them, and from my soul pity those miseries, [which] it is neither in my power to relieve or prevent."

Is it any wonder those soldiers were willing to endure almost any hardship for a leader like that?

Practicing Perseverance

Can people train themselves to persevere, to see tasks through and not give up when the going gets tough? We believe they can. We believe that perseverance can be developed over time until it becomes habitual—that is, a virtue. The key is to identify those areas of your life, both personal and professional, where you have a natural tendency to give in, or at least procrastinate, and then address those specifically. The following exercises may help.

Revisit your dreams. Think back on some of the dreams you had—personal or professional—five, ten, twenty years ago. Have they come true? If not, why not? Maybe the answer is that those dreams were not practical to begin with. You may be a guy who wanted to play in the NBA when you were growing up, but you are only 5'7" and not possessed of extraordinary leaping ability. Or perhaps circumstances intervened, events beyond your control. Maybe you found yourself expecting your first child while still in graduate school and had to drop out and get a job without finishing. Or maybe, looking back, you can admit to yourself that you probably *could* have achieved that goal; you just did not work hard enough at it.

In some cases, there will be nothing you can do now about those broken dreams. Say you had the physical tools and perhaps could have played in the NBA if you had worked harder. If you are now 45 years of age, that ship has sailed. In other cases, however, the fact that you have not already realized those dreams does not mean they are off the table. What is to stop you from going back to grad school? Or taking guitar lessons? Or pursuing a new market for your product? Recognizing that a dream may still be viable can be wonderfully empowering. Pursuing it will require just as much perseverance now as it would have years ago if not more; however, you are a stronger person now, with more determination—otherwise, you would not be where you are.

So go ahead. Grab hold of one of those old dreams. Make it a new dream. But this time, see it through.

Develop a stubborn streak. Maybe you are one of those people who has always gone along to get along. Perhaps it has worked out well enough for you, so far, but going along to get along usually entails some compromise. Compromise can be both good and necessary, an indispensable means of getting things done in any large organization. It is when compromise begins to involve core values and not just details that problems can arise. Are you really going to sacrifice ideals you believe in deeply just to advance some agenda? If you have become accustomed to giving in, you may find it difficult to dig in your heels.

Do it anyway. We know that is easier said than done, but you have to start someplace. A good place to start is by developing a little bit of a stubborn streak—some may call it growing a backbone—when it comes to things that are truly important.

At this point, having some sort of personal mission statement that lays out your personal values and priorities can come in handy. Go back to that mission statement—or create one, if you have not already—then examine the things you are being asked to do, at work or elsewhere. If they do not align, it may be time to stick to your guns, regardless of the consequences.

For example, let us say you are an admissions officer at an institution, and one of your personal values is diversity. For that matter, the institution claims it as a value, too. But you notice that the institution's policies do not actually promote diversity; in fact, they do exactly the opposite. Do you keep quiet? Or do you launch a crusade (a one-person crusade, if necessary) to change some of those policies? The latter will require a great deal of perseverance, not to mention courage, but it may be worth that for you and your institution to move forward.

Increase your endurance. A great deal has been written about the health benefits of exercise, but we are going to suggest another benefit that perhaps you have not thought of. There is something about consistent exercise, and in particular endurance exercise (such as distance running, biking, or walking), that helps us develop our perseverance "muscles." To put it another way, practicing not quitting, especially when your body really wants to quit, can help you train yourself not to quit in other aspects of your life. So start that walking regimen you have been resolving to start for years now—and then keep it up. Go ahead and train for that marathon or triathlon, and then follow through and compete. You will find that you become a tougher individual, not just physically but mentally.

And it is not just intense physical exercise that can help you develop perseverance. Learning to play a musical instrument or learning a new language requires similar determination and self-discipline. So do many hobbies. Choose something that interests you; then stick with it.

Pick up a dropped task. Look around your home and office. What tasks have you begun in the past year or two that are still waiting to be finished? It could be anything from remodeling your kitchen to overhauling your organization's website. The point is that the project seemed worthwhile to begin with, but for some reason you did not see it through. Whether that reason involves circumstances beyond your control (can you say "excuses"?) or laziness on your part does not really matter. You cannot undo the past; you can only resolve to do better in the future.

So resolve to do better. Identify a specific task you started but did not finish, and make a plan to finish it. Be realistic about the time frame, but this time see the task through, no matter how long it takes and no matter how many times you want to quit. You will be amazed at the confidence and renewed sense of purpose you gain from finishing that abandoned task—not to mention the sense of renewed confidence others will feel toward you.

Stick up for the tenacious. Perhaps there are others in your organization who are doing what we advocate here. They are standing on principle, digging in their heels in the furtherance of some worthwhile cause, and suffering as a result by being marginalized or even persecuted within the organization. Maybe they are on the verge of losing their jobs. Nevertheless, you recognize that they are in the right. If you are in a position to do so, come to their aid.

Such aid can take several forms. Maybe you will have the opportunity in a meeting to defend those people vocally when others are attacking them. You can lend moral support, letting them know you are on their side; you may even be able to provide direct support in the form of resources. And if they work directly for you, you can run interference with the higher-ups, which may be the best thing you could possibly do for them.

Although many leaders may not appreciate tenacity or determination even in a good cause, you do not have to be one of those leaders. Virtue is virtue, wherever it is found, and virtuous leaders both recognize and reward it. That is how virtuous leadership ultimately translates into a virtuous organization. Meanwhile, if you claim to value perseverance but do not support and reward those who persevere, you actually are promoting the opposite of this virtue, and your organization will come to reflect that.

9. Hope

DR. VIKTOR FRANKL, A SURVIVOR OF BOTH AUSCHWITZ AND DACHAU, argues in his highly regarded book *Man's Search for Meaning* that human beings are motivated primarily by a quest for meaning in their lives. This was no different for inmates of the concentration camps, he observed, than for anyone else. Even though the inmates ostensibly had little to live for, they still sought to imbue their lives with some meaning, because, according to Frankl, what kept them all going was the hope of something beyond the fences.

In fact, he writes that, in the camps, you could tell who was going to die soon because they often would light a long-hidden cigarette. What does that have to do with dying? Well, prisoners were granted a ration of cigarettes, but most refused to smoke them as a silent protest against the way they were treated and the conditions in which they were held. When someone lit up, that meant he had given up hope. He was going to die anyway, so why not enjoy a smoke? And die he did, usually within a day or two.

Frankl's story illustrates both the power of hope and the danger of hopelessness. While as a leader your organization will never face the extremes that Frankl describes, difficult times are inevitable. The question is, how will you collectively get through these difficulties? And the answer is that, as a leader, you have to create a climate of hope.

Hope Versus Despair

To understand what a climate of hope feels like, let us first look at its opposite. A climate of despair is characterized by apathy, lack of accountability, low morale, a desire to escape, and even a lack of meaning. Sometimes those negative attitudes arise in response to the situation itself, and sometimes they are the result of the way leaders react to the situation. The irony is that when leaders see qualities like apathy and lack of accountability in the people they lead, their first reaction is often denial or assertiveness. Denial is turning from the problem, pretending it is not there or hoping it will go away. Assertiveness in the face of apathy often looks like "cracking the whip": "Things are good, you're not appreciative; get onboard and show some initiative—with a smile." This type of assertiveness only makes the situation worse while lowering morale even further and ratcheting up everyone's desire to abandon what seems to be a sinking ship.

Karl's experiences with a client a few years ago illustrate this dynamic perfectly. He was working with the dean of a professional school at a large research university where everyone, it seemed, had become mired in a climate of despair. Faculty members had stopped caring about their work or the university's reputation, there was a perceived lack of accountability on the part of administrators, and a number of people were openly looking for other employment. The situation was bad enough that most employees did not even bother filling out the organizational climate questionnaire Karl sent as a prelude to his visit, an attempt to gauge the atmosphere of the unit. They just did not care.

That state of affairs was explained somewhat when he received an e-mail from the dean outlining the questions he wanted Karl to explore with the department chairs in their upcoming meeting. The list included questions like these: What do you think is your role in facilitating change necessitated by external and internal pressures? What is your role in holding faculty accountable in their responsibilities during times of change? What is your role in defusing situations that contribute to negative morale?

Do you see a theme here? All the questions focused on the chairs and what they were doing or not doing that had led to the current mess. Certainly, the chairs had responsibilities in those areas, but the environment had become one of blame. Senior leadership transferred all of the responsibility for the situation to the chairs: What are you doing wrong? What can you do better? The dean wanted to hold them accountable—and expected them to hold faculty members accountable—but he was unwilling to hold himself accountable or take any of the blame. The environment was so toxic that people wanted to leave, and many did.

Compare that dean's approach to the one demonstrated by Dr. Martin Luther King Jr. in the very last speech he gave, popularly known as "I've Been to the Mountaintop." Rarely has one person served as such a beacon of hope for so many, and King did not disappoint on that spring day in Memphis, less than 24 hours before his assassination. Perhaps foreseeing that event, as some have suggested, he left his followers with these inspirational lines:

Like anybody, I would like to live a long life. Longevity has its place. But I'm not concerned about that now. I just want to do God's will. And He's allowed me to go up to the mountain. And I've looked over. And I've seen the Promised Land. I may not get there with you. But I want you to know tonight, that we, as a people, will get to the Promised Land!

Those words of hope and inspiration galvanized the people who looked to him for leadership and empowered them to carry on after his death.

As a leader, one of your primary responsibilities is to foster a climate of hope within your organization. Unless you are extraordinarily unlucky, times will not always be bad; but unless you lead a charmed life, they will not always be good either. Virtuous leaders plan for both, and a large reservoir of hope is one of the main things that will enable you to make it through those difficult times.

Faith

The New Testament draws a connection between hope and faith by defining the latter as a function of the former: "Faith," wrote St. Paul in his epistle to the Hebrews, "is the substance of things hoped for, the evidence of things not seen." With all due respect to St. Paul, we would like to suggest that hope also is a function of faith—faith in other people, in our organizations, in ourselves, and in something beyond ourselves.

Remember those concentration camp inmates that Dr. Frankl wrote about? When he said they had hope that something existed beyond the barbed wire fences surrounding their prison, what did he really mean? After all, most of them had very little real hope they would ever see the outside again, much less return to the lives they had known before the war. Furthermore, whatever hope they may have had at the beginning was no doubt slowly drained from them as the weeks turned into months, and they saw friends and family members die from hunger or exposure—or saw them marched off to the gas chambers.

What characterized the survivors, however, was an unflagging belief that there *was* a world beyond those fences, a world worth living in, and that there would be a time when order was restored and life was good, even if most of them would not live to see it. No doubt that is what kept them going, long after they should have given up, lit up one last smoke, and lain down to die. Having faith that such a world existed, or would exist again, gave their lives and their current suffering meaning. It gave them hope.

When we, as individuals or as organizations, face difficult times, what keeps us going if not the belief that, at some point, things will get better and, at that point, all our suffering will have been worthwhile? To be clear, we do not mean to compare a career setback or a financial downturn to the Holocaust. The examples of others in extreme situations teach us lessons that we can apply in circumstances that are far less dire. Frankl devoted his life to teaching us how to apply in our daily lives what he had learned in the cruelest of worlds. One of those lessons: faith—the "evidence" of things we have not seen—is what carries us through.

Faith in what? Let us start with faith in the people we work with, the other members of our organization. When faced with a crisis, groups—be they businesses or nations—find comfort in the faith they have in their leaders. We have seen this time and time again in our nation's history, as the American people, in times of trouble, have rallied around leaders like Franklin D. Roosevelt, John F. Kennedy, Ronald Reagan, and George W. Bush. History has not been kind to all these presidents nor all their policies, but at the moment of truth, they did what great leaders must do: they gave the nation hope that everything would, in the long run, be okay. The nation, for its part, was able to withstand adversity and persevere because it had faith in its leaders.

As a leader, you have to earn people's faith, or at least be worthy of it. We all hope that, when dire circumstances raise uncertainty and anxiety, our record as a leader will inspire faith in our ability; most of us strive to be that type of leader. This kind of faith is something you have to work at constantly, even while things are good, by practicing all the virtues that we talk about in this book. You cannot just step up during a crisis and expect people to trust you if you have not earned that trust all along the way. At the same time, we all make mistakes. But when the time comes, if we have worked to be worthy of their trust, we hope that the people we lead will overlook our weaknesses, show faith in our leadership, and take heart.

This is important to keep in mind not only in your role as a leader, but also as a follower. Perhaps you are blessed to have complete confidence in the people above you on the organizational chart, and you can easily communicate that trust to others by word, deed, and attitude. But even if you do not have much faith in those people, perhaps with good reason, the time may come when you must give them the benefit of the doubt, along with your vote of confidence—just as we tend to rally around our head of state in time of crisis, regardless of our political persuasion. Faith, in that way, is a little like respect: if you expect your leaders to have faith in you, sometimes you have to demonstrate faith in them.

By the same token, leaders must show faith in the people they lead. Some leaders, when times get tough, tend to develop a bunker mentality. Like the dean at the professional school Karl was working with, they blame those who report to them and others for the institution's current trouble and respond by withdrawing decision-making power from them. "You screwed up," they say in effect, "so from now on I'll be making all the decisions."

That approach is generally a mistake. Even if some people have made bad decisions in the past—and even if those decisions did contribute to the current crisis—at this point, everyone is in it together, and there really is nothing to be gained from pointing fingers. Probably, the people who made those bad decisions are as aware of their mistakes as anybody—perhaps painfully so. If they are worth anything at all (and why would you have hired them if they were not?), they want to do everything in their power to make up for those mistakes. The fact that you show your faith in them, even when they do not necessarily merit it, could be a powerful motivating factor. They will not want to let you down again. That dynamic will last long after the current crisis has passed. Nothing creates allies for life like showing faith in someone, especially when he or she has no reason to expect it.

Likewise, we should have faith in the organizations we serve. All too often we become jaded and cynical about the places we work, like those professional school faculty members. But if we are going to help the organization succeed and not bail at the first sign of trouble, we have to believe both in its mission and in our role in helping it fulfill that mission. We may not always agree with the way the organization is run, and things may not always be done to our satisfaction. No one is suggesting that we bury our heads in the sand and ignore the issues that need to be addressed. But at the end of the day, we must have faith that the organization has the potential to be better than it is and that perhaps we can make a positive difference through our own courage, perseverance, and hope. That kind of generous, positive attitude enables us to see beyond current difficulties, giving us and others a positive vision of the future.

We also need to have faith in ourselves. One of the most common causes of despair in the workplace is coming to the conclusion that, as an individual, you can do nothing to positively affect your situation. At that point, there seems to be little to do but give up, succumb to apathy, and start looking for another job. As leaders, we cannot allow ourselves to go there—right up to the point, at least, when things really *are* that bad. Sometimes work environments become so toxic that you have little choice but to move on, for your own mental and physical health. Certainly, you should never stay in an environment where you are being exploited or abused. But short of those situations (which are thankfully both extreme and rare), maintaining faith in yourself and believing that you really can make a positive difference will be critical components to your success.

Having this kind of self-confidence does not mean that you are arrogant or an egomaniac. In reality, it just means you have the same kind of belief in yourself you have in others: a belief that, if you consistently do the right things, everything will generally turn out well in the long run. Such faith is based not on a sense of superiority but rather on a firm conviction in the rightness of your guiding principles. To have faith in yourself means recognizing that, although you will make mistakes just like everybody else, in the end you will do the right things for the right reasons more often than not. Many times, the key to getting through a rough spot is simply to believe in yourself and keep pressing forward, with an unwavering hope in the likelihood of a positive outcome.

Finally, you should ground your faith in something beyond yourself. You can place this in a religious context if you like. Many people take great comfort in the belief that a higher power is in control and that, if we do our part, eventually that higher power will see to it that everything works out for the best.

But if you are not religious, you can certainly believe in something greater than yourself—even if that something is as abstract as a set of personal values or guiding principles, or a belief in some form of ultimate right and wrong, or an abiding hope in the basic goodness and indomitability of the human spirit. We sometimes call this a moral sensibility, and most human beings have it, whether based on a religious tradition or not. Too often, the cynic in us looks at the world, with its wars and hunger and suffering, and concludes that things are generally awful and not likely to get better. But we cannot allow ourselves to fall into that mindset, for in that direction lies ultimate despair.

In Nathaniel Hawthorne's great short story "Young Goodman Brown," set in 17th-century Salem, Massachusetts, the title character stumbles one night upon what he believes to be a witches' meeting involving members of his own church congregation (we say "believes" because it never is entirely clear whether he saw what he thought he saw). And he hears, or thinks he hears, the Satan character say the following to the assembled devotees: "Trusting in one another's hearts, ye had believed that virtue were not all a dream. Now are ye undeceived. Evil is the nature of mankind." Brown emerges from the forest a very different person from the innocent, hopeful young man who entered, and the story tells us that, although he lived a long life, "his dying hour was gloom." Why? Because he had lost all hope in humanity—and, ultimately, all hope in himself.

If you are going to cultivate and practice the virtue of hope and inspire hope in others, you cannot allow yourself to become a modern-day Young Goodman Brown, however tempting that may seem at times. You must hold stubbornly to your faith, in others and yourself—and in doing so, you almost always will be rewarded in the long run.

Vision

Much has been written over the past few decades about vision in leadership and how important it is to organizations. These days, it seems if there is one thing all leaders want engraved on their tombstones, it is that they were "visionary." We equate vision, in that sense, with being innovative and transformational, with pushing the envelope and taking an organization or even an entire industry to places it has never been before.

Given its importance, then, does that mean vision is a virtue unto itself? We propose that you should think of vision as an outer manifestation of a deeper virtue. It is another function of hope.

Consider the case of Steve Jobs, arguably one of the greatest business leaders of our time. Although few who knew Jobs would call him humble and some even questioned his wisdom at times, there is no question about the strength and power of his vision. In 1996, after a ten-year hiatus, Jobs returned to Apple, the company he had helped start almost two decades before, and found it on the verge of bankruptcy. Within a few years, he had turned the company's fortunes around, creating a new, hipper image and introducing products like the iPod. By 2006, Apple was worth more than competitor Dell Computers. Jai Singh quoted Dell CEO, Michael Dell, as having said in 1997 that if he owned Apple he would "shut it down and give the money back to the shareholders."

How did Jobs accomplish this turnaround? He explained his approach in a keynote speech delivered at the Macworld Conference and Expo in 2007: "There's an old Wayne Gretzky quote that I love. 'I skate to where the puck is going to be, not where it has been.' And we've always tried to do that at Apple. Since the very, very beginning. And we always will." Gretzky, like Magic Johnson in basketball and Joe Montana in football, was an athlete whose success was often attributed not so much to his physical gifts as to his uncanny ability to see two or three plays ahead, to understand what was going to happen in the game before it happened—and certainly before anybody else realized it. "Skating to where the puck is going to be, not where it has been": that's vision.

In leadership, vision is based on hope and, correspondingly, faith. Jobs was able to turn Apple around because he believed in the company, he generally believed in the employees, and most of all he believed in himself and his ability. He had a clear sense of what the company could accomplish if it did certain things; he thought he knew what those things were, and he set out to do them. Jobs's vision, in turn, inspired hope in others—namely, Apple employees, stockholders, creditors, and customers. They believed in him, just as he believed in them and in himself. Together, they were able to restore Apple and then build it into a giant of American innovation and industry.

The truth is that one person's vision, while perhaps powerful enough to set necessary changes in motion, rarely is sufficient to sustain progress and move an organization forward over time. In order for that to happen, the vision must be shared by a majority, if not all, of the people in the organization. Jobs acknowledged as much when he told *60 Minutes,* "Great things in business are never done by one person; they are done by a team of people."

So it is not enough for a leader to have vision; he or she also has to be able to communicate that vision effectively, so that others, both inside and outside the organization, buy in. We will discuss that concept in more detail later in this chapter, when we address inspiring hope in others.

One other point before we move on to the next section: vision without humility can, in the long run, be counterproductive, perhaps even destructive. Without humility, we may find it easy to declare our vision the only viable one—which smacks of audacity and arrogance. That sort of thinking also can create a tremendous backlash, as followers conclude they have been disenfranchised and shut out of the decision-making process. They may very well fail to buy in or may even become obstructive, in a worst-case scenario.

Plus, there is always the possibility that the leaders' vision may be wrong for the organization, and we just do not understand it. That is why our chapter on humility is so important and the reason we placed it first among the Nine Virtues. No other virtue can be fully achieved without it. And that includes hope, or in this case, vision as a function of hope.

Optimism

Have you ever known someone who was always cheerfully optimistic? A perpetually glass-half-full kind of person?

Annoying, isn't it?

Well, such optimism *can* be, particularly if it is Pollyanna-ish. Most of us are not perpetual optimists. Even if we consciously try to be optimistic, on our darker days we may tend to gravitate towards pessimism. At other times, we view ourselves as neither optimists nor pessimists but as realists—seeing the situation clearly for what it is or how we imagine it is. For that reason, people who are unfailingly optimistic tend to annoy us. We do not think they are being realistic. Sometimes we even think they are faking: no one can be that cheerful all the time, right? But mostly they annoy us because they force us to acknowledge a deficiency we sense in ourselves. Or maybe they remind us of a time in our own lives when we were more innocent or naïve, as we may describe it now. But what we really mean is a time when we too were perpetual optimists.

We are not suggesting that you wear rose-colored glasses. A certain amount of realism, or pragmatism, is certainly required to see the world clearly and make correct decisions; we will discuss that shortly. But all too often, saying "I'm a pragmatist" is simply an excuse for not taking a more hopeful, positive, and forward-looking view of things.

The 19th-century Romantics believed that human beings are at their most perfect state at the time they are born, a state the Romantics described as innocence. At that point, they said, we all begin a lifelong journey toward experience, which for them was something negative. They equated experience with pessimism, cynicism, and loss of hope. As human beings, our goal in life, according to the Romantics, should be to recapture the innocence of our childhood, tempered by the experiences we have had along the way.

With this example, the two of us are suggesting that perhaps most of us have been looking at this question wrong. We tend to see the opposite of hopefulness as pessimism. Or, more accurately, we draw a continuum with hopefulness at one end, pessimism at the other, and pragmatism as a halfway point. As long as we are not all the way at the pessimistic end of the spectrum, then we assume we are doing okay, even if we can hardly call ourselves optimists. Sometimes we even take that idea a step further, concluding that since optimism and pessimism are extremes, we are better off falling somewhere in the middle. And so we glorify pragmatism to the detriment of optimism.

But what if the opposite of optimism is not really pessimism, but cynicism? That is what the Romantics were suggesting: that as we grow older and encounter more and more life experiences, many of which are negative, we become more and more cynical. What is cynicism if not the loss of optimism—the loss of hope? If the perpetual optimist is sometimes annoying, what about the perpetual cynic? Think about the person in your organization who seems to greet every new idea with some darkly sarcastic remark, which might provoke a little nervous laughter but also serves to isolate that person, as colleagues almost perceptibly withdraw. Now imagine if more people in the organization were like that. Or if *you* were like that. What we are suggesting is that a sustained emphasis on pragmatism over optimism may be a first step down that road to cynicism.

There is no question the confirmed cynic often plays a valuable role in an organization and any set of deliberations. The cynic can be the one who brings us back to reality when we get a little too starry-eyed or the lone dissenting voice in a chorus of self-promoting sycophants. For these reasons, the wise and humble leader will always tolerate the cynic. However, an entire *organization* of cynics, of people who have allowed themselves to be so beaten down and become so jaded by their life experiences they simply cannot see the good, would be an organization that never accomplished anything.

As leaders, we cannot allow such negativity to happen. We can prevent this pervasive cynicism in two ways. The first is that we must become optimists ourselves, which is another way of saying that we must cultivate the virtue of hope. Even if we do not always feel optimistic—and of course we will not—we must work constantly to project an air of overall optimism about the organization and its future. That will not be easy, of course, but remember our lesson from Chapter 1: if you want to become something, act as if you already are.

If you continue to approach each situation, and especially each negative situation, with a positive attitude—with hope—then eventually you will become the optimist that your actions suggest. Optimistic leadership will have a powerful impact for good on the people around you.

Being an optimist also does not mean that you have to ignore reality. You can see your situation quite clearly and even recognize that it is a very dire situation indeed—as Frankl and his fellow prisoners certainly did—without losing hope in a better tomorrow, in the basic goodness of people, and in the rightness of your own core values. In this sense, pragmatism is not really opposed to optimism at all. To put it in Romantic terms, it is just innocence tempered by experience.

The other way to fight cynicism within an organization is by fostering a climate of hope, as opposed to a climate of despair. And we do this by sharing responsibility and accountability and by offering a vision of the good we can achieve if we all work together. In fact, personal optimism on the part of the leader can be one of the most powerful forces for creating this kind of climate. When leaders believe in their organizations, believe that what they are doing has great value, believe in the people around them, and believe in themselves (without arrogance or narcissism), others are much more likely to believe as well, especially when they perceive the leader's optimism is genuine and not based on fantasy. Conversely, when leaders become cynical, it is only a matter of time before everyone else starts to share that cynicism—and that is essentially a death-knell for any organization.

Whatever you may think of their politics, both Ronald Reagan and Barack Obama serve as prime examples of the power of optimism. Both were elected by significant margins at a time when America was going through very difficult periods economically. People were understandably cynical and pessimistic. But that state is not natural for most human beings. Most people do not want to be cynical; they just feel driven to it, as if cynicism is the only rational response. What they really want is to feel optimistic. They want to have hope. This hope is what both Reagan and Obama offered them. Obama even incorporated the word into his winning slogan, "Hope and Change." Reagan promised people that, after the long, dark night of economic recession, it was "Morning in America." Both succeeded in inspiring the American people, and both won not only their first election but a second term. They won because few things inspire followers like optimism on the part of their leader.

Pragmatism

With optimism as a given, there is still a place in the leaders' lexicon for honest pragmatism. In fact, pragmatism is not so much a lack of optimism as a reality-based version of it.

Yes, sometimes a leader has to appear optimistic—even if he or she is not, particularly—in order to rally followers. Can you imagine the coach of a small-college football team, before a big game against a major-college opponent, telling his team in the locker room they have no chance to win? On some level, he probably knows that, and so do the players. History is not on their side, as major upsets happen so rarely they make big news when they do occur and are remembered for years afterward. But he is not going to say, "Okay, guys, there's no way you can win, but go out there and do your best, anyway." No, he is going to tell them, "Listen, if you go out there and give it your very best shot, if you execute every play just the way we've practiced it and follow the plan to the letter, we can win this game."

Upsets do happen. They may be extremely rare, but rarity does not mean they are nonexistent or impossible. The pragmatist in that coach knows the team is probably not going to win. He is just hoping for a good showing, one that will demonstrate to the players what they are capable of accomplishing the rest of the season when they play in their own division. He is looking for something they can build on. But he also is not being completely disingenuous when we says, "We can win," because he knows they *can* win—but only if they really try.

The players understand this. They know the history of the game. They know an upset, however unlikely, is not impossible. In other words, they know their coach's pep talk is not based on fantasy. When followers conclude the leader has lost touch with reality, that is when they begin to distance themselves from the vision and abandon hope.

Imagine a leader whose ambitious vision for the organization initially creates an almost palpable atmosphere of hope and inspires people to achieve far beyond their normal capacity. But over time, as he begins to believe his own press and concludes he can do literally whatever he wants, his vision for the organization becomes more and more divorced from reality, or at least from what the majority of his followers think is feasible. In fact, many think some of his more extreme ideas will hurt the organization rather than help. In the hallways, people whisper, "I think he's lost his mind." At that point, they begin to get off the bandwagon; some even became obstructive as they attempt to thwart what they believe to be a dangerous, unrealistic agenda.

Losing touch with reality is exactly what we were referring to earlier in this chapter when we stated that vision without humility can be counterproductive, as can vision without wisdom. All the virtues work together, in the sense that a leader cannot truly acquire one without acquiring all. Hope without wisdom is fantasy; vision without humility is arrogance. Neither fantasy nor arrogance is likely to inspire people and will probably have the opposite effect.

Conversely, a good working definition of healthy pragmatism may be hope tempered by both wisdom and humility. We could also define it as confidence. A college coach Rob knew described the difference between confidence and arrogance this way. Confidence, he said, "lies in knowing that if you do the right things and always give your best effort, then you have an excellent chance of achieving the desired result. Arrogance, on the other hand, involves believing that you'll get what you want just because of how wonderful you are." The latter attitude, by the way, is exactly why upsets happen in sports. The superior team believes it is going to win just because it is superior; all the players really have to do is show up. But when facing an opponent that has hope, evidenced by a quiet confidence, the supposedly superior squad might find that they have their work cut out for them.

This principle is just as true for individuals as for sports teams. Confidence, pragmatism, realistic optimism—call it what you will—trumps arrogance on one hand and cynicism on the other every time. That is especially true when it is both modeled and communicated effectively by the virtuous leader.

Inspiration

At the beginning of this chapter, we noted that part of a leader's job description is to cultivate a climate of hope. We then discussed the way some people manage to create—or at least contribute to—just the opposite, a climate of despair. Now we would like to go back and address the question: how exactly do leaders cultivate a climate of hope? The answer, we believe, can be summed up in a single word: inspiration.

Many of the chapters dealing with the individual virtues have ended with a section on inspiration: how to inspire people to be honest or have courage or persevere. But in this particular case, inspiration is more than just an aspect of hope; inspiration is the very essence of hope. In any organization, one person's optimism, vision, or faith is never enough. Others must also embrace, embody, and reflect those qualities; if not, the organization is probably doomed. Inspiring hope in others may be a leader's most vital function, especially during difficult times.

In order to inspire hope in others, leaders must first develop that virtue for themselves. Leaders who are cynical or even pessimistic will not inspire hope in others. They are much more likely to elicit those same negative attitudes in everyone around them, to the detriment of all. Likewise, leaders who constantly find fault, point fingers, and assign blame—while refusing to accept any blame themselves—will create an environment in which everyone is looking to deflect responsibility.

Although we occasionally find it necessary to understand who is responsible for a particular decision or situation and why it happened, playing the blame game is a backward-looking strategy, focused on the past. Hope is just the opposite: forward-looking and focused on the future. Virtuous leaders are humble enough to acknowledge their faults and take responsibility for their own actions and decisions, while at the same time giving the clear impression that they are looking primarily to the future, intent on continuous improvement. This attitude sets a tremendous example for those they lead.

Beyond the practice of hope, effective leaders also communicate their vision to others in such a way as to make them want to adopt the same vision. Think again about King's "I've Been to the Mountaintop" speech. His followers understood that he knew exactly where he wanted to go—where he had every intention of going—and, more important, he believed he would get there and they all would get there with him. However, he also made clear that, even if he never made it "to the mountaintop," he had complete faith his followers would. Those inspiring words probably kept the movement from dying with the man. (Note, by the way, that his hope was not just in himself or even his followers, but in something greater than all of them: the principles of liberty and equality.)

Of course, none of us are in King's class when it comes to oratory or the written word. Some leaders, in fact, may not be particularly charismatic, have great skill as writers, or feel very comfortable talking to large groups. To those leaders, we would say that if one or more of these skills is a weakness of yours, work on it. The importance of being able to communicate effectively with those you lead cannot be overstated. However, you may find that there are others in your organization who *do* have those skills, and you can enlist their help to make sure you are reaching people as you should. Some of you may recall the story of Moses in the Old Testament book of Genesis. According to the Biblical account, when Moses was commanded by God to petition Pharaoh for the release of the Hebrew slaves, he objected that he was not a very good speaker. God then told him to take his more articulate brother Aaron along as a spokesperson.

In the final analysis, the true power of hope will lie not in your words but in your actions. If you give people both a voice in the decision-making process and a stake in the outcome; if you accept responsibility and deflect credit (rather than the other way around); if you show faith in others by the way you treat them and faith in the organization by the way you talk about it; if you consistently project an attitude of confidence and realistic optimism in the future of the organization—then your peers and employees will be inspired to follow suit. They will reflect the same qualities, and the climate in your workplace will be overwhelmingly one of hope.

Practicing Hope

Can a person really *develop* hope? Is it something you either have or you do not have? And is it not determined, to some extent, by circumstances? After all, some situations are just hopeless, right?

Well, maybe—but not necessarily. In many cases, even the most lost of causes is not nearly as hopeless as it seems. If the inmates of Dachau and Auschwitz can find some ray of hope in a genuinely bleak existence, surely the rest of us can manage to keep despair at bay when faced with more mundane crises.

Some people are more optimistic by nature than others. That is true of all the Nine Virtues. Some people are inherently courageous, some are naturally more humble, and some seem wise from birth. Hope is not unique in that regard. The bottom line is that people *can* develop the virtue of hope. They *can* train themselves to approach the world more optimistically, to have more faith in themselves and others, to expand their vision of what is possible. In that endeavor, the following exercises should help.

Have some faith. If you have people who report directly to you, make a list of them by name. Then, rate each person on a scale of 0 to 5, with 5 indicating you have complete faith in them and 0 meaning you have no faith in them at all. With luck, you will not have any zeroes in your organization, but take a close look at the people who received a 1, 2, or 3.

Now ask yourself a couple of questions. First, why do you not have much faith in those people; what is it specifically that you do not trust about them? Then ask yourself what you can do to help them become more trustworthy, to earn (or re-earn) your faith. Perhaps the response will be as simple as showing a modicum of faith in them, even if they have not particularly earned it, by giving them assignments you normally would entrust to others you deem more reliable. You can start with smaller, less important tasks and then build up to larger and more critical tasks as they gradually earn your trust. Your step of faith, by showing faith in others, may not make a difference; but it may turn those people's lives and careers around. In fact, your show of faith could even make a noticeable difference in the entire organization.

Take the plunge. Next, take inventory of your own strengths and weaknesses, focusing especially on those areas in which you lack confidence. Maybe you are a reluctant (or even poor) public speaker, and that deficiency is limiting you professionally. Maybe you have hesitated to take on some specific responsibility in the organization, even though you know others would like you to do so. Maybe you have not tried moving up the career ladder because you are afraid you lack the ability to succeed at the next level.

Whatever that area of weakness is, resolve to address it. Learn what you need to learn, formally or informally. Take whatever courses or get whatever training is necessary to acquire the skills you need. Talk to the people you need to talk to. And then, again take a step of faith—in this case, faith in yourself. Note that doing so may require a great deal of courage, but remember the example of people like Frankl and King. In a very real sense, hope is a form of courage. Neither virtue can be very effective without the other.

Draft a personal vision statement. Write a statement that reflects your own personal vision. What are your fundamental values? Perhaps you have already articulated these values from the mission statement exercise in Chapter 6. Think of your mission as your life's purpose and vision as the destination. What are your goals in life, both personal and professional? What is it that you most hope to accomplish during your time on this earth? What constitutes a well-lived, successful life for you?

You can start simply by jotting down one- or two-word answers to each of these questions and then over time develop your short answers into a more complete and polished document. You will probably need several drafts to get it right, and you will want to revisit your vision and mission statements from time to time, as you will likely find that your values, goals, and priorities change as you go through different phases in your life. We cannot emphasize enough the importance of having all this written somewhere, preferably in hard copy, as a document you can access regularly and read often. In other words, do not try keeping all that information in your head. There is real power in having it in writing.

Once you are satisfied with your personal vision statement, pull all the members of your organization together, and invite them to participate in creating a vision statement for the group. (You may want to suggest they start by crafting their own personal statements as you have done.) Then, when you have collectively produced a document that reflects the mission, shared values, priorities, and goals of the organization, each of you individually can compare your personal vision to the group's vision and see how compatible they are and whether any adjustments need to be made on either side.

For example, if most members of the organization agree that family should be a personal priority, but that priority is not reflected in the group statement, then maybe the group statement needs to be revised accordingly.

Cut back on the sarcasm. A sense of humor is a good quality in a leader. Members of an organization especially appreciate self-deprecating humor or humor that gently satirizes the unpleasant circumstances in which all occasionally find themselves. If you are a successful leader, chances are you have made your share of those kinds of jokes.

Sometimes, however, we can go overboard, to the point where our gentle satire becomes not so gentle, where it becomes cynicism. Clearly, there is a line between a good joke, shared by all—which lightens the mood, eases tension, and helps put a difficult situation in perspective—and a darkly sarcastic remark that makes things seem even worse and makes people feel uncomfortable. Many of us, perhaps, as we deal with our daily frustrations, cross that line from time to time. The question is: how often are *you* crossing it?

To determine that, begin taking note of the jokes that you make, the remarks intended to be humorous, especially when dealing with colleagues or subordinates. Actually go back to your office after a meeting, and write them down. Do this for several weeks; then, take a few moments to read over what you have written. Are you being humorous, or are you being cynical? Are you lightening the mood, or darkening it? How would you react if it were someone else saying these things? Be honest with yourself, and adjust your behavior accordingly.

Practice being practical. Go back and read through your personal vision statement as well as your organization's statement. As you consider the hopes, dreams, and aspirations reflected in both documents, attempt to evaluate them objectively—in "the light of day," so to speak. Here is a list of questions to ask about each item to determine how practical they are:

1. What is the likelihood that this could actually happen in the real world? Rate each item on a scale of 1 to 5, with 5 being very likely and 1 being very unlikely.
2. What will each item cost, in terms of time, money, and staff hours? What will be the likely return on the investment?
3. What are the major obstacles that could prevent this from ever happening? Are they obstacles that you and/or the group realistically can overcome?
4. Why is this item on your list? What is your investment in it? Will it benefit others or just you?
5. Exactly how much buy-in does this idea have from others? If it is part of the group statement, was it something everyone embraced right away, or was there a lot of debate? If it is part of your personal statement, will you have the needed support from family and friends?
6. What specific actions need to be undertaken for this idea to come to fruition? Who will have to undertake them? Do you, or does your organization, currently possess the necessary talent and skill? If not, is that likely to change in the near future?

Conspire to inspire. Finally, resolve not only to be more hopeful, optimistic, and forward-looking yourself, but to inspire others to be the same way. If your default response to most situations is a kind of cynical pragmatism that in reality borders on pessimism, discipline yourself to keep those thoughts to yourself. Make a conscious commitment to try seeing the glass half-full all the time, even if that is not your natural way of looking at the world. Then, actively set out to convince other people that the glass is half-full, too.

Work on your body language. Leaders who hang their heads, wring their hands, or scowl angrily rarely inspire confidence in followers. Work on your language, with the goal of using positive words—and avoiding negative ones—as much as possible. Then, make sure you align your behavior with your words, so that people see you acting as though you actually are optimistic about the future. Finally, actively seek out opportunities to encourage others to be optimistic—in e-mails, in one-on-one conversations, in group meetings.

Even if you do gain a reputation for being a perpetual optimist, at least you will not be alone.

10. Charity

WE SUSPECT THAT FEW PASSAGES IN ALL OF WESTERN LITERATURE have been cited more often, or in a wider variety of contexts, than St. Paul's discourse on love in I Corinthians, Chapter 13. It is quoted, in whole or in part, on Valentine's Day cards, wedding announcements, church bulletins, even obituaries. The Greek word that Paul uses in that passage is *agape*, which was translated into Latin as *caritas*, from which we get our English word "charity." The King James version actually uses that word although most modern translations replace it with "love." Thus, the terms "love" and "charity" tend to be equated, at least as far as Paul's discourse is concerned.

But do they really mean the same thing, in practice? Think about how we use the word "charity" in conversation. Most commonly, it refers to the act of giving to those in need or to organizations that perform that function. We even use the term as an adjective: to be charitable means to be generous or giving.

The word "love," on the other hand, usually refers to a feeling and in some contexts to a particular kind of feeling that includes sexual attraction. The latter is a type of love that in Greek would have been translated as *eros* (from which we get our word "erotic") and in Latin as *cupiditas* (note the reference to the cherubic match-making archer). Of course, as with the ancient Greeks and Romans, we recognize other types of love, as well: love for family members, love for friends, even love of self. But what all of those have in common is that they are based on emotions.

Charity, on the other hand—*agape* or *caritas*—is something a little different. As Paul describes it his iconic sermon, charity is an action word, defined more by what we do (or do not do) than by what we feel. Charity, says Paul, demonstrates patience, or "suffers long." It is "kind." It "doesn't envy." It "doesn't exalt itself, is not puffed up"—in other words, it shows humility. Charity is not selfish and does not mistreat others ("does not behave itself unseemly, seeks not its own"). Nor is charity "easily provoked" or prone to assuming the worst about others ("thinks no evil").

By personifying charity, Paul is saying that the charitable person is one who exhibits all these traits. What do they all have in common? They require us to practice specific behaviors or avoid others. We should be patient, kind, and humble. We should treat others well. We should not be selfish or lose our tempers.

In other words, being charitable goes far beyond feelings. It involves action. Whereas the physical attraction and/or fondness that we normally associate with love is often involuntary, charity, as we are defining it here, is a rational choice.

For this reason, we chose charity as both the title and the focus of this chapter, rather than simply talking about love. When we use the word "love" in this chapter, think of the term as synonymous with the way we are describing charity. When we say "love," what we literally mean is *agape*, or charity.

We do not mean to discount or undervalue love. However, while it is important for virtuous leaders to feel love—for others, for their work, even for themselves—charity cannot end there. Emotions, as we all know, are ephemeral, subject to change on a daily and sometimes even hourly basis. If we behave charitably only when we feel like it, then we are not actually being charitable at all—and we certainly are not exhibiting the kind of love that rises to the level of a virtue. *That* kind of love will enable us to maximize our potential as human beings while also helping others to maximize theirs and in the process, as leaders, move important and worthwhile projects forward.

Love of Self

Let us start off this chapter by talking about love (charity), specifically the kinds of love a leader must have in order to be effective. We mentioned those briefly above: love of self, love of one's work, and love for others.

We list love of self first, not necessarily because it is most important but as a nod to the popular notion that, to love others, you must first love yourself. The idea is debatable; one could argue the truth is actually the other way around—that learning to love others and treat them accordingly is the first step toward developing a healthy self-love. But if we do not have the appropriate regard for ourselves, having that kind of regard for anyone or anything else is difficult.

Perhaps the key word here is "healthy." As we noted earlier, the ancient Greeks tended to see virtue as a mean between two extremes, and nowhere is that definition more useful than in talking about love—in particular, about self-love. Please note that we are avoiding the often-abused phrase "self-esteem." What we are talking about has a lot in common with self-esteem, but we believe the modern concept of self-esteem is too often based on emotions that may not be warranted, rather than on substantive, positive behaviors that lead to true self-love.

At one end of the spectrum lies narcissism, an extreme and unhealthy form of self-love that we often equate with arrogance and lack of humility. Narcissists think—or at least give the appearance of thinking—that they are simply smarter, better, and all-round more wonderful than everyone else. The rest of us should do whatever they say without question because we are in awe of their superiority; or so they think and indicate. While narcissism is a characteristic of some notable leaders, we do not believe it is a sustainable quality in a leader. Leaders need followers, and narcissistic leaders have a way of alienating followers over time.

At the other end of the spectrum is self-loathing, which if anything is even more destructive than narcissism. Self-loathers are, first of all, miserable, and as the old adage goes, "misery loves company." People who hate themselves tend to hate others, too, especially those they perceive as happy or successful. As a result, whether consciously or unconsciously, they often try to pull down happy, successful people. Thankfully, obvious self-loathers rarely find themselves in positions of leadership, but when they do, high achievers should beware.

Achievers should also beware when narcissists are in charge as they tend to view other high achievers as threats and competitors. We would be remiss if we failed to note that narcissism and self-loathing are sometimes two sides of the same coin. Neither of us is a psychologist, but we have both known enough narcissists in our professional lives to conclude that extreme and conspicuous self-love is is a means of compensating for, and perhaps covering up, deep-seated feelings of inadequacy and self-hatred.

The happy medium between these two extremes is a kind of healthy self-regard based on justifiable pride in one's accomplishments, balanced by a frank recognition of the role that others—as well as circumstances beyond one's control—have played in those accomplishments. That kind of self-love is bolstered by an honest and consistent focus on acquiring all the virtues we have been discussing in this book: humility, honesty, perseverance, courage, and so forth.

In other words, you feel good about yourself because you have reason to feel good about yourself. You work hard. You honestly try your best to do the right things and treat people the way you would like to be treated. At the same time, you acknowledge you can improve and resolve to keep working to become a better person—that is, to acquire all the virtues. You recognize that, whatever you have accomplished, you have had a lot of help and that you will continue to need help from others as you strive to accomplish even more.

This concept of healthy self-love, by the way, has much in common with the "authentic leadership" approach espoused by Harvard business professor and former Medtronic CEO Bill George, among others. The essence of authentic leadership is recognizing what you uniquely have to offer as a leader, which requires a fair amount of introspection and objective self-analysis.

For instance, Karl is a philosopher by both inclination and training, and that particular skill set is a large part of what defines him as a leader. Other members of his organization offer their own talents, such as marketing and financial management, but Karl's analytical skills and ability to think abstractly, along with his love of learning, are indispensable to the company's success. The fact that he can frankly acknowledge the benefits of these traits does not mean he lacks humility; it enables him to lead authentically, with a healthy appreciation for and attention to what he personally brings to the table.

In fact, that kind of self-love is extremely beneficial in leaders because it gives them a clear sense of purpose and vision. And those qualities positively impact the entire organization because people who see the best in themselves also tend to see the best in others. They are secure enough in their own identity to be decisive and proactive, but at the same time humble enough to listen and learn. They seek not to pull down but to build up, helping others develop the same kind of self-confidence they have. In addition to respecting themselves, they respect others, as well their organizations and jobs.

Love of Work

Respecting oneself and respecting others segues neatly into the next type of love that we want to examine: loving the work you do.

As Rob has noted often, one of the things that continues to surprise him most after nearly 30 years in the teaching profession is how many of his colleagues do not like to teach. Quite a few seem to actively hate it. And we are not referring to only those burned-out types who have been at it for 40 years and become jaded and disillusioned along the way. A shocking number of young teachers have an equal disdain for the profession, prompting Rob to wonder, more than once, as he eavesdropped on some conversation in the faculty lounge, "Why in the world did you become a teacher? And why stay in teaching if you hate it so much?"

This matter concerns not only an individual's dissatisfaction with his or her chosen profession because the individual is not the only one who suffers. Can you imagine a teacher who hates teaching being effective? In giving advice to new teachers, Rob has often said that an effective teacher really needs only two things: love of students (which we will address in the next section) and love of teaching. We cannot overstate the difference it makes to a classroom when students see how much the teacher enjoys what he or she is doing. That kind of love, which we sometimes call passion, can be positively infectious: students are more likely to enjoy the class and to get more out of it. No doubt all of us can recall teachers like that and how much they inspired us— perhaps even to go into the profession we chose.

That same dynamic applies in almost any organization. People who love what they do—and especially leaders who love what they do— inspire others to love it and to want to do more and achieve more. In this case, loving what you do means enjoying your work to the point that you probably would do it as a hobby if it were not your profession. If you won the lottery today, you still would go into work every day (well, maybe not *every* day) and do what you do because you are that passionate about it. You cannot imagine *not* doing your work.

This is a concept that psychologist Mihaly Csikszentmihalyi has explored in his highly regarded book *Flow: The Psychology of Optimal Experience.* According to Csikszentmihalyi, what makes an activity genuinely satisfying is a state of consciousness that he refers to as "flow." People "in the flow" typically experience enhanced creativity, deep enjoyment, and a sense of total involvement with life—of being completely in the moment.

There is a great scene in the film *Chariots of Fire* in which English sprinter Eric Liddell's sister Jenny is trying to persuade him to forget about the Olympics and go to China as a Christian missionary.

Liddell, a deeply religious man, is torn. He says to Jenny, "God made me for China. But He also made me fast, and, when I run, I feel His pleasure." That is flow.

Moreover, Csikszentmihalyi argues in his book that flow is not something we have to wait around for. We can control it, to some extent, by putting ourselves in situations where it is likely to occur. In other words, we are much more likely to feel flow when we are engaged in activities we enjoy and believe are important, as opposed to tasks we regard as both menial and meaningless.

Of course, we are not always blessed to be in that position. Obviously, people sometimes get stuck in jobs they do not like for economic reasons because they have obligations. But we respectfully suggest that if you do not love your work or if you do not find it fulfilling, you should figure out what you would be passionate about and formulate a plan to do that instead of what you are doing now. Although you may be an effective manager, there is no way you ever will be a great *leader* unless you truly love what you do. Also, there is no way you will reach your full potential until you put yourself in situations in which you can experience flow.

Loving your work is not just about feeling good. It also means believing deeply in what you do. It means you are absolutely convinced that what you do for a living is beneficial to others: that society in general and many individuals in particular are better off because of your organization and the job you do in that organization. In other words, you believe you make a difference in the world. Feeling fulfilled in work is difficult for people if they are convinced their presence every day does not really affect much one way or the other—and people who feel that way cannot inspire others to believe that *they* can make a difference.

If you do not believe deeply in your work or your organization, you should take time for a serious self-inventory. Perhaps you need to reconsider your approach to your job or your attitude toward the organization. Maybe you need to find another job.

Finally, loving what you do includes loving the organization you work for. Consider how many people constantly criticize their employer, whether around the water-cooler or in the presence of clients— or even on Facebook or Twitter. Sure, you probably recognize that your organization, like all organizations, has faults. But, as a loyal employee, you should be committed to addressing those faults: to being part of the solution rather than part of the problem. That attitude is a lot different from hating the organization and trashing it every opportunity you get.

Loving where you work means you enjoy working there, you believe in the organization and its mission, you understand where you fit in the grand scheme of things, and you feel a sense of loyalty to your team. As a leader, you cannot expect other people to feel that way if you do not exhibit those sentiments on a consistent basis. If you talk the organization down, you can bet those you lead will do the same, and over time they will lose respect not only for the organization but for you as well.

You must balance the organization and its needs with those of the employees. One of the most common complaints workers have is that their managers do not value them as individuals but see them only in terms of their worth to the organizations, their contribution to the bottom line. If you are going to be an effective leader, you must put others before the organization and certainly before yourself.

Love for Others

This section is one of the few sections in this book that comes with its own subheads because love for others consists of a number of specific behaviors we want to address individually.

Before we get into those, however, please note our use of the term "behaviors" in the paragraph above. That was intentional, and it refers back to the key point we made at the beginning of this chapter: that love, or *caritas*, is not about feelings but rather about actions. Loving others, whether friends or coworkers or even members of your family, must not depend entirely on emotions. There are certainly times when we do not feel a lot of love for those people—when we are angry or frustrated or annoyed with them, when they are doing things we do not approve of or not treating us the way we would like to be treated. But the essence of charity, as St. Paul made clear, is that we have to love them anyway, whether we feel like it or not. Loving them in this case means behaving in specific ways toward them.

Service. Perhaps the highest manifestation of love for others is serving them. That certainly meets the threshold established above—that is, it requires action—and is completely independent of emotion. You do not have to like someone to serve them, but you probably do have to love them. Or, to look at the matter from another angle, not only do we serve those we truly love, but we ultimately come to love those whom we truly serve.

Think about your own family. Why do you love your children so much? Yes, because they are your flesh and blood; but what about parents who adopt children and come to love them as if they were biologically related? Is it possible that we love our children so desperately because we spend so much time and effort serving them, especially when they are young?

Perhaps our intuitive understanding of the connection between love and service is why we do not question people like Dr. Martin Luther King Jr. or Mother Teresa when they profess their love for humanity. Those rare individuals who spend their lives in the service of others demonstrate their love by their actions; undoubtedly, they actually come to feel love for the people they serve, completely independent of whether they *like* those people or even know them personally.

As a leader of an organization or unit, if you are to demonstrate and epitomize the virtue of charity, you must learn to serve the people you lead. This is a concept that has come to be known in recent years as "servant leadership," a term coined by Robert K. Greenleaf in his seminal 1970 essay, "The Servant as Leader," and popularized by Ken Blanchard's book *The Servant Leader*. According to Greenleaf, "the servant leader is servant first ...[which] manifests itself in the care taken ...to make sure that other people's highest priority needs are being filled....Do those served grow as persons? Do they, while being served, become healthier, wiser, freer, more autonomous, more likely themselves to become servants?" "Yes," is the unequivocal answer to both questions.

For all of Greenleaf's noteworthy contributions to the current literature on this topic, the concept of servant leadership itself is an ancient one. Practically every civilization and certainly every great religious tradition has had its own ideas about the role of the leader as servant, dating back at least to the fifth century B.C.E., when the Indian philosopher Chanakya wrote that the "king (or leader) shall consider as good not what pleases himself but what pleases his subjects (or followers)." The Koran asserts that "the leader of the people is their servant." And Jesus taught his disciples, as recorded in the Gospel of St. Mark, that "whosoever would be the greatest among you must be your servant."

Note several common themes here. First, the servant leader is one who puts the best interests of others and of the whole, above personal interests. On a practical level, as a leader you must know enough about the people you lead to understand their needs. Far too many leaders remain aloof from the day-to-day problems facing the people under them, or else they see themselves as being above those petty concerns. Soldiers, faculty members, cubicle dwellers—these lower-level employees have a reputation for complaining about the clueless people at the top, and often with good reason. To make an obvious point, you cannot expect to meet people's needs if you do not even know what their needs are to begin with.

Second, after coming to understand people's needs, the servant leader must seek to fulfill those needs, often at some personal sacrifice. In fact, if there is no sacrifice, in a very real sense there is no service.

Because simply meeting people's needs is not enough; to exhibit real virtue, you have to put those needs ahead of your own.

What do you want or imagine you need? A raise? A promotion? A bigger office? More prestige or respect? Whatever it is, the concept of servant leadership says, "Forget that. Think about what other people need, and then seek to give it to them." The paradox, of course, and what all those great philosophers and religious leaders have been trying for so many millennia to teach us, is that by meeting other people's needs first, you will find, in the long run, your needs have been met, too.

Third, note that the real purpose of servant leadership is not to give people only what they need on a physical or mundane level—better working conditions, more appreciation, perhaps better pay—but to help them grow as individuals. That is, to enable them to become, in Greenleaf's words, "healthier, wiser, freer, more autonomous." Being an organizational leader is not about building your own career, enhancing your own credentials, or making yourself look good, and it certainly is not about using others to accomplish those goals. It is about helping *other* people look good, helping them to acquire the skills they need to build their careers and enhance their credentials. Leadership is about giving them responsibility so they can develop their own leadership skills, along with the support and the tools to enable them to be successful. If, as a leader, you consistently are doing those things, then your career will take care of itself because their success will become your success.

Finally, the ultimate goal of servant leadership is to create more servant leaders. As you model the behaviors described above, you will find more and more people in your organization emulating you, seeking to put others' needs ahead of their own. When an organization reaches the point at which every member is operating that way—when all self-interest has been set aside in favor of the greater good—then, and only then, can it reach its maximum potential and function at its highest level. This organizational ethos is what every leader should strive to achieve.

Of course, few organizations achieve that level of selflessness. But that does not mean it is a completely unattainable goal. One person exhibiting true love by serving others can make a tremendous difference, and there is no reason that one person cannot be you.

Before closing this subsection, we should note that it is possible to serve people *too* much, to the point at which they lose all initiative and desire to do anything for themselves, much less for others. Think again about your children. If you constantly are doing their chores, are you really serving them? Or are you denying them an opportunity to serve and to learn and grow from the experience? Sometimes the way we can best serve others is to allow them to serve, to put them in positions where they are required to perform service for others, including (sometimes) you. This service not only benefits the people who are served; it also benefits the ones performing the service.

Forgiveness. Perhaps Don Henley of Eagles fame said it best when he sang, "I think it's about forgiveness." What's about forgiveness? On an interpersonal level, practically everything—and leadership is nothing if not an interpersonal skill. You cannot hope to lead many if you cannot lead the one; you cannot lead the one unless you can love the one; and you cannot love the one until you truly can forgive.

Forgive for what? Well, for everything. For anything. Because inevitably, in every single interpersonal relationship—and that includes professional relationships—something is going to come up that requires you to forgive.

Let us be completely honest: no matter how good and how virtuous a person you are, no matter how humble or how wise or how inspirational, people are sometimes going to irritate you. While occasionally that may be more your fault than theirs—maybe you are having a bad day or feeling grumpy for whatever reason—most of the time you are going to be perfectly justified in feeling irritated because what those people did was genuinely irritating. And that might be putting it mildly. People do bone-headed things. They behave selfishly. They say things they should not say. They have bad days, too, as well as days when they feel grumpy for no particular reason or maybe for a reason that you do not happen to be privy to.

To be an effective leader, you have to love those people anyway. Loving them means forgiving them—regardless of whether they ask, whether they deserve it, whether they even know you are forgiving them. They may be unaware they have done anything wrong or offended you in any way; if they *are* aware, they may not care. They may be completely unrepentant. None of that matters. Forgiveness is not primarily about them; it is about you.

A quote often attributed to the late American actor, writer, and politician Malachy McCourt goes like this: "Harboring resentment is like taking poison and expecting the other person to die." What that means is something all of us understand intuitively or perhaps have come to learn the hard way: allowing ourselves to remain angry at people, refusing to forgive them, really hurts us more than them. It may not even hurt them at all, either because they do not care how we feel or they are not aware of it. But resentment, as McCourt suggested, is a kind of poison, a cancer that if allowed to metastasize in our system ultimately will kill our moral character, not to mention our happiness.

The most important reason we have to learn to forgive is for our own sake. We can never become the kind of virtuous leaders (not to mention virtuous people) that we are capable of becoming as long as we are unable to forgive. Anger and resentment, over time, turn us into the worst versions of ourselves: bitter and cynical, the kind of people no one wants to be around, much less follow.

Another good reason to forgive, however, is that we want to be forgiven ourselves. As certain as it is that others will irritate, disappoint, and even hurt us throughout our lives, it is equally certain that we too will irritate, disappoint, and hurt others from time to time. No matter how hard we work to internalize, exemplify, and practice the virtues described in this book, we will occasionally—and perhaps regularly—fail because we remain human and therefore imperfect. We too sometimes do boneheaded things, behave selfishly, say things we should not say. At those times, when we have failed people and damaged relationships, we will want to be forgiven. Experience shows that others are much more likely to forgive us if we have previously demonstrated a kind and forgiving spirit. What goes around comes around, as they say—or, as Jesus put it in the Lord's Prayer, "Forgive us our trespasses as we forgive those who trespass against us."

The final reason to forgive is that people need to be forgiven. Sometimes, people who have wronged us can be oblivious or even apathetic, either not knowing they have damaged a relationship or simply not caring. In most cases, however, people know when they somehow have failed us, and they feel bad about it. They may not come to us and ask for forgiveness; they may not say anything at all. But they know it and we know it, and they know we know it. Forgiving someone in a situation like that can go a long way toward removing the heavy burden of guilt from their shoulders (not to mention drawing the poison from our own veins) and putting the relationship on more solid footing.

Conveying forgiveness may be tricky. If the wrong done to you by another person has remained unspoken, then simply going to that person saying and "I forgive you" is likely to do more harm than good. The person may well respond defensively—"Forgive me for what?"—causing the hurt to deepen, the resentment to grow, the alienation to increase.

But there are ways you can show forgiveness without actually coming out and saying it. First of all, you have to resolve in your heart that you have forgiven that person. Then, you need to treat him or her, as much as possible, as if the wrong never took place. Acting like the wrong never took place is not always possible; sometimes, even if you forgive, trust has been lost and the relationship can never again be what it once was. However, if you have truly forgiven, you must attempt to restore the relationship as much as possible and behave toward that person as if there is no rancor between you. If you have been acting with malice toward that person, such as by shunning or retaliating against him or her, then stop. There is no other way to move forward and grow. Otherwise you have not forgiven; and without forgiveness, you cannot claim to love.

Sometimes people will come to you, apologize for their behavior, and ask for your forgiveness. Those cases are rare, but when they *do* occur, you must of course forgive immediately and unconditionally. Such forgiveness does not mean that everything automatically goes back to being the way it was, that trust is always restored or position regained. The new relationship will depend on the severity of the offense. The person seeking forgiveness may have much work to do before things get back to normal. But forgiveness in this case means that you let go of whatever animosity you feel toward that person and allow him or her to begin the process of restoring the relationship. As much as possible, you meet the repentant party at least halfway.

What about forgiving people who do not even know they need to be forgiven, who are completely oblivious to your hurt, disappointment, or irritation? Perhaps they have done something genuinely wrong and just do not know it or do not recognize it. Or perhaps the wrong they have done is more a matter of perception on your part: they have offended you or hurt your feelings by saying or doing something they never thought would cause offense.

Unrecognized offenses happen all the time in interpersonal relationships. There is a story about a newly married man who became deeply offended because his wife was always giving him the heels of the bread loaf. He had grown up in a large family with several older siblings, and getting the heels meant you were lower in the pecking order. The older, bigger children got the soft, middle pieces; the younger kids got what was left. After finally expressing his hurt to his wife, however, he was amazed to learn that, in her home, the heels were considered a great prize and always reserved for the child who was best behaved. Saving the heels for her husband was to her a great sign of love and respect.

We cannot always know other people's motivations. All we can do is forgive—even if they do not ask for it, even if they do not know they need to be forgiven. We have to let go of whatever bitterness or resentment we feel toward others before it eats us up, poisons our relationships, and makes it impossible for us to lead.

Acceptance. In a presentation Rob gave to a group of academic administrators based loosely on this book, he used the word "tolerance" to describe what we are talking about in this section. That term did not go over well with at least one attendee, who visibly bristled at it. Being tolerant, she said, implies that other people are doing things that you have to tolerate—things that are wrong on some level or at least not as good as what you are doing. Tolerance is a patronizing term, she argued, implying that you are superior to those whom you must merely tolerate.

Point taken. We did change the word for this section. On the other hand, we are not backing away from the concept of tolerance. We all have our biases, our own ways of looking at the world, our preferred ways of doing things. Of course, if we think our way of doing, speaking, or thinking is *the* right way, then it follows that other people are doing it wrong. Even if we have the self-awareness to recognize this mindset is not entirely logical, it is still difficult to overcome.

Such differences are why loving others—being truly charitable—requires a certain amount of tolerance. Tolerance does not mean we think that we are better than anybody else or that we are always right and they are always wrong. Or at least it *should* not mean that if we are practicing the foundational virtue of humility. Rather, tolerance means that no matter how much patience and humility we have, other people, including (sometimes especially) those closest to us, are going to do things we do not like and say things with which we do not agree. If we love those people, we simply have to put up with those things (at least to a point, something we will come back to in a moment).

"Acceptance" is the more precise word for the idea we are conveying here: taking others as you find them and accepting them for who they are and what they are, despite what you may regard as their faults or flaws.

Remember one of the things St. Paul said about charity: that it "seeks not its own." A large part of what he meant is that charity is not selfish and therefore does not try to gratify itself at the expense of others. He also could have been suggesting that charitable people do not attempt to remake others in their own image. Insisting that everyone has to be just like us and want exactly what we want so that, in the end, we get what we want is another type of selfishness. Being charitable means we acknowledge differences even if we do not like them; that we do not force everyone else to conform to our worldview; that we do not withhold our love from them when they fail (as we may see it) to do so.

This concept has profound implications for organizational leaders. One of the surest ways to kill creativity and genuine innovation in any organization is to promote what is usually called "group-think." That means to foster an environment in which everyone is expected to have the same outlook, the same opinions, and the same interpretation of reality (which is to say the leader's outlook, opinions, and interpretation). In our cultural climate, the term "diversity" has become a heavily overused buzzword, to the point at which it has unfortunately taken on political overtones that are offensive or tiresome to many. But in an organization, true diversity—including diversity of opinion, diversity of perspective, diversity of ideas—can be a tremendous source of strength, provided the leader values it.

In most organizations, what the leader values generally is what he or she gets from followers. If you want everyone to think the same way— the way you think—then they will probably default to your opinion, whether or not they actually believe it, and that will greatly decrease the number of good, new ideas generated. In contrast, if you expect people to be different and you value those differences, they will oblige you by being different. As a leader, you then will have many more ideas to choose from, thereby significantly improving your chances of making good decisions in any given instance. In addition, the people you lead, because they *are* valued, will *feel* valued, which is another way of saying they will feel loved. As a result, they likely will work harder, demonstrate more loyalty to you and to the organization, and become more personally invested in its success.

In closing this section, we note that being tolerant or accepting does not mean that you have to tolerate or accept *everything*. Some behaviors, such as sexual harassment, discrimination, and serial dishonesty, are simply intolerable. Such extreme examples are easy to identify. The real test of your tolerance comes when people exhibit behaviors, display habits, or embrace beliefs or ideas that you personally find objectionable but which are not objectively wrong. As a leader, you must have the wisdom and discernment—not to mention the humility—to differentiate between things that actually are harmful to others or to the organization and things you just do not like. The latter you simply have to accept if you wish to embrace the virtue of charity.

Generosity

Perhaps the most common definition of charity, which is related to its adjective form, "charitable," is generous. If practicing the virtue of charity means loving others in an active and meaningful way, then to love others is to give—of our money, of our time, and ultimately of ourselves. That is why we admire people such as Mother Teresa and Dr. King, who gave so fully and completely of themselves to others, as well as great philanthropists, including Andrew Carnegie and Bill Gates, who have given millions of dollars to worthwhile causes.

When we think of generosity, giving financially is probably one of the first things that comes to mind. Those who would be examples of charity must be willing to give generously of their substance. It is hard to imagine, for instance, an organizational initiative to support the United Way or organize a walk-a-thon that did not begin with a pledge or donation from the leader. As always in leadership, you cannot ask people to do something you are not willing to do yourself, and that probably applies to giving money as much as anything. Of course, even organizational leaders who enjoy sizable salaries do not always have a lot of disposable income. But our obligation is to do what we can with what we have.

Perhaps a bigger problem is that, in many cases, being too open in our financial giving can become counterproductive. If we are not careful, giving can take on a "look at me" aspect that is contrary to the essence of charity, not to mention humility. More bluntly, people can interpret our charitable actions as mere bragging or showing off; and if we are not careful, they might be right.

That said, there are times when it is perfectly acceptable for leaders to step up and be the first to support a worthwhile cause, inviting others to do the same. Plus, if you are genuinely a charitable person— giving of your substance as you are able and not just pretending to be charitable so everyone will say how wonderful you are—people will be able to tell. Most will admire you for it; many will follow your lead.

Do not forget the old saying "Charity begins at home." In your case, "home" means your organization, where no doubt you will have many opportunities to demonstrate your charitable urges by donating to various office collections for weddings, retirement gifts, philanthropic events, and so forth. Depending on the organization and your position in it, you may also show your generosity in other areas: funding people's worthwhile projects, for example, allowing them to travel to attend conferences or other meetings, and sharing the organization's good fortune in the form of raises or bonuses with those who made it happen.

Another way leaders can be generous is to share their time. In some cases or to some individuals, that may be more important than money. Everyone knows that leaders are busy. As a leader, you probably got where you are by putting in long hours, taking on extra assignments, and working meticulously on each project to make sure it was done right. As you climb the organizational ladder and take on more and more responsibility, the more precious your time becomes. At some point, time may well be the most valuable commodity you have.

Nevertheless, you have to understand that no one likes to work with somebody, much less *for* somebody, who is always complaining about how busy he or she is or—worse yet—wearing their busyness like a badge of honor. Rob once interviewed for an administrative position with a vice president who informed him that she had not taken a vacation in several years. He looked her in the eye and said, "You won't have to worry about that with me." She turned out to be a good boss, but that inauspicious beginning left Rob wondering what he was getting himself into.

What people *do* appreciate is a leader who, although busy, is never too busy to talk to them, hear their complaints, give them advice, or help them on a project. After years in the corporate and academic worlds, we both have heard lots of leaders loudly proclaim, "My door is always open," but sadly that seldom turned out to be true. Great leaders, virtuous leaders, leaders who truly love others, do indeed have open door policies. They are always willing to give generously of their time to those who need it, even if it is inconvenient.

Finally, the last—and perhaps the most important—type of generosity to discuss is being generous with one's self, a quality sometimes referred to as generosity of spirit. This is closely akin to humility, which we already discussed at some length, except that it is more active in nature. If being generous is the opposite of being stingy, then generosity of spirit means that you are not stingy with praise, with encouragement, or with credit. Just as philanthropists recognize people's physical needs and take steps to meet them, so do the generous in spirit recognize people's emotional needs and take steps to meet them.

For example, one of the things people need most from a leader is recognition of their legitimate contributions—in other words, praise. Most workers are eager to please the boss, regardless of what they think of him or her personally; and nothing validates their efforts more or encourages them to continue those efforts like a word of praise from the one they are trying so hard to impress. Good leaders look for opportunities to praise their followers when it is warranted—and even sometimes when it may not be fully warranted but when a word of praise can accomplish far more than a rebuke. Such praise should not be delivered condescendingly. It must be sincere, measured, and specific. But that does not mean praise has to be meted out sparingly, like Halloween candy to a child. For most people, there is no such thing as too much praise. (Just think for a moment about how you feel when your boss praises *you*.)

Something else that needs to be spread around with a snow shovel rather than a teaspoon is credit. One of the biggest complaints most people have about their leaders is that they take the lion's share of the credit when things go well and then deflect blame when things go wrong. Virtuous leaders do exactly the opposite: they accept responsibility for failure and make sure to share the credit for success. Again, this is a form of humility, but it is also a matter of generosity of spirit—of giving something you value greatly to others.

The best leaders for whom Karl and Rob have worked, or worked with, were invariably people who not only shared credit when things went well, but often saw to it that others received *all* the credit, keeping none for themselves. They understood one of the fundamental truisms of leadership: when your followers succeed, you also succeed. They also understood that people are more likely to commit themselves to the success of the organization—and therefore your long-term success—if they know they will be recognized and appreciated for their hard work.

While you may sense we have wandered far afield from our original topic of charity, remember the assertion with which we began this chapter: charity is an active form of love, a love that goes far beyond how we feel and focuses rather on what we *do*. Loving people does not always involve feeling fondness for them; it may not even involve liking them very much. Instead, we show our love for the people we lead—that is, we demonstrate the virtue of charity—by what we do for them that they cannot do for themselves and by what we give them that they cannot acquire for themselves. That may be money, but in a professional setting it is more likely to be fulfillment, a sense of accomplishment, and pride in their work. Meeting those needs for the people we lead is, as St. Paul may have put it, the very essence of kindness.

Practicing Charity

Since the kind of love we are examining in this chapter is based not on feelings but on actions, it is developed through practice just like any other virtue. You cannot necessarily control how you feel, but you can generally control how you act; and how you act, over time, may well influence the way you feel about yourself, about your work situation, and about others. That is the key to understanding this particular virtue: normally, we expect behaviors to follow emotions, but the concept of charity teaches us that, in reality, emotions often follow behaviors such as these.

Make a list. Actually, start by making two lists. On one, put all the things you like or value about yourself. Go back to the idea of authentic leadership we mentioned earlier in this chapter: what is your unique contribution to your role? On the other, list all the things you do not like, the things you want to change, about yourself. Be as honest and exhaustive in both cases as you can. After all, unless you leave the lists lying around, no one but you is going to see them—or needs to see them.

Once you have written all your thoughts in both categories, compare the two lists, not just to see which is longer but to see which is more substantive. This exercise is not about weighing your positive and negative attributes to determine whether you are a good or bad person. If you have gotten this far in a book about embracing virtue, that is not an issue. You already have a desire to improve yourself and to become a better leader. (Put that on the first list, if you have not already.) The point is that looking at these two lists should help you appreciate yourself more—help you feel good about the things you ought to feel good about—while at the same time reminding you that you are not perfect, that you still have room for improvement. That is the pathway to healthy self-love: legitimate and substantive acknowledgement of your own virtues and accomplishments paired with, and mitigated by, humility.

Make another list (or two). Now make a couple more lists, these having to do with the things that you like and do not like about your current job and the organization for which you work. On the first list, focus especially on the things your organization does that benefit others. Then, as you compare the two lists, ask yourself how many of the items on the second—the complaints list—are relatively petty compared to the good things itemized on list one. A doctor, for example, may realize that all the ways in which her practice helps patients far outweigh the red tape she has to deal with.

Ideally, this exercise will give you a much greater appreciation for the work you do and for your organization or department. If it does not, perhaps because list two is much longer than list one, then some serious reforms may be in order, reforms that perhaps you can initiate and lead. Either that, or the time may be right to look for a new job (a realization that would also be a worthwhile outcome of this exercise).

Serve someone. Identify an individual in your organization, ideally someone who is either below you on the organizational chart or at your level, whom you can serve in some meaningful and specific way. This may be a subordinate who is in over his or her head with a particular project. Instead of letting that person "sink or swim," try pitching in and offering a hand. You do not have to usurp that person's authority or take the responsibility for the project out of his or her hands. You can make clear that you just are helping out, as a colleague, perhaps by taking on some of the grunt work, like doing basic research or making copies.

Or perhaps the leader of another unit needs your cooperation to fulfill some task or assignment. One's default mode, in situations like this, may be to give in to competitive urges and allow that person to fail because his or her failure is not our fault (or so we rationalize) and, anyway, it makes us look better. But is that person's failure better for the organization? Is it better for that individual? Is it even better for you, in the long run? Those are all questions worth asking, but in a sense they are beside the point. The point is that true charity requires us to serve people, whether we like them or not and whether we want to or not. That service must be its own reward, even if other rewards manifest themselves as the entire organization benefits from your self-less act of service.

Forgive someone. Talking about forgiveness in the abstract is easy. We all know forgiveness is something we should do more often. But forgiving a specific individual who has wronged us (as we see it) is something else altogether. Yet that is what charity requires.

Think of someone who has wronged you. If you are like most of us, you will not have to think very long. Now resolve to forgive that person, and begin making a concerted effort over time to demonstrate true forgiveness. This effort might mean, among other things, you stop plotting to get even with that person, or you stop shunning or retaliating against him or her. Whether you actually go to that person and express your forgiveness is up to you and may well depend on the circumstances. If the person has asked for your forgiveness and you have withheld it, now is the time to fix that. But if the wrong has gone unacknowledged, there is not necessarily any reason to acknowledge it now. Forgiveness is more a state of mind. It has to do with how you behave toward that person and even more with what you think about him or her. If you are honest with yourself, you will know whether you truly have forgiven.

Forgiveness may well take some time. Just remember that behaving as if you feel a certain way will, over time, help you to actually feel that way. If you treat people *as if* you have forgiven them, eventually you will find you have *in fact* forgiven them.

Strive to accept. Think about someone with whom you work—either at your level or below—whose beliefs or habits or characteristics you find objectionable for some reason. We are not talking about people who have done genuinely bad things at work, but people who are different from you in some way and with whom you would not normally associate for that reason. Now the time has come for a little introspection: have you discriminated against that person in any way, perhaps in assigning projects or giving raises, based on your negative perceptions? Have any of your decisions been unfair or biased where that person is concerned?

If you answer "yes" to either of those questions, take steps to rectify the situation. Resolve to evaluate that person based on what he or she brings to the organization and not on other, irrelevant factors. This process may, in fact, involve more than one person if they share a group attribute. Re-examine the way you assign projects, give raises, or make other work-related decisions to make sure you are not exhibiting any bias.

Remember, as you think about your response to this assignment, to focus on an actual individual or small group. Because acceptance of others is much easier in the abstract, challenge yourself to demonstrate acceptance of a specific person you do not like very much.

Shower praise. Finally, resolve that as a leader, from now on you will be slower to criticize and quicker to praise. This will require you to think carefully before you speak and in some instances to hold your tongue. Remember: to offer praise only when it occurs to you or solely at times when others expect it of you, such as at department meetings or award ceremonies, is probably not enough.

No, you will have to go out of your way to look for things you can praise—for qualities and behaviors in the people you lead and work with that are praiseworthy, even if they are not necessarily eye-catching or sensational. You do not have to limit your praise to the big sale or the impressive publication. You can praise someone's work ethic, meticulousness, and tenacity. You can praise people for being selfless, for being team players, for their daily contributions to the organization's success. You do not have to wait for a special occasion. You can praise them in private anytime and whenever possible within the hearing of others. There is no need to be ostentatious. Just be sincere and matter-of-fact. That will mean more to most people than lavish praise served up at some annual celebration.

As you actively look for reasons to praise people, a funny thing will happen: you will find those reasons, many of them; far more, perhaps, than you ever would have thought. Then, you may discover that praising the people you lead, serving them, accepting them, loving them—well, it is not nearly as hard as you thought.

11. Balance

THE CONCEPT OF BALANCE MAY SEEM LIKE SOMETHING OF A MISFIT among the Nine Virtues. Balance is unique in that this virtue is highly personal; it certainly is not one-size-fits-all. This virtue is about your well-being and happiness.

According to the popular media, most of us lack balance, and we should be devoting significant effort to achieve it. Fewer voices, but perhaps a growing number, tell us that balance between work and other aspects of life is simply unattainable. The challenge facing all of us, especially leaders, is to balance our many and various interests, needs, desires, and responsibilities—including all the things we ought to do but probably are not, like exercising more, eating better, and spending more time with our families.

What exactly is balance? Is it attainable?

Karl likes to tell about the time he took his then-seven-year-old daughter fishing at a local lake. Of course, he had brought his cell phone along—just in case one of them landed a trophy fish and a quick photo was in order. But as they sat on the dock, not catching anything or even getting any bites, Karl's mind began to wander to his work. He had a big program coming up in a couple of days, and he suspected he had some important unread e-mails. The temptation to pull out his phone and start checking was almost overwhelming.

Then, out of the blue, his daughter asked him a question: "Dad, when you were my age, what did you want to be when you grew up?" Sensing an opportunity to throw a curve ball, Karl answered, "A philosopher." His daughter answered, "Sure. Right!" Karl smiled, and they began to talk about a child's dreams, his aspirations, and now hers at seven years old. The conversation ended, and they again turned their attention to lines and bobbers until she broke the hypnotic spell of water lapping against the dock a second time: "What was the worst thing you ever did when you were my age?" That necessitated another lengthy discussion, during which Karl dissembled shamelessly. In spite of a temptation to check his e-mail, he returned with his daughter to the spectacle of bobbers riding up and down gentle waves. Then, that little girl dropped this bombshell: "Dad, some people think that when you die, you no longer exist. What do you think?"

Karl does not recall specifically what he said to her. However, he remembers well the feeling that silenced every distracting thought in an instant. He remembers the two of them, father and daughter, had a wonderful time together, sitting on that dock, not catching any fish, talking about life. If he had been checking e-mail during that time— if he had not been *present* in the moment—that conversation never would have taken place. The urgency of the awaiting e-mails would have faded quickly had he turned to them. He did not. Instead, he captured a memory that will last a lifetime. In that moment with his daughter, Karl was in perfect balance: right where he should have been, when he should have been there, doing what he should have done.

Too often our concept of balance evokes mental images of a circus performer spinning plates—dozens of plates on multiple rods, all spinning precariously, constantly in danger of crashing to the ground. We sometimes feel as though, to keep our lives in balance, we have to run frantically from one thing to the next, making sure one set of plates is not going to fall before immediately rushing over to another set.

We suggest that is not what balance is about—and it certainly is no way to live.

Instead, balance is about being fully aware in the present. It is not simply an external template for ordering our lives, but rather a virtue that can be developed and internalized over time. Like Karl with his daughter at the lake, those who cultivate the virtue of balance become mindful of where they are at that moment. They are content with what they have, even while striving for more—more growth, greater accomplishments, better relationships. They are "comfortable in their own skin," as the saying goes, which takes us back to Chapter 10 and the idea of healthy self-love or authenticity.

Another popular misconception about balance is that it is something attainable, not to mention desirable. But that too is false. In an absolute sense, it is neither.

We know what you are thinking: "What? You just said balance is a virtue that can be developed over time. Now you're telling us it's not attainable or even desirable? Why devote an entire chapter to it then?" Remember our disclaimer at the beginning of this book: none of the Nine Virtues is fully attainable. This of course does not mean that we should not strive to attain them. True virtue, to whatever degree we humans can attain it, is found in the pursuit.

Balance is a special case. Again, most people think of balance as a kind of equilibrium: if they are not exercising enough or spending enough time with family, then they are out of balance. If they can bring everything into balance, they think—equal out the time they spend at work and with family, carve out 30 minutes a day for exercise, read more, and watch less TV—then everything in their lives will be perfect.

The fact is that being a little out of balance is not a bad thing. It is what makes us human—and, more important, what drives us. For example, if your health is in perfect balance already, if your weight and cholesterol and blood pressure are all exactly where you want them to be, why would you need to exercise more or eat healthier food? The fact that you perceive some imbalance in your health or your diet is what makes you want to strive for something better, which leads to better health. Similarly, if your knowledge is already in balance, if you know everything you need to know when you need to know it, why bother to keep learning? And how about relationships? If your personal life is completely in balance, in perfect equilibrium, why continue to work on your relationships or build new ones?

As Darwin noted, evolution (defined for our purposes as ongoing, necessary change) is about struggle. One of the great paradoxes of existence is that we are always seeking and striving for balance; yet if perfect balance were ever achieved, life would cease to be as meaningful. As Viktor Frankl put it in *Man's Search for Meaning*, "What man actually needs is not a tensionless state but rather the striving and struggling for some goal worthy of him. What he needs is not the discharge of tension at any cost, but the call of a potential meaning waiting to be fulfilled by him."

As you read the word "balance" throughout this chapter, keep this basic premise in mind: balance is a *pursuit*, not a destination.

Organization

Balance is not simply a matter of organizing and arranging our lives in order to schedule adequate and appropriate amounts of time for every activity. On the other hand, without some sense of organization, which includes scheduling and prioritizing, most of us are extremely unlikely to achieve any sort of balance.

The essence of balance in regard to organization can be expressed in the following motto: "A time and place for everything, and everything in its time and place." That evokes our idea of being in the moment. Achieving organization is not simply a matter of scheduling your day down to the last minute, with 30 minutes set aside for exercise and an hour marked "family time." If anything, that kind of rigidity, although perhaps convenient, is inimical to true balance.

Instead of thinking of organization in terms of a schedule, think about the meaning of the word as it appears in the following passage from Ralph Waldo Emerson: "For poetry was all written before time was, and whenever we are so finely organized that we can penetrate that region where the air is music, we hear those primal warblings and attempt to write them down." Here, Emerson clearly uses the idea of organization to mean something much akin to harmony. When our minds, bodies, and spirits are in harmony, we then can experience the poetry of the universe.

Please note that harmony by definition is not based on sameness. In fact, the opposite is true: in a choral arrangement, the singers achieve harmony as each executes his or her assigned part. All of the parts are different, even to the point (in many cases) of not sounding anything alike. They do not necessarily incorporate the same notes. At any given point in the arrangement, one part may be emphasized over others; then, the emphasis may shift. Each singer forms exactly the notes assigned, at exactly the right time. The result is beauty. It is perfect balance.

So it is with organizing our lives. Laying out a daily schedule and attempting to follow it is just part of the battle. Although scheduling our days may well be necessary, so that we get to places on time and do the things that require doing, the real challenge lies in being where we are supposed to be, when we are supposed to be there, doing what we are supposed to do—mentally and spiritually as well as physically.

On a practical level, on some days we may need to spend more time at home. Other days we need to devote more to work. Some activities may require us to set aside time each day. Karl, for instance, finds he is much more likely to exercise by setting aside the time from 6:30 to 7:15 each morning for that purpose. At the same time, we need to remain flexible and sensitive to our own needs and, more important, to the needs of those around us. Scheduling can take us some distance in that direction, but it is not sufficient by itself. If you do not schedule time for exercise, for instance, you may not exercise regularly; yet there will be days when you have to cross out "exercise" on your calendar and instead attend an important, impromptu meeting or finish that document before the deadline or show up at your child's school for a parent-teacher conference.

The key point is being where you are supposed to be, when you are supposed to be there, doing what you are supposed to do. A time and a place for everything, and everything in its time and place. Think back to Karl's fishing trip with his daughter. He had scheduled the time to be with her; he had taken the day off and set aside other priorities to be dealt with another day. But none of that would have mattered if he had been there only in body. If he had been merely ticking items off his weekly planner, he would never have achieved what he needed to as a father. Despite his best scheduling efforts, his life would not have been in balance.

That said, we have to start somewhere. Some of us live such scattered lives that a little physical organization—some daily-planner-type scheduling—can be a good first step toward finding balance. Again, the emphasis should be not so much on fitting everything in or on uniformity, but rather on deciding what is important and making sure we set aside the necessary time for those things. Deciding what is important, of course, comes under the topic of prioritizing, which we will address in the next section.

Before moving on to that point, we want to focus on one more aspect of organization, and that is organizing our *stuff*. Again, remember our mantra: a time and a *place* for everything, and everything in its time and *place*.

Despite popular (and often contradictory) perceptions that a clean desk must belong to a lazy person or a cluttered desk represents a cluttered mind, the reality is that we cannot make such sweeping generalizations. While most people probably function best in a relatively ordered environment, others seem to thrive on apparent chaos. Consider the manager whose office, to the casual eye, looks like nothing but a mass of clutter, with tall stacks of reports and papers covering every available surface. Nonetheless, she can put her hands immediately on any document or piece of information she needs. The key is that, contrary to appearances, she actually *does* have a place for everything. Not necessarily the place most people would have chosen, but her place. What looks to everyone else like an episode of *Hoarders* represents, for her, perfect balance.

For most of us, however, a cluttered office may well be an impediment to balance. If we always feel stressed because we are surrounded by piles of papers or we are spending inordinate amounts of time looking for things we should be able to locate quickly, then perhaps we ought to spend some time organizing our environment in the same way we organize our calendar. Organization is not necessarily the same as balance—but it can be an excellent place to start.

Prioritizing

Given the constraints on our time faced by all of us—leaders and others—trying to fit in all the things that need to be done in a given day, week, or month can be a distinct challenge. Constructing a schedule that reflects some degree of balance is a matter of prioritizing: determining which areas of our lives deserve the most time and attention, and then deciding how much time and attention they require relative to other areas.

One tool that can be immensely helpful in this regard is the kind of personal mission statement that we recommended developing in Chapter 6. Once you understand what is truly important to you and the order in which you place various priorities, you will be much better equipped to make difficult decisions about how you spend your time.

In Karl's story of being with his daughter at the lake, the salient point is that he had decided long before that day, at the time his daughter was born, that his role as a father was going to take precedence over being a consultant or an entrepreneur. So when he was tempted to step out of the moment on the lake and check his e-mail—to stop being a father and become a businessman, even though he was not at work—it was easier to stifle that desire because he had already defined his priorities.

Of course, as with all of us, Karl has plenty of other days when he has to set aside being a parent for a number of hours and do his job. Supporting his family financially is important to him, and the personal fulfillment he finds in his work makes him a better parent and role model in the long run. The trick is in knowing when to be a parent, when to be a businessperson, when to be a student, when to be an athlete, when to be a couch potato, and so on. As the Hebrew sage put it in the Book of Ecclesiastes—a passage many of us remember thanks not to our Sunday school days but to The Byrds—"To everything there is a season, and a time for every purpose under heaven."

We also appreciate Stephen Covey's approach to setting priorities: a rubric in which "Important" and "Urgent" are placed on x and y axes to create four quadrants. Some things, he explains, are important but not urgent, meaning we must devote adequate time to them, but should not drop everything else in order to attend to them immediately. Most relationships and many of our work responsibilities fall into this category. Other things are urgent but not necessarily important, like the ringing phone, the e-mail that pops up just as you are closing your laptop, or the colleague who pokes his head into your office just to "shoot the bull." Those things seem to demand our immediate attention, but they are not necessarily important. Of course, some things are both urgent *and* important: they need to be taken care of, and they need to be taken care of *now*. Then, there are those things that are neither urgent nor important—another category into which many of our daily activities can fall if we are not careful.

Understanding these four quadrants and identifying where our various responsibilities and activities lie within them can take us a long way toward prioritizing our schedules: things that are important and urgent come first, followed by those that are important but not urgent, those that are urgent but not important, and those that are neither. We should aim to spend most of our time in the "important but not urgent" quadrant.

To determine where your activities fall on this rubric, ask yourself a series of questions about each one:

1. Does this need to be done?
2. Why does it need to be done?
3. When does it need to be done?
4. Do I have to be the one to do it?
5. How does it fit into my personal mission statement?
6. What may be the consequences of neglecting it or putting it off?
7. Who is relying on me to do this?

Note that there are two principles of prioritizing implicit in this list that we have not addressed yet: delegating and responsibility. Something may very well need to be done, and it may need to be done right away; but that does not mean you have to be the one to do it. As a leader, you may be able to assign the task to someone else who is better equipped or has more time to deal with it. The matter might not even be your responsibility at all.

At the same time, there may be things that are not high on your personal list of priorities that you have to do simply because they are your responsibility. You have made decisions over time that led to your being in a particular position—as a spouse, a parent, a manager, or a community volunteer—that requires you to do certain things whether you want to or not. People are counting on you.

One last point about prioritizing is that, as a leader, your priorities naturally will influence the priorities of the people who report to you. In fact, you will find they generally will modify their behaviors to reflect what they see as your priorities. Rob had an experience with this several years ago when he was directing a large center for his college. Initially, the program was internally focused, but a new president came on board who strongly emphasized community engagement. In response, Rob and his colleagues began to look for opportunities to serve members of the community and develop partnerships with other local organizations. As a direct result of their leader's stated priorities, they became more externally focused.

This dynamic brings with it a tremendous responsibility as well as a wonderful opportunity. If you are spending all your time on things that are urgent but not really important or on things that are neither, you will find the people you lead behaving much the same way—with the result that strategically key activities do not get done. Moreover, leaders who do not make time for family, friends, and personal development are not only likely to be unhappy; they are also setting a terrible example. Our experience over the years is that no one wants to work for leaders like that: people who see their jobs as the most important thing in the world and expect everyone else to feel and act the same way.

On the other hand, if you as leader model the right priorities—aiming for an appropriate balance between work and life—then the others in your organization probably will do so as well. Seeing you make time for family, exercise, and personal development, even while working hard and devoting yourself to the success of the organization, will empower them to live more healthy and balanced lives. And the organization almost certainly will be better and more productive as a result.

Work-Life Balance

One of the most important types of balance you should pursue, even while understanding its total achievement may not be attainable, is balance between your professional life and your personal life: what we call work-life balance.

In the *Nicomachean Ethics*, Aristotle distinguishes between two types of work: work that is economically necessary (work for which we are paid) and work that is morally obligatory (things we ought to do as human beings). He called this second category "leisure." To use leisure well can be hard work! Included in his concept of leisure are activities such as reading and learning, exercising our creative energies, and engaging in family or community activities. Even leisure activities should be engaged with balance. Karl leads a "Great Books of the Western World" club he thoroughly enjoys. He benefits from reading timeless books and from the friendships developed with other members over the years. He enjoys this leisure activity *so* much that he disciplines himself to restrict the amount of time he devotes to these studies. As Shakespeare put it in *Henry IV*, "If all the year were playing holidays, to sport would be as tedious as work." The trick, as always, is to find and maintain some equilibrium between the two.

Finding this balance can be especially challenging for people in leadership positions. You almost certainly got to this point in your career by working long hours and going the extra mile. You are used to this extra effort; moreover, other people expect it of you. Chances are that you have come to expect extra effort of other people, too.

Yet, as you get older, your priorities tend to change. If you have children, you see them growing older, and suddenly one day you realize they are not going to be kids forever. Family members and friends age. You are not always going to have them around. Perhaps you begin to see the negative effects of your long absences from home, due to all those hours at the office, in the way your children behave or the way they relate to you—maybe the way your spouse or friends relate to you, too. You begin to think maybe you should be home more, spend more time with your family, more time with friends.

You may also look at yourself and wonder what happened: you have put on weight, you are out of shape, your health is not what it could, or should, be. Or maybe you have hobbies or interests you have neglected for years while devoting yourself to your work, trying to climb that corporate ladder. So you resolve to start spending some time at the gym, to get back into cycling, to take a day off every now and then to go fishing.

Resolutions like these are typical for people in their late 30s or early 40s who have spent the last decade or two building a career and now find themselves very successful in it—but perhaps not as successful in other aspects of their lives. They perceive a gross imbalance, and their natural inclination is to seek to bring everything back into harmony. The effort can be very difficult, but not impossible.

Unfortunately, by the time we see just how out of balance our lives have gotten—well, it may not be too late to change course, but certain things may have passed us by. Our children are young for only a while; we get just one chance to watch them grow up. And you can always hit the gym and lose weight in your 40s since it is never too late to improve your fitness; but you still will not be as healthy as if you had developed the habit of exercising as a young person and stuck with it all those years.

If you are in your late 20s or early 30s, we advise you to begin your *quest* for work-life balance now. Do not make the mistake of thinking you can devote all your time to one thing at present—building your career, for instance—and then balance things out later in life, after you have achieved financial security or other work goals. For one thing, you probably will not ever be financially secure enough to be satisfied if it is such a priority that you are willing to sacrifice everything else to it. And second, although you can always change your mind about what is most important, there will be consequences for your earlier decisions. By and large, whatever you miss, you will not be able to get back.

Plus, habits are easier to create when you are young. You can form habits then that will stick with you throughout your life. Establishing a new habit when you are older may require changing a behavior that has become ingrained at that point. So seek balance while you are young. You will not regret your efforts when you are older.

Of course, if you are beyond your mid-30s, you still should seek balance. Prioritizing and scheduling are critical to this attempt. Once you determine your priorities are out of order—that you want to spend more time with your children, for instance, and less time at the office—you may find cutting back on your workload difficult. After all, you have created certain expectations among your supervisors, your subordinates, and your clients; people are counting on you. What you *can* do, however, is rearrange your life to make more time for the things you think are important, perhaps without spending less time at work.

Making time for the priorities can be as simple as getting up half an hour earlier each morning (which may necessitate getting to bed half an hour earlier each night), so you can spend that time on the treadmill. Or working through lunch so you can get to your daughter's dance recital. Or scheduling that important meeting so it does not conflict with your family's long weekend.

Also, do not forget to take the vacation time allotted to you. No one, not even you, is indispensable; the organization will survive if you are not there with your hand on the wheel at every moment. Go back and reread some of the earlier chapters about trusting the people who work for you and helping them build their careers by giving them more responsibility. Vacation time is your chance to do just that, while also paying attention to the other important things in your life and refreshing yourself in body and spirit.

Whatever you do, if you do not start trying to put your life in order, to find some acceptable balance between what you do for a living and how you actually live, you almost certainly will regret it down the road. As Aristotle put it in *Nichomachean Ethics*, "Work is for the sake of leisure as war is for the sake of peace. And happiness depends on leisure more than anything else."

Work-Work Balance

Another type of balance that most of us do not really think about when we are young but probably consider more as we grow older is something we call "work-work balance." Even when confining your attention to your professional life, you have to seek some balance among your various work-related activities.

All of us, regardless of our jobs, have tasks we hate and tasks we do not mind and tasks we really enjoy. Actually, one of the things that distinguishes a higher level, professional position from menial labor is that it is, well, not menial; it entails more of the kinds of tasks that professionals enjoy enough to have studied for many years in order to pursue. A college professor, for example, may enjoy teaching classes, being in front of and interacting with students. A lawyer may thrive on being in the courtroom. A marketing director may enjoy putting together a campaign. What would you do even if you were not paid for it? Would you still want to teach a class or two? Represent a worthy cause? Design a story board?

However much you may daydream of quitting your job and spending every day on the golf course or the beach, the simple truth is that, beyond merely allowing us to make a living, work is ennobling and fulfilling. In *The Doctor and the Soul*, Viktor Frankl observed that "the existential importance of work is most clearly seen where work is entirely eliminated from a person's life, as in unemployment." We fear losing our jobs because of the financial consequences, of course; but we also fear being without work because, for many of us, it helps define who we are. We would not know what to do with ourselves if suddenly we were not working, whether by choice or otherwise.

In other words, we work because we need to, but also because we like to. There are some parts of our jobs we like better than others. When we start out in a profession or are new to a specific job or in a low-ranking position, the more routine aspects of the work tend to predominate, leaving us less time to do the things we enjoy. In almost every profession, the junior people have to do the bulk of the "grunt work," which is to say the tasks the people with more seniority do not want to do. We commonly call this "paying your dues."

As we advance in our professions, however, one of the things most of us try to do, perhaps without even being aware, is to find more balance: to divest ourselves of some of those less pleasant tasks and spend more time working at the parts of our job we actually like. One of Rob's good friends, a partner in a Big Four accounting firm, laughed recently when Rob joked with him about sitting around looking at spreadsheets all day. "I don't have to do much of that anymore," he said.

"I have people to do it for me. Now I spend most of my time talking with clients, which I really enjoy." As a young associate, he explained, he spent most of his time performing the grunt work involved in conducting an audit. Now that he has seniority, he gets to do what he likes: work with people. That is the main reason he became an auditor in the first place.

Chances are, you are already working toward this kind of balance, whether deliberately or unconsciously. But if not, perhaps it is something you should consider for your own professional satisfaction and mental health. You can begin by taking inventory of your current position and your prospects for the future within your organization. If you see no potential other than doing the same job ten years from now and that is unsatisfactory to you, perhaps you should start looking for a position that will give you more flexibility, an opportunity to move from "doing my job because I have to" toward "doing my job because I want to."

Unfortunately, one of the paradoxes of leadership is that you may find you have unintentionally gone backwards on the work-work balance scale. In other words, as a manager, you no longer get to do some of the things you enjoy, while at the same time finding yourself having to perform more and more duties you do not enjoy. The dean attends budget meetings instead of teaching classes. The managing partner never sees the inside of a courtroom, instead spending all her time supervising the firm's other attorneys. The marketing director never gets to roll up his sleeves and dive into a campaign because he is overseeing five or six campaigns at once.

If you get to a point in your career where you find this is the case, and as a result you no longer enjoy your work as much as you once did, then you have some important decisions to make. Basically, you have three choices. You can make peace with your new reality and try to find more satisfaction in the important role you now play, which is different from but not necessarily inferior to the role you used to play. Or you can figure out how to bring more balance to your current position by doing more of the things you like. (Who says the managing partner cannot second-chair a case occasionally?) Or you can give up your leadership role (assuming your organization allows for that) and go back to doing what you love. That last choice probably will have financial consequences, but depending on your frame of mind, that may be a small sacrifice.

The important principle to remember is the work-work balance you are striving for is the work-work balance that best suits you. It will be different for everybody, because it is based on your own distinctive preferences and idea of what constitutes balance. As you seek your point of balance, do not allow yourself to be overly influenced by popular conceptions of power or success or by what other people think you ought to do. Only you can decide what works for you.

Encouraging Balance

As a leader, one of the best things you can do for the people you lead is to help them pursue balance in their own lives, both personal and professional. Pursuing balance will not only help them as individuals, reducing mental stress and stress-related illnesses among your workforce while at the same building loyalty; it also will help your organization function better and more efficiently. After all, an organization is only as good as the individuals who comprise it. If those individuals are consistently and severely out of balance, the organization will be out of balance as well.

To help those you lead maintain a healthy work-life balance, for instance, you should enact, support, and promote balance-friendly policies, such as flex-time, family leave, job-sharing, and health and wellness initiatives. Unless you are in senior management, some or all of those policy decisions may not be entirely up to you. Also, some professions are more conducive to work-life balance than others. But you certainly can advocate for such policies where appropriate, make promoting balance a personal priority, and do what you can within your sphere of influence. If the people you lead feel that you have their back where their efforts to build a life apart from work are concerned, they are much more likely to make the effort.

Something else you can do for your people, as a leader, is to respect their personal time. One of Karl's clients had the reputation of constantly calling employees—late at night, early in the morning, on weekends, even while they were on vacation—about matters that were often unimportant and seldom urgent. This leader was one of those people for whom her work was her life; thus, she expected everyone who reported to her to feel the same way and be on call 24/7. Not only does nobody want to work for a leader like that, but being that kind of boss is not healthy for your organization since anyone with a modicum of work-life balance, or any sense of personal boundaries, will leave sooner or later.

Perhaps most important, you can help those you lead by setting a good example of work-life balance. A leader like the one described above does not need to verbalize her belief that all members of the organization should put their jobs first. People see the way she acts; they know how she feels; and they automatically feel pressure to act the same way, even if they do not agree with her priorities. This unspoken expectation ultimately leads to resentment and a decline in job performance. On the other hand, when people see a leader who obviously has some sense of balance—who takes time off from work for family, who has hobbies and interests apart from work, who takes the job seriously but does not mistake it for life itself—they feel much freer to pursue the same kind of balance in their own lives, without fear that doing so will somehow make them look bad at the office or negatively affect their career.

This kind of modeling works just like a dress code: if you show up for work your first day wearing a suit and see the boss is in khakis and a button-down, you will probably adopt a more casual style from then on.

In promoting work-work balance, your goal as a leader should be to let the people who work for you—and especially the junior people—see that there is a light at the end of the tunnel. That is, you need to give them hope they can advance in their careers, and a part of advancement should include greater enjoyment of their work—and of their lives outside of work.

Sure, somebody has to do the grunt work, and sometimes everybody has to pull together to make sure a project gets done. But as a leader you can often distribute those burdens by divvying up the tasks as much as possible, while at the same time providing all staff members (based on experience and qualifications) with opportunities to stretch their wings, to be involved in those aspects of the job that drew them to the profession to begin with. New accounting associates may spend all their time making copies or correcting spreadsheets. But eventually, for those individuals to grow professionally—and for the organization to grow as people move up or retire or otherwise move on—they must have an opportunity to sit down with clients.

More to the point, that new associate needs to believe that, whatever drudgery the job entails today, there is the realistic hope of moving, over time, toward more responsibility and a more balanced work life. That hope is what keeps people motivated, what keeps them happy and healthy, and what keeps organizations moving forward.

Practicing Balance

As with all the other virtues, balance is something you have to work at constantly while acknowledging you will never attain it completely. Remember, the point of seeking balance is that the pursuit forces us to improve ourselves: our minds, our health, our job performance, our relationships. If we did not feel out of balance, we would not make the effort. But make the effort we must, and here are some practical suggestions for doing just that.

A few of your favorite things. Make a list of the things you enjoy doing most outside of work. These could include exercise, hobbies and other interests, and spending time with family and friends. Now, next to each item on the list, jot down an estimate of the amount of time you spend engaged in that activity each week. Then, total up those hours or minutes as the case may be. Below that, write down the average amount of time you spend at work each week.

Now compare the two numbers. Is a significant imbalance apparent? If so, then perhaps you need to take steps to correct it.

Make a schedule. One way you can address work-life imbalance is to set aside time for the activities you enjoy away from the office. We are talking about literally making a daily or (we recommend) weekly schedule in which you designate specific times for family or exercise or reading or whatever. Yes, we realize this may detract from the spontaneity of the moment. But be honest: if you have become a corporate or academic drone, just how spontaneous has your life been?

The sad truth is that if you do not set aside, say, an hour a day on three days a week for exercise and hold that time sacrosanct, you probably will not exercise. If you do not resolve to leave the office by 6:00 every night so you can be home for dinner with your family, you are going to miss a lot of family dinners—and maybe, eventually, find yourself without a family with whom to eat dinner. If you do not schedule some "me-time," even if it is just an hour a week, for reading or reflection or watching television—whatever recharges your batteries—then there is not going to be any "me-time." Just a lot of run-down batteries.

Read over the list you made above; figure out which items on that list are truly important in terms of your health, happiness, and sanity; find some time for them; and schedule it in your weekly planner. Then, barring some sort of code-red emergency, hold yourself to the schedule.

Make another list. This time, write on one side of the page all the things you like most about your job. On the other side, write all the things you like least. Then, underneath each list, jot down an estimate of the amount of time—perhaps expressed as a percentage—that you spend on both sets of activities. Do you see an imbalance?

Chances are that you do. If you are like many people, you probably spend an inordinate amount of time at work doing things you enjoy least—especially if it is still early in your career or if you are a manager. At least you know now what the problem is. You just need a plan.

One more list—and a plan. For this final list, write down the work-related activities you would still enjoy participating in even if you were retired. Maybe, when you think about retirement, all you can picture is yourself on a beach or a golf course. But chances are, if you are a little more mature and do not completely hate your job, you recognize how unsettling it would be not to have any real reason to get out of bed in the morning, and you have given some thought to what you would like to do that would be interesting and fulfilling. Perhaps that activity is something completely different from what you do at work every day, but probably not. Most likely, you have thought about ways to use the skills you have spent a lifetime acquiring and which you enjoy putting to good use in the right context. If not, the time may be right to think about it.

Once you have defined what parts of your job you would still want to do even if you were not paid for doing them, the next step is to begin making a plan that will allow you to eventually do more of those things on a daily basis. That way, you do not have to wait until you retire to achieve some degree of work-work balance.

Putting together such a plan may require some tough decisions on your part. You might even need to look for a new job. Maybe you will have to give up some of your leadership duties, along with the power, perks, and salary that come with them. There may well be financial consequences. But if you find your work life seriously out of balance and it is making you unhappy or even unhealthy, any sacrifice necessary to pursue balance will be worth considering.

Get to know your people. If you do not already, get to know all of the people who report directly to you—or as many as possible. That may take some time, and it certainly will require you to come out occasionally from the executive suite, but building connections with your reports will be worthwhile in the long run.

By getting to know your people, we mean getting to know them on a fairly personal basis—personal enough, at least, that you know about their family, their hobbies, their interests. What is their spouse's name? Their children's names? What do they like to do when they are not at work? Simply engaging in casual conversation with people can provide answers to a lot of those questions, especially as you share personal information of your own, perhaps by talking about your kids or your hobbies. You will find, when you do so, that others tend to open up about their own lives.

You also can ask questions, as long as they are reasonably spontaneous and do not sound like an interrogation. While in a subordinate's office talking about a project, you may notice a family photo on the desk. In that situation, to ask a question like "So, how old are your kids?" is perfectly appropriate, not to mention human.

As you collect this information, be sure to keep track of it. You may need to take notes or keep a file on each person in your office. Yes, we know that may sound a little creepy. However, if you cannot keep track of the information in your head, you need to record it somehow and review it often. Knowing about the people who work for you is that important.

Spread the work-life balance. Once you know the people you lead well enough that you are conversant about their lives, talk to them about their interests and activities every chance you get. Obviously, depending on the situation, it will not always be appropriate to bring up someone's hobby. There are certainly times when you should be professional and focused on the task in front of you. On the other hand, you are not an automaton—or at least you should not be. In a typical workday, there are plenty of opportunities to chat with people about their families, hobbies, latest vacation, and so on, without taking anything away from the work environment. As a leader, look for those opportunities and take advantage of them when they come along.

The result, over time, will be that people feel comfortable talking to you about their lives outside of work—which is another way of saying that they will come to feel comfortable about *having* a life outside of work. By showing interest in their non-work lives, you are sending a clear if subtle message that you *expect* them to have non-work lives and you encourage it. Expecting people *not* to devote all their time to work promotes balance, just as expecting them to devote all their time to work creates a *lack* of balance.

Share the work-work balance. Finally, in the same way you learn about your employees' personal lives, you also must come to know what they enjoy and value, as well as what they are good at doing, in terms of their work. Just as you seek, over time, to move more of your daily activities and responsibilities out of the drudgery category, so do they. Most people expect to have to pay their dues, but no one wants to be doing the same things, day after day, year after year, until old age and retirement beckon.

As a leader, there are specific steps you can take to help those you lead become more engaged and interested in their jobs and to help them pursue work-work balance. For one thing, you can spread the less pleasant tasks around, as much as possible, so that nobody gets stuck with all of them, all the time. You also can look for opportunities to give people more responsibility or allow them to take on new tasks. We understand that leaders have to take things like qualifications and seniority into consideration. But sometimes, if you want people to grow, you have to allow them to branch out. If you want them to enjoy a healthy balance at work—or at least to move toward that—then you must offer them opportunities to reach for that balance.

In the end, balance is an individual consideration, but it is not just about individuals. Workers who are out of balance make for an organization that is out of balance. Just as unbalanced people cannot function at peak effectiveness, neither can unbalanced organizations. Your goal as a leader should be to seek balance in your own life—both at the office and away from it—while at the same time doing everything in your power to help those you lead seek balance, too. Then, your organization will run like a well-oiled machine.

Or, at the very least, maybe it will stop making strange grinding noises.

12. Wisdom

AMONG THE MANY REMARKABLE PAINTINGS THAT GRACE THE VATI-
can, one of the most visually complex and intellectually challenging
is Raphael's *School of Athens*, depicting the great thinkers of antiquity.
In the center of the painting stand Plato (represented, interestingly, as
Leonardo Da Vinci) and Aristotle, turned slightly toward each other
as if conversing. Plato holds his book *Timaeus* in one hand and points
toward the sky with the other, while Aristotle holds *Nichomachean
Ethics* and points to the world in front of him. Many commentators
have observed that the two great philosophers seem to be having a debate, perhaps over the nature of knowledge—what exactly constitutes
wisdom and where it can be found.

That interpretation certainly fits because, for the ancient Greeks,
there were basically two types of wisdom or rather two words that we
may translate as "wisdom." *Sophia* has to do with abstract or theoretical wisdom, what Aristotle referred to as knowledge of first principles.
Obviously, *sophia* is the root of our word "philosophy," which actually
means "love of wisdom." The second Greek word commonly translated as "wisdom" is *phronesis*, which refers to a more practical kind of
knowledge, especially the application of that knowledge. This practical
knowledge is what Aristotle is talking about in *Nicomachean Ethics*
when he describes virtue as a habit of character. For Aristotle, virtue
was always a mean between two extremes, with both ends potentially
fraught with peril. The person of wisdom is one who is able to consistently find that mean and thus make good choices.

In Raphael's painting, what we see is indeed a debate. Plato, clutching his densely theoretical tome *Timaeus* to his chest, points toward the sky as if to suggest that truth and wisdom are in another realm and other-worldly. Aristotle meanwhile holds *Nichomachean Ethics* at waist level, the cover toward him—as if he may actually open and use it—and points forward as if to say, "No, the truth is right here in front of us." We propose that these two figures from antiquity represent the contrast between *sophia* and *phronesis*: between theoretical wisdom and practical wisdom.

Keep in mind that even though these two great thinkers seem in the painting to represent opposing viewpoints, the connection between them is actually much more complex. Aristotle was Plato's pupil, just as Plato was the student of Socrates before him. So perhaps what Raphael was attempting to depict was not merely a debate, but rather the evolution of our thinking about wisdom. Aristotle may have disagreed with his teacher about the nature of wisdom, but that does not mean Plato was entirely wrong. Rather, the pupil saw things differently. In some ways, they both were right: true wisdom requires both theoretical knowledge and an understanding of how to apply that knowledge in real world situations.

This dual framework for knowledge has profound implications for virtuous leaders (just in case you were wondering where we were going with this little art history lesson). Knowledge by itself is not sufficient—brilliant people without common sense are practically a cliché—but at the same time, wisdom cannot exist without knowledge. To be effective, leaders must devote themselves to learning as much as possible, not only about their field but about people and about the world around them, as we discussed in Chapter 3. At the same time, they must strive to apply their knowledge in ways that will benefit not only themselves but their organizations, the people around them, and to some extent their entire communities. After all, we do not necessarily describe the people who have a great knowledge of their field as "wise"; that term is used more to refer to those who know how to use their knowledge and use it well.

One other aspect of wisdom suggested by Raphael's painting, which we intend to explore in this chapter, is the idea of mentoring—passing wisdom on. That is what Socrates did with Plato, Plato with Aristotle, and so on. But these great thinkers did not become clones of each other. Each in turn took the wisdom handed down to him and expanded on it through his own efforts and the power of his own mind. And although each became in a way more famous than the one before, in no way did his accomplishments diminish the stature of the mentor. If anything, they *added* to it. This is a tremendous lesson to be learned as leaders work not only to build their own careers but to create the next generation of leaders.

Knowledge

Knowledge by itself is not wisdom; yet wisdom cannot exist without knowledge. To be wise, leaders must learn as much as they can about their field of endeavor, about human behavior and motivations, about the way the world works, and about themselves.

One of the main reasons people become leaders in their profession or industry is the depth and scope of their knowledge—or at least that is what generally happens. The fact of the matter, as we all know from experience, is that many times people rise to positions of authority for other reasons, such as their connections or their political ability. Such leaders are almost always resented, especially by those with more knowledge and experience who were passed over. In higher education, for instance, many recent presidential appointments have gone to well-connected business leaders or former politicians. What does someone like that know about teaching or research, some faculty members demand to know.

To be fair, there are different types of expertise and different areas of knowledge that can apply in any given leadership situation. For instance, the CEO of a technology firm should know more about running a business than writing code. (Not that the two are necessarily mutually exclusive.) Maybe what a college needs, if it has been having financial problems, is indeed someone with real-world experience in saving struggling organizations or someone with ties to the state legislature and its purse-strings.

If you find yourself in a position where, as a leader, you obviously know less about the industry than the people around you, the first thing to do is acknowledge your ignorance. Do not act as if you know more than everybody else; your ignorance will be obvious to everyone, and others will come to deeply resent you for it. Instead, resolve to learn as much as you can about the industry and the organization as quickly as possible. Listen, seek advice, and learn from the people who really *are* experts. Over time, rather than despise you for your ignorance, they will come to admire your humility and respect your desire to learn. More important, they will teach you much of what you need to know. The rest you can find out from researching and reading on your own.

Even if you are a bona fide expert in your field, there is still plenty to learn. Others in the organization may still know more than you, and there may be multiple job skills and functions that are only tangentially related to yours. In some cases, you must nevertheless become knowledgeable if you are to lead effectively. When Rob served as a department chair, for instance, he supervised several faculty members who were teaching online. He was an experienced teacher and a subject matter expert—but he had never taught online. In order to evaluate those courses and instructors and best serve the needs and represent the interests of the online faculty, he had to learn a great deal about what online courses are supposed to look like and how people teach in a virtual environment. He could not hope to make wise decisions about distance learning if he did not have sufficient knowledge about it.

Besides becoming subject matter experts, good leaders also need to have a solid understanding of human nature. Why do people behave the way they do? What motivates them? There are plenty of academic books and research studies that address such questions, from psychology and sociology to biology and business management. Even studying history and literature can help, perhaps more than most people think, because those disciplines teach us not only what people did at various points in the past but what they were thinking at the time. If you really want a crash course in human behavior and motivation, read Shakespeare's plays. Studying his characters may be roughly the equivalent of earning a bachelor's degree in psychology!

We can also learn a lot about people from reading nonfiction works, such as popular leadership and management books like *The Seven Habits of Highly Effective People* and *Who Moved My Cheese?* as well as the articles in *Forbes* and *Inc.* on this book's reference list. One of the best nonfiction writers today is Malcolm Gladwell, whose keen insights into human behavior are both fascinating and illuminating. If you have not yet picked up *Outliers* or *Blink*, you are in for a real treat.

Perhaps the best teacher, when it comes to learning about people, is experience. The value of experience is why leaders tend to be older, with a number of years in the industry or at the organization. Age does not necessarily make us wise, but it does expose us to a broad range of difficult situations. If we are able to deal with those situations successfully, then presumably we have learned something—assuming, of course, we are humble and teachable. The observation of the two of us is that people do not necessarily learn from experience; some people make the same mistakes, the same bad decisions, over and over again. However, experience *can* teach us, if we will let it, especially when it comes to dealing with people.

Another lesson that experience can teach us better than any other method—and another reason leaders tend to have been around the block a few times—is how the world works. This kind of knowledge is often called common sense, and though many praiseworthy leaders are famous for having it, others have become legendary for their lack of it. Common sense is something you cannot get from a book, even though we can read about people who have shown copious amounts of it, such as the founders of the United States. We can also learn from leaders like Louis XVI and others whose lack of common sense led to disaster. Mostly, however, we have to learn about the world around us by experiencing it first-hand, becoming keen observers, and actively seeking to learn the lessons life freely offers whether we want them or not.

Finally, effective leaders must have a great deal of self-knowledge. Self-knowledge has much to do with what we described in Chapter 4 as reflection and introspection. As a leader, you have to know your own strengths and weaknesses, as well as recognize what motivates you. You also have to be aware of your own biases, always questioning your assumptions. Self-knowledge is probably the most important kind of knowledge there is, and it can be gained only by actively and earnestly seeking it.

Try as we may, we will never fully come to know ourselves, any more than we come to understand fully why other people do what they do or how and why things happen. For that matter, even if we spend our whole lives studying, we never will become perfect masters of our own disciplines. That is why our emphasis in Chapter 3 was on *lifelong* learning. Gaining knowledge, and thus acquiring wisdom, is an ongoing process, one that never ends. The important thing is to recognize our own ignorance, our need to know more than we do. Then we must strive, throughout our lives, to learn everything we can. Lifelong learning is the first, indispensable step toward becoming wise.

Common Sense, Conventional Wisdom, and Collective Wisdom

Having previously mentioned common sense or what philosophers call practical wisdom, we would like to expand on that discussion. As we noted earlier, common sense is really not all that common. A surprising number of people, even those in important positions of leadership, seem to lack it. Sometimes, to the rank and file at the bottom of the organizational chart, there is an inverse relationship between people's position in the organization and the amount of practical wisdom they possess: the higher up the ladder they climb, the less common sense they appear to have. Maybe that is because, at the top of the ladder, there is less oxygen, and people do not think as clearly. Or perhaps the absence of common sense has to do with business guru Lawrence J. Peter's famous "Peter Principle"—the idea that, in any organization, people tend to rise to their level of incompetence and then stay at that level.

In any case, people with genuine common sense are rare enough that they stand out in any organization. Those who stand out that way are generally regarded as wise, and their advice and input are frequently sought out. The need for and appreciation of common sense are reason enough for a leader to cultivate practical wisdom.

Unfortunately, what passes for common sense is sometimes not really sensible or even true. When that happens—when what seems perfectly reasonable actually turns out to be false—we call such an idea counterintuitive. For example, the assumption that raising the price of something people use a lot will increase a company's revenues seems reasonable. But what if, as a result of the price hike, people stop buying that product or start buying less of it? That reaction might cause revenues to plummet.

We see this sort of thinking frequently in education. Surely, if we want to increase college completion rates, make college more accessible to students by offering more online courses, right? Well, that might be true—assuming a sufficient number of students complete online courses. But studies show that completion rates in online classes are far lower than in comparable face-to-face courses. Once we understand that, we can see that simply increasing the number of online offerings may not have a positive effect on completion rates. It may do just the opposite.

These examples underscore the importance of knowledge in the wisdom equation. Practical wisdom is not simply something that is inborn, a matter of intuition. It must be based firmly in knowledge, acquired through diligent study. When the data contradict what we may otherwise intuit, we have to set intuition aside in favor of evidence. The ability to recognize, objectively, when your beliefs or instincts are belied by the facts and then act on those facts rather than "going with your gut" is also a form of wisdom—and a rare form at that.

These examples also illustrate the precarious nature of what we often refer to as conventional wisdom or what "everybody knows" to be true: that the current generation does not work as hard as their predecessors, that real estate is always a solid investment, or that crime rates are steadily rising year after year. A little research will show that none of those statements is true, which is exactly the problem with conventional wisdom: just because everybody knows it does not make it so.

Conventional wisdom can be problematic because it seduces us into going along with the crowd. If everyone else believes something and we *do not* believe it—if we contradict common beliefs or opinions or make decisions contrary to them—then we run the risk of appearing foolish. Knowing that we will be proven right eventually does not help much when we are faced with the prospect of ridicule, loss of respect, or worse. Recall how Copernicus defied the conventional wisdom of his day—everybody knew the Sun revolved around the Earth, right?—and the price he paid for his insolence. This dynamic explains why so many leaders tend to go along with the conventional thinking on an issue. They are afraid of the impact on their careers if they try to swim against the tide.

And yet, this tendency to go along with the crowd is responsible for a great deal of the problems this world has seen, from human tragedies like the Holocaust to your organization's failure to adapt to new technologies. In some ways, knowing the wrong things can be worse than not knowing anything. As the 19th-century American humorist Josh Billings once put it—in a statement famously paraphrased by Ronald Reagan—"It ain't ignorance that causes so much trouble; it's folks knowing so much that ain't so."

Clearly, if leaders want to be wise, they cannot rely on conventional wisdom. But that does not mean they have nothing to rely on besides their own knowledge and whatever wisdom they have acquired. Within every organization lies collective wisdom (not to be confused with conventional wisdom): the accumulated knowledge and experience of every person in that organization. As we have stated many times, no one can know everything. Wise leaders acknowledge that. They recognize there are people in the organization who know more than they do about a particular topic or have more experience than they do. They do not hesitate to dip into that well of collective wisdom and draw out what they need in order to make good decisions, always making sure to give credit where credit is due along the way.

Decision-Making

For leaders, the most obvious and practical application of wisdom lies in decision-making. That is, after all, what leaders are, especially in a professional setting: decision-makers. We often use the word "executive" to describe such leaders. But what is it that they are executing? They are executing, or carrying out, decisions—sometimes decisions made by others, but often decisions they have made themselves. In that sense, the terms "executive" and "decision-maker" are practically synonymous.

A leader's day often seems to consist of hundreds of decisions, large and small, most minor but some momentous—although of course, all too often, decisions that seem minor at the time turn out later to have been momentous. If nothing else, the cumulative effect of all those minor decisions can become immensely more important than the individual decisions themselves, setting the tone and course for the organization in ways the leader may be only vaguely aware of, if at all.

Leaders are judged primarily by their decisions. If their decisions appear over time to advance the organization's goals, they are considered successful and gain all the rewards associated with success: raises, promotions, recruitment by bigger firms or organizations. When a corporation is looking for a new CEO or a university for a new president, they look for someone with a reputation for having made good decisions that benefited the last place they worked. Meanwhile, those leaders—and former leaders—whose decisions are viewed as having harmed their last organization find themselves demoted or out of work, perhaps even unemployable.

Clearly, it is in a leader's best interest to make wise decisions.

Besides such financial and career considerations, leaders also have a moral obligation to make the best decisions possible for the people they lead. If the captain of a ship runs the vessel aground, not only will he or she probably be demoted (and perhaps dismissed), but the lives of the ship's passengers and crew are also at stake. Good leaders feel this obligation to decide wisely as an ever-present responsibility, part of the burden of leadership.

Leaders often are held responsible not only for their own decisions but for those of their subordinates. The captain may not have been at the helm when the ship ran aground, but he or she will still be blamed. Remember Harry S. Truman's famous motto: "The buck stops here"? That is true whether the leader is willing to accept it or not. Few people are more despised in professional life than those who happily accept the perks of leadership, along with the credit when things are going well—which may or may not be their doing—yet do not want to take any of the blame when things go wrong. Instead, they point fingers at subordinates. Those who will not take responsibility for their own decisions, along with the decisions of those under them, really are not leaders at all and certainly are not virtuous leaders. This point highlights the key role leaders play in helping those they lead cultivate wisdom, a subject we will examine later in this chapter.

How do leaders make wise decisions? Again, there are two parts to the wisdom equation: the theoretical and the practical. The former is primarily a function of all the things we talked about regarding lifelong learning: formal and informal education, reading, study, reflection. To make good decisions that impact their organizations, leaders should be as knowledgeable as possible in their field, which means gaining the necessary education and then continuing to learn and stay current.

However, not all organizational leaders can be experts in all the areas over which they have responsibility. Karl is the president of a company that provides consulting and professional development services primarily to health professions education and businesses in health care. With a background in humanities, he does not possess the technical knowledge of a physician, a nurse, a dentist, or a hospital CEO. Nevertheless, his responsibility is to help these health professionals solve problems, develop into better leaders, plan successful careers, and become master teachers. The only way he can manage these tasks effectively for his company's clients is to assemble a team of people who *do* possess both content and process knowledge, as well as compatible values. He listens to these experts, trusts them, learns from them, and depends on them to advise him and engage AAL's clients.

There is no way leaders can know or learn everything. But what they *can* do, first of all, is accept the fact that they do not know everything (recognizing that not knowing everything is hardly a character flaw; *pretending* to know everything is); and second, they can listen to those who *do* know more about a given area. In fact, they should do more than just listen: they should seek out those people and actively consult their advice on an ongoing basis. Our experience is that weak leaders have a problem seeking advice—no doubt because they fear it will expose their weakness—but great leaders never do. The significance of this point thus relates to our discussion of humility in Chapter 5.

The other side of the decision-making equation involves practical wisdom. Once you have learned everything you can about the issues at hand, either through your own knowledge and study or the advice of others or, most commonly, some combination of the two, you still have a decision to make. The quality of that decision will rest primarily on your wisdom.

The pursuit of virtue itself is essentially a kind of decision-making process. Recall that Aristotle often spoke of virtue as a mean between two extremes, both of which represent, in different ways, the opposite of virtue. Take courage, for example. At one extreme on the continuum we have cowardice; at the other extreme we have foolhardiness, which also is, in its own way, antithetical to courage. True courage, Aristotle would say, is obviously not cowardice, but neither is it foolhardiness. Rather, it is the mean—the happy medium we may say today—between the two.

The same reasoning would apply to a virtue like perseverance, with quitting at one extreme and self-destructive bull-headedness at the other. Or love, the opposite of which either could be hatred or, at the other end, unhealthy obsession.

A large part of practical wisdom, as it applies to decision-making, lies in understanding the extremes of any situation and then choosing a path that falls somewhere in the middle (or at least avoids either extreme). So many leaders jump right to one extreme or the other because those extremes tend to represent the most obvious answers and thus do not require as much study or consideration. They either want to cancel the program because it does not seem to be effective or they want to drastically increase its funding, hoping it eventually will pan out—throwing good money after bad, as we sometimes say. Perhaps, in some cases, the answer is to increase the funding slightly, while modifying the program's goals and the criteria for success.

Remember the wisdom of Solomon: when two women came to him, both claiming to be the mother of a certain child, he offered to split the child in half. One woman rejected his proposed solution immediately, thus revealing herself as the child's true mother. The woman who was lying expected a strictly either-or resolution: either she would get the child, or her rival would. Solomon showed that one could serve the child's best interest while at the same time meting out justice to both women.

Of course, there will be times when, as a leader, you do have to cancel a program or project because it is simply not working. In some cases, where the two extremes are "we keep the program" and "the organization goes down the tubes," cutting off the anchor to save the ship from sinking may well be the best choice. Decision-making is the application of both knowledge and practical wisdom. We even have a term for this combination: we call it *good judgment*. Those who have it are considered wise and usually succeed over time, while those who lack it—regardless of their other gifts—ultimately fail.

Mentoring

A key element of wisdom, as suggested by the Raphael painting, is the idea that wisdom must be passed on. Not only that, but as it is handed down from generation to generation, wisdom expands and increases. Remember, Socrates was Plato's teacher, and Plato was Aristotle's—and though all three of these great philosophers are revered, each made contributions beyond those of his teacher.

Leaders who wish to gain wisdom must spend a fair amount of time learning from those who came before: what Ralph Waldo Emerson referred to as "the mind of the past." We do this by reading and pondering the great thinkers throughout history, by studying history and literature and art and philosophy, and by not turning our noses up at those opportunities when they come along. As a college professor, Rob encounters many students—most of them, in fact—who chafe at the notion of taking a literature or philosophy course, wondering out loud what relevance such topics have for them. Those students are probably too young to understand, but in order for leaders to be effective thinkers—in other words, to be wise—they must learn as much as they can about what people have thought in the past. This knowledge will help them find firm intellectual footing as they make important decisions, prevent them from making the same errors others have, and enable them to construct a solid foundation for their own emerging world view.

Of course, wisdom is not limited to Raphael's subjects, the great thinkers of antiquity. Modern history has produced its share of the great and wise, many of them still alive and working today. As we not-ed earlier in this chapter, wise leaders will expose themselves as much as possible to the best thinking and writing, not just in their own field but in multiple fields. Obviously, no one has time to read everything while still maintaining some sort of life balance, but wise leaders will make ongoing learning, in the form of reading, study, and reflection, a personal and professional priority.

Then, there is the kind of learning that takes place between two people in a professional (and sometimes personal) setting: what we of-ten refer to as mentoring. For most of us, some of the wisest people we ever encounter will be those who work right down the hall, colleagues who are often older, more experienced, and willing to share what they have learned. Some of us are fortunate to meet people like that early in our careers, people who take us under their wing and do all they can to help us succeed. Those of us who have been in that position will attest to the positive impact such a relationship can have. Others have to work a little harder to find the Plato to their Aristotle. But those who desire to cultivate wisdom will seek out mentors wherever they can find them.

In other words, if you are a leader but no one has volunteered to serve as your mentor, go find someone you respect and ask him or her to fulfill that role. Most of the mentors the two of us have had over the years are people whom we approached first. Do not wait until some-one comes to you.

Accepting mentorship requires a certain amount of humility, rec-ognizing you do not know everything and you want to learn from someone who has more experience. Not wanting to appear weak or ignorant, many leaders early in their careers make the mistake of re-jecting the idea of having a mentor. But in reality, the best leaders tend to establish such relationships when they are young and maintain them throughout their professional lives, even after they have reached a point at which others may view them as being on the same level as their mentor. No matter how many years you have been in leadership, there are still those who have been at it longer; if nothing else, you can always benefit from having someone whose judgment you trust to use as a sounding board.

In Karl's case, he grew as a leader through his relationship with Jack, a successful executive, father, and civic leader. Karl first met Jack as a fellow employee and a senior staff colleague. Jack was two decades older than Karl and had a depth of wisdom that came through study, experience, and deep reflection. Jack and Karl spent countless hours discussing, exploring, and often disagreeing about a range of topics, from business to family, from theology to world travel. When hundreds of miles separated them because they no longer worked in the same organization, the two were in frequent contact by telephone and e-mail. Karl sought Jack's sage advice often. Although Jack died several years ago, Karl has consciously worked to exhibit the kind of mentorship he experienced with Jack in the lives of others, to pay it forward.

Mentoring others is the wise leader's ultimate responsibility: to pass on the wisdom that he or she has gained—be it through learning, experience, or trial and error. We wish that all great organizational leaders could record what they have learned for posterity, but most labor in relative obscurity and have neither the time nor the inclination to write a book. What they *can* do, however, is seek out young, talented leaders within their own organization and take those people under their wing. This process is how wisdom is passed on: how the next generation improves on the performance of their predecessors, learns from their successes, and avoids their mistakes. Having sung the praises of collective wisdom, perhaps we should note here the term "collective" is not only sociological; it also is historical. And within an organization, the most efficient way of sharing that common history is through one-on-one mentoring relationships.

Wisdom and the Other Virtues

As we have implied all along, wisdom bears a unique relationship to the other virtues because it underlies all of them. To explain that statement, we need to go back to the concept of wisdom as a mean between two extremes, which suggests that wisdom is a prerequisite for practicing any of the other virtues.

We already used courage as an example, but let us revisit that point for a moment. We all have heard the saying paraphrased from Shakespeare, "Discretion is the better part of valor." If you think about it, that saying is a reference to the continuum with cowardice at one extreme and foolhardiness at the other. Lack of courage is not a virtue, but it certainly could be argued that having too much courage—that is, taking foolish risks—is not a virtue either. The virtue of courage is found in the middle, as the mean between those two extremes.

Without wisdom, though, how are we to know where that mean lies? If it is true that sometimes the wisest course of action is no action—which is what the proverb really means after all—how do we know when that is the case and when it is not? Obviously, we could engage internally in the kind of sophistry that may equate cowardice with wisdom. Yet there are times when the courageous person must act, regardless of the consequences. Knowing when action is necessary and when it is not—or even when it might be counterproductive—requires wisdom.

Let us take a look at how the other virtues fit into this discussion.

Humility. Can you be *too* humble? People who rise to positions of leadership and authority typically have substantial egos, which—assuming they are striving to be virtuous—they must constantly fight to keep in check. At the same time, achieving humility does not require us to annihilate the self, only to control it. We all have probably known people who were so self-effacing they never really reached their potential or influenced others to the degree they could have. Developing the proper humility without losing ourselves altogether requires wisdom and especially self-knowledge.

Honesty. We know what you are thinking: "Shouldn't people be honest all the time? Isn't that what honesty means?" Yes, that is true—

and yet, as we discussed in Chapters 4 and 6, there are times when honesty can be used to injure. Although we should always be honest when put to the test, sometimes it is better to say nothing at all than to speak the truth and hurt someone's feelings (or worse) unnecessarily. Then again, there are times when we must speak the truth when nobody else is willing to do so. But how do we know when to speak and when to remain silent? Once again, we need wisdom to make these judgments.

Perseverance. The two extremes here are giving up versus self-destructive stubbornness. Conventional wisdom suggests that displaying the virtue of perseverance means never, ever giving up—right? Not necessarily. True wisdom would dictate that there are times when we need to re-evaluate and perhaps make needed changes. After all, a pilot who knew he was off course yet continued traveling in the same direction would not be considered virtuous because he had persevered. He would be called incompetent. There are times when what we are doing is not working, and we need to stop and try something else. That is not quitting. Knowing when to stop and reconsider is exercising practical wisdom.

Hope. Hope is another case in which the two extremes are fairly obvious: despair versus self-delusion. Developing the virtue of hope requires us to have a healthy optimism about the future, but it does not mean we have to wear rose-colored glasses. We must exhibit a certain amount of faith in human nature, without assuming that people will always live up to our expectations. We need to have faith in ourselves as well, while at the same time recognizing our limitations. Hope as a virtue is confidence without being unrealistic; understanding the difference is where wisdom comes in.

Charity. If we are supposed to love everybody, can we love too much? The answer lies in how we show that love. When the family members of a drug addict refuse to take the necessary steps to help that person, perhaps out of a surfeit of love, we call them enablers. They may love that person more than life itself, but they are not doing what is in his or her best interests. They actually are doing the opposite. You could say they love that person too much. And while we have to learn to love ourselves, it certainly is possible to go overboard with the self-love. As with everything else, there is a balance to be found, a balance dictated by wisdom.

Balance. Speaking of which, the whole concept of balance is based on the idea of the happy medium. In fact, true balance involves taking all the extremes in our lives—such as neglecting family versus neglecting work—and finding the virtuous mean. We can make those decisions only as we gain sufficient knowledge and apply practical wisdom.

Justice. The last virtue is justice, which we will discuss in the next chapter. As a brief preview, remember that justice is often represented in our culture as a set of scales, suggesting that it involves finding a balancing point between two equally problematic extremes. Clearly, justice requires wisdom, just as being wise requires us to be just.

Practicing Wisdom

No one is born wise. The wisdom we acquire over the years is based on the sum total of our life experiences. But wisdom also depends on the extent to which we actively attempt to acquire it, by gaining knowledge and seeking out the wise, as well as how diligently we seek to apply that wisdom in our decision-making and our relationships. As with the other virtues, wisdom can be developed over time; but it does not automatically accrue merely because we have been alive a certain number of years. Having gray hair does not mean you are wise; it just means you are aging. Here are some exercises you can practice to help develop your capacity for wisdom.

Make a reading list. Take some time to put together a list of the books you would like to read, or at least recognize that you need to read, for professional reasons. Some titles probably will come to mind immediately, but you may need to do some research to fill out the list. Ask people you respect for recommendations. Of course, keep your eye on the literature in your profession—periodicals, online publications, and books that deal specifically with your field—because new research and insights are being published all the time and you will want to add some of those to your list. Remember that a good reading list is a lot like a list of home improvement projects: you may not live long enough to complete it, in part because you keep adding to it, but as long as you remain engaged on an ongoing basis, you make progress.

Once you have a good list of at least 10 books, prioritize them based on either which ones you would most like to read or which you most need to read or some combination of those two criteria. Then, develop a plan for working your way through them on a systematic basis. If you commute by rail or bus, you can use that time to read. If you usually eat lunch by yourself, at your desk or elsewhere, you should have that 30- or 60-minute time block. You can get up 15 minutes earlier each morning and use that time to read, or else put the book on your nightstand and read for 10 or 15 minutes before going to sleep each night. Even if you read for only 10 minutes a day, you will be surprised at how fast you get through a book you probably would not have read otherwise.

Address your knowledge deficiencies. What areas of your organization do you know the least about? In particular, what functions are you charged with overseeing that you do not have any personal experience with? Those are areas you should consider taking some time to learn more about.

There are various ways to go about this learning. You could seek out formal training, in the form of a course or workshop. Perhaps your institution or company offers these on an ongoing basis for people who perform certain jobs and need to improve their skills. (A common example would be an online course that teaches people how to use a software application.) Even if it is not part of *your* job, if you manage people who are engaged in that activity on a regular basis, you should consider taking the course and learning all you can about it. Note that, if you are a beginner, you may need to back up and take some basic courses before taking the latest one being offered.

Another way to learn more about a particular function is to apprentice yourself, informally, to people who perform that function on a regular basis. As a leader or manager, you need to be careful how you approach others. Whoever you ask to help you learn more about that particular function probably will be someone who reports to you, in which case they may be a little nervous about having you look over their shoulder. They might even feel threatened, fearing that your reason for wanting to learn how to do what they do is so you can criticize them or even take over that function yourself, putting them out of a job.

However, if you approach them with an attitude of humility and explain clearly why you want them to teach you—because you have a significant lack in your knowledge base, which may prevent you from making good decisions, and you regard them as experts—you most likely will find that they are happy to help. Everyone likes being an expert at something, and most enjoy the opportunity to share their expertise with others.

Be the voice of reason. Identify three or four policies in your organization that strike you as not particularly logical. Perhaps they are based on data you believe are invalid or on conventional wisdom that on closer inspection turns out to be incorrect. Choose one of those policies that makes you particularly grind your teeth, and do some research on the issue so you have the facts. Note that this research may involve traditional research of the literature and available information, but it may also involve polling or surveying people to get a more accurate representation. Say, for example, your organization is communicating with clients and customers primarily via e-mail, but you believe most of them are not reading those e-mails. Can you find studies that support that view? Could you conduct a survey of your own to see if using e-mail is effective for your clients?

Once armed with reliable information, you can approach the necessary decision-makers, present your findings, and recommend a needed change. If you are well prepared regarding the issues that affect your organization, you could contribute your ideas in a meeting and offer wise counsel that will prevent your boss from making a bad decision. And to whatever extent you *are* the leader, and the decision is up to you, having that information will enable *you* to make wise decisions.

Tap into collective wisdom. Remember that, in addition to employing many wise individuals, your organization also has an impressive store of collective wisdom, which is the sum total of all the experiences of everyone in the organization. As a leader, you should tap into that collective wisdom as much as possible. Often, one person, however wise and learned, simply cannot know enough to make an informed decision. Even everyone put together probably does not know everything; but collectively, they know a lot more than any individual.

With collective wisdom in mind, identify a specific professional problem or challenge you currently face, something you have to make a decision about. Then, begin seeking out information from the people who report to you and others in your organization. You can go to them personally and ask for advice, you can pull them together into a meeting, or you can solicit input electronically, or any combination of these. The important thing is that you communicate with as many people as possible, ideally all those who have any stake in the decision—and that includes the naysayers and curmudgeons. One of the biggest traps into which leaders sometimes fall is listening only to people who tell them what they want to hear. Creating such an echo chamber may make you feel better about yourself, but it will not make you any wiser in the long run. If anything, it will have the opposite effect.

Of course, if you seek input from a wide range of people, you will get plenty of conflicting opinions and advice, which is where your own judgment becomes critical. As you talk to more and more people, you will probably see a clear consensus begin to emerge. Although the consensus view is not always the correct view, it often is. By following collective wisdom—especially when you do not know what to do—you are more likely to make the right decision. Additionally, you will earn a reputation as a humble leader who genuinely listens.

Seek out a mentor. If you are a mid-career professional, especially one who has been in leadership positions for several years at this point, you may think you do not need a mentor. You are beyond that, right?

Maybe not. No matter how much knowledge and experience you have, there are people who have more. Recognizing that others can guide you is an expression of humility. Doing something about it is a function of wisdom.

Regardless of where you are in your career, if you do not already have a mentor, take the time to seek one out. It could be someone from within your organization, perhaps a person who is above you on the organizational chart or who simply has more years working there, with whom you have a good working relationship (and perhaps a friendship as well, although that is not necessary) and who is willing to serve as an informal advisor and sounding board. A mentor also could be someone from outside your organization who is in the same or a related field.

If you do not know where else to start looking for a mentor, you can go back to someone who played that role earlier in your career—perhaps one of your professors in graduate school or an older colleague with whom you once worked. Reach out to that person if you have lost track of each other, and see if you can re-establish your relationship. You do not even have to call it "mentoring"; the engagement can be simply renewing a friendship. The chances are good, if you once respected that person's opinions and perspectives, that will still be the case; and he or she once again will become a kind of mentor, whether or not the two of you choose to call it that.

Pay it forward. Finally, remember that, in the long run, wisdom is only valuable if it is passed on. No doubt you are grateful for all the wonderful mentors in your own life and career. Perhaps there is very little you can do to return the favor, but one thing you can do is pay it forward by becoming a mentor to someone else—or even more than one person.

At the very least, if you are not currently mentoring someone—

probably a younger individual who may or may not report to you but probably falls below you on the organizational chart—then you owe it to the organization and to yourself to seek out a likely candidate. Otherwise, whatever wisdom you have accumulated throughout your career goes out the door with you when you retire or leave the organization. The ideal candidate is someone in whom you see potential, with whom your personality is compatible or complementary, and who is humble enough to accept you as a mentor. You do not have to start by walking up to that person and saying, "Hi, I want to be your mentor." Just take advantage of the opportunities that come along to offer advice, constructive feedback, and praise where warranted (but do not be stingy with your praise). As you offer your wisdom in an unobtrusive manner, you will find that person will begin to seek you out more and more over time.

One dynamic we have observed that prevents some leaders from becoming more active as mentors is what we may describe as "the law of the jungle"—the fear that if they give too much of their hard-earned wisdom away to the younger generation, one of their protégés will replace them. That is a possibility, of course. But the more likely outcome is that being generous with your knowledge and the benefit of your experience will foster loyalty within the ranks. In addition, it will help the people under you make better decisions, which in turn will reflect well on you. So in the long run, becoming a good mentor is to your advantage.

But your personal benefit is not really why you should mentor someone. You should do it because it is the right thing to do—and because wisdom that is not shared, when all is said and done, is not really wisdom at all.

13. Justice

OF ALL THE VIRTUES WE HAVE EXAMINED IN THIS BOOK, PERHAPS none is as controversial or as politically fraught as this last one. Almost everyone agrees on the basic definitions of courage, honesty, perseverance, and charity, even if we do not always see eye to eye as to how those virtues ought to be practiced. But when it comes to justice, people cannot even seem to agree on a definition. Historically, justice has meant different things to different people; that remains the case today.

Perhaps, for our purposes, we can best sum up this diversity of opinion by referencing Mortimer Adler in *The Syntopicon: An Index to the Great Ideas*. In his introduction to the chapter on justice, Adler notes that, going back to Plato (at least), there have been two main views of justice, which he terms political justice and natural justice.

Political justice is the belief that might makes right and justice is whatever the government deems it to be. As the character Thrasymachus puts it in Plato's *Republic*, "Justice is nothing else than the interest of the stronger....And this is what I mean when I say that in all states there is the same principle of justice which is the interest of the government; and as the government must be supposed to have power, the only reasonable conclusion is that everywhere there is one principle of justice which is the interest of the stronger."

This view is what we may call a purely law-and-order concept of justice. The government—that is, the people in charge—makes laws designed to further the interests of the body politic, which is to say their own interests; and everyone else—the governed—must follow those laws. Anyone who fails to follow the laws, however they were made and by whomever, is by definition a lawbreaker and therefore has behaved unjustly.

The questions raised by this concept of justice are immediately obvious to all of us who have been brought up and educated in the Western democratic tradition: Who makes the laws? Who says they are good laws? What about the interests of the governed—are they being promoted as well? If might makes right, what about those who lack might? Are they simply in the wrong? Would true justice not demand that the rights of the weak be protected along with those of the strong?

A more enlightened view, or at least one that is more consistent with our democratic values, is that justice is not based on physical or political might but rather is a natural law. Political justice is relative, based on the whims of those in power. Natural justice is an absolute, which exists for all people in all circumstances. This is what the 17th-century British philosopher John Locke referred to as the "law of nature" that "teaches all mankind who will but consult it that, being all equal and independent, no one ought to harm another in his life, liberty, or possessions....Everyone, as he is bound to preserve himself and not quit his station willfully, so, by the like reason ...ought he, as much as he can, to preserve the rest of mankind." Locke had a tremendous influence on Thomas Jefferson and the other Founders of the United States, as seen in the Declaration of Independence, where the term "natural law" becomes the "inalienable rights" possessed by all humans.

As heirs to the Jeffersonian tradition, we recoil at the suggestion that might makes right and that justice is only what the government declares it to be—even though, as a practical matter, that is often the case. Witness any number of laws passed in the United States in recent years without popular support, not to the mention the power of regulatory agencies to bypass the legislative process altogether.

For our purposes in this chapter, since this is a book specifically aimed at organizational leaders, we would like to borrow a page from Plato's *Republic*—except that instead of talking about the Just Society and the Just Person, we want to focus on the Just Organization and the Just Leader. What exactly would those look like? What does justice mean as it applies to leadership? And how can leaders develop and practice the virtue of justice? Those are the questions we intend to address in the following pages.

Fairness and Equality

At its most fundamental level, justice is understood often as simple fairness. But that definition leads us right back to the same problem: what exactly is fair, and who decides? Is it fair that some people have more than others? What if they have worked harder or managed their money more wisely? And then there are all those accidents of nature over which we have no control. One person is born into a wealthy family, while another is born into poverty. One child grows up in an industrialized nation, with all its creature comforts and technological advantages, while another faces a life of scarcity and hardship in one of the world's underdeveloped regions.

Is any of that fair?

The only possible answer is no. And the obvious conclusion, at which most adults long ago arrived, is that life is not fair. We cannot control those kinds of circumstances. All we can do is try our best to treat people fairly within our narrow sphere of influence.

Still, we are left with the question: what do we mean by treating people fairly? There are those who would argue that treating people fairly means treating them all the same. But that definition does not hold up to scrutiny. Most school systems recognize, for instance, that holding the best students back because some of their classmates struggle to keep up is not fair. For this reason, they create special programs for gifted students and offer Advanced Placement courses in high school. If you are coaching a Little League baseball team, you cannot play all the kids in the infield. Besides the fact that there are only four positions, some of those players are simply not capable of fielding a sharply hit ground ball. They would get hurt if you put them that close to the batter.

What we *can* do as leaders, however, is to evaluate everyone by the same criteria and treat them as equally as possible within those parameters. When a student who is not initially pegged as gifted turns out to show promise, the school can give that child a chance to participate in the program. If you have six or seven players who can field a ground ball without getting hurt—something you have determined through trial and error during practice—you may want to rotate your lineup to give all of them an opportunity to play in the infield occasionally.

The key word here is opportunity. Adler distinguishes between what he calls "equality of condition" and "equality of opportunity," illustrating his point with the example of a footrace "in which individuals all start out with no one affected by circumstances more or less favorable to winning the race. Their equality of opportunity consists in an equality of the initial conditions under which they enter the race. When the race is run, these same individuals end up unequal. According to the speed with which they ran the race, one comes in first, another second, another third, and so on." Providing people with the same opportunity will not guarantee that everyone achieves the same degree of success; the leader's job is to make sure all the people who report to him or her have the same chance at succeeding and that they all are treated more or less the same, given similar circumstances.

Years ago, when Rob was serving as chair of a large academic department, one of his faculty members asked permission to miss the first two days of the spring semester. He had been presented with the opportunity of a lifetime: a friend was paying his airfare to visit Australia. He was going to be there for two weeks over the holiday break, but he would not be getting back until two days into the new term. The two days in question were not even class days: they fell during the first week of registration, when faculty members normally would be on duty to advise and help enroll students. Rob told the faculty member to enjoy his trip, assuring him that he would personally cover for him as needed those two days.

A week or so later, another faculty member came to see Rob, incensed that he had given her colleague permission (as she saw it) to shirk his duties. "Are you going to give me permission to miss those two days, too?" she demanded.

"Sure," Rob replied. "If you have a friend who pays your way to take a trip abroad, and the only way you can go is if you miss a couple of days of work, by all means, go for it. We will cover for you."

That faculty member was upset because she felt she was not being treated fairly: was not being dealt with exactly the same. Rob's point was that, under the same or similar circumstances, he would have done for her the same thing he did for her colleague. Life does not get any fairer than that.

This example also highlights another aspect of fairness that leaders must keep in mind: what's often referred to as equality under the law. Being treated the same in a legal sense, regardless of race, gender, economic class, or any other factor, is one of our most cherished and fundamental rights and indeed one of the guiding principles of our democracy. Perhaps our society does not always live up to that high ideal, but it is something we aspire to—something that is in fact codified in the founding documents of the United States.

For organizational leaders, the term "law" can be taken to mean rules or policies. The just leader must ensure that rules and policies are applied in the same way to everyone: that there are no unwarranted special exceptions, that some infractions are not ignored while others are punished, and that violators receive comparable penalties. There are few things leaders can do that will engender more resentment and open hostility than appearing to crack down on some while letting others slide.

That said, justice does not demand that everyone be treated identically. The rules may be the same for all, but circumstances vary. Even the normally hidebound Professional Golf Association recognized this a few years ago when they agreed to allow professional golfer Casey Martin to use a cart in tournaments because he had a documented medical condition that prevented him from walking long distances. Was that fair to the other competitors, who all had to walk the course as the rules had long required? We would argue that it was fair because if any of those other golfers had developed a similar condition, they too would have been allowed to ride in a cart. The bottom line is that, without the cart, Martin would not have had the opportunity to compete. Getting to use a cart did not mean he would win; it just meant he had as much of a chance to win as anyone else.

So how does a leader know when to make such exceptions? Leaders need sound judgment—which is to say, wisdom. Everyone will not always agree with your decisions, of course. But if you strive to use wisdom in your deliberations, while at the same time doing everything in your power to make sure all the people in your organization have the same opportunities to achieve and excel, you will earn a reputation as a wise and just leader. Your team will be willing to overlook what they may regard as an occasional lapse in judgment because they believe your heart is in the right place.

Sharing Power

At the beginning of the last section, we posed two questions: what does "fair" mean, and who decides? But we went on to answer only the first. In this section, we would like to address question number two: who decides what is fair?

If Thrasymachus was correct and might makes right, then the answer is that those in power are the ones who decide what is fair. Which leads us naturally to another obvious question: fair for whom? Well, if the powerful are the ones making the rules, unless they are extraordinarily wise and humble, then what they regard as fair is probably whatever serves their own interests—that is, what is fair to them. Even if they honestly attempt to do what is best for the majority, that lofty ideal does not necessarily guarantee fairness for any individual. History is rife with regimes that have ostensibly sought justice for the many by taking the property and even the lives of a (relative) few. No doubt to those few, that did not seem fair.

The idea at the heart of our modern democratic societies is that justice is best served by allowing those who must live under a system to decide for themselves, collectively, what is fair. Of course, that does not guarantee everyone will be happy with every decision. However, democracy posits that decisions are most likely to be fair to the most people if everyone has some say in the matter.

Obviously, this belief applies to the law. If the rules we live under are to be fair and just, then the people who must live under them should have some input in their creation. And since the United States (like many other countries) is too large for people to vote individually on every law that comes up, we have devised a system by which people elect representatives to protect their interests. What we would call a democratic republic offers individuals some degree of control over their circumstances, without which they quickly can come to feel they are being dictated to and treated unjustly.

There is an important lesson here for organizational leaders. We understand that corporations and many other types of organizations are not really democracies. Either they have owners or they have executives who answer to the owners—in many cases, shareholders. Those executives, and the management teams they lead, are responsible for the decisions made on behalf of the organization; thus, they tend to provide the lion's share of the input when the rules are made. Their jobs are on the line, after all.

Even so, when organizations operate too much from the top down, and the rank-and-file feel they have little or no say in the policies and procedures they are required to follow, the results can be employee dissatisfaction, low morale, and high turnover rates as people seek a fairer working environment elsewhere. Excessive top-down management is especially problematic for organizations that consist of large numbers of intelligent, well-educated, independent thinkers, such as higher education institutions, technology companies, and professional services firms. People who work in those fields often have strong opinions, in many cases backed up by data, and they expect to be listened to. For this reason, most colleges and universities employ some sort of shared governance model, allowing faculty members to have meaningful input on matters that directly concern them.

Smart, capable people have a high degree of mobility, as their skills and experience tend to be in demand. So the leaders' best interest is to create some mechanism for sharing power, for allowing lower ranking but still valuable employees to play some role in governing themselves and the organization. Remember the lesson of democracy: people are much less likely to believe they are being treated unfairly if they have some input into the decision-making process.

We recognize that organizational leaders cannot, as a practical matter, put every issue up for a vote. Sometimes leaders have to make the call and take the hit if the decision turns out to be a bad one. There also are some rules or policies that are non-negotiable, regardless of majority opinion, such as those regarding financial accountability or sexual harassment. Matters such as these fall under the heading of natural justice: it is always wrong to lie, steal, or assault someone.

Such issues rarely are points of contention. No responsible employee objects to reasonable policies designed to prohibit pilfering or unwanted sexual advances. Grumbling begins when leaders appear to arbitrarily reduce their staff members' vacation time, create overly restrictive telephone policies, or add another layer of bureaucratic paperwork to an already complex process. Perhaps those leaders should learn what every competent second-grade teacher knows: rules for the group are more likely to be followed, with a minimum of dissent, if they are made and agreed upon by the group. Those leaders may also be surprised, as any good second-grade teacher can attest, at how closely the agreed-upon rules resemble the rules they would have made themselves. If anything, the group's list might even be a little stricter.

The bottom line is that leaders should look for any and every opportunity to share power with those they lead. They can create committees or other governance bodies, ideally with representation from all affected departments or units, to address issues of concern to all. Not only is such power-sharing conducive to fairness and good policy; it also can allow leaders to deflect anger and resentment by spreading the responsibility for difficult decisions. Generally, once employees understand the company has a choice between cutting vacation days and laying people off, they are a lot less likely to feel ill-used because they lose some vacation.

Sharing power obviously requires a great deal of humility, as we discussed in the chapter devoted to that virtue. But justice—defined here as basic fairness—demands that those expected to follow the rules should have an opportunity to shape those rules. Anything less is a form of tyranny, however well intended.

Justice As a Duty

Much of Plato's *Republic* is devoted to his description of the just ruler, which he also refers to as the Philosopher King—one who rules with fairness and wisdom, always with an eye toward the common good. Although perhaps an unattainable ideal, the Philosopher King nonetheless serves as an excellent role model for the just leader in today's often-cutthroat business environment.

According to Plato, the soul or essential self of every individual is comprised of three parts: appetites, emotions, and reason. Those three elements are constantly at odds, striving for mastery within each of us. The result is that some people end up being dominated by their appetites, others by their emotions. The just person is one who is ruled primarily by reason and thus succeeds in keeping his or her appetites and emotions in check. Such individuals, says Plato, must be the ones in charge of things if we are to have a just society—which is another way of saying that those who are in charge must strive to master their

appetites and emotions and not allow their decisions to be overly influenced by those elements. Reason must prevail.

Consider, for a moment, what happens when leaders are ruled by
their appetites. We all have known people who fall into that category. They want what they want—sex, money, power—and they want it
now, everyone else be damned. In particular, such leaders tend to become megalomaniacs, addicted to power and willing to do or say anything to acquire and maintain it. They will step on others on their way
up the corporate ladder and use their coworkers to make themselves
look better. Clearly, that kind of behavior is not just.

Or what about those who are dominated by emotions? They may
be well-meaning; they may even serve a useful role in society. As Plato
points out, strong emotions are often key to doing many things well.
But in the end, those who are guided primarily by emotions do not
make good leaders because their feelings cloud the decision-making
process. We all know people like this; we even may have worked for
them. They might desire to do what is right, but they are too blinded
by their emotions to see clearly what right is. Because of this blind-
ness, even though they mean well, they end up treating some people
unfairly. The writings of Daniel Goleman and others on the topic of
emotional intelligence teach us that emotions provide vital information and that effective leaders listen to their emotions. But emotions
should *inform* a rational process of leading; they do not dictate the
process.

The best leaders are those who base their actions and decisions primarily on reason. That does not mean emotional considerations such
as compassion should not factor in; we devoted the entire chapter on
charity to that premise. But if the ultimate goal is justice, such considerations must be subordinate to reason. Otherwise, what seems like
compassion for one person could very well be injurious to another.
Only those guided by reason can see clearly all sides of an issue and
make the call that is most beneficial to the largest number of people. If
you are not by nature that sort of person (and most of us are not), then

your task is to seek to acquire the virtue of justice by mastering both your appetites and your emotions. This self-mastery is good practice for any organizational leader—it is also your *duty*.

As a leader, you have a duty to ensure that all the people in your organization or unit have, within their sphere, the same opportunities to excel and advance. You have a duty to see that all are treated fairly, including in the area of compensation. You have a duty to make sure they are evaluated based on the same standards, that those who are affected have some say in what those standards are, and that there is no discrimination. You have a duty to communicate clearly and regularly with those you lead and to make sure the lines of communication flow both ways. Above all, you have a duty to model the kind of behavior you expect from those you lead, especially in the area of fairness.

In the end, there is perhaps no greater praise for a leader than to say he or she treated everyone fairly. We all *hope* the people we work for will have courage, perseverance, wisdom, humility, and so forth. We *expect* them to be fair.

Fairness Is a Two-Way Street

At the same time as the people within the organization have a right to expect fair treatment from their leaders, the organization has a right to expect certain behaviors from its members. And since virtually all leaders are also followers, it is important to keep this fact in mind as you seek to internalize the virtue of justice.

What does the organization have a reasonable right to expect from you as an employee? Primarily that you put in a day's work for a day's pay. As long as the organization is living up to the terms of its agreement with you—paying you the salary you agreed to, providing the agreed-upon benefits, and so forth—then you have an obligation to give your best effort while on company time. Rob likes to recall a conversation he overheard years ago at the college where he worked at the time. In this conversation between the men's head basketball coach and an assistant coach, the assistant, who was a part-time employee, made the comment that he was not going to devote a lot of time to a certain aspect of his job because, as he put it, "They aren't paying me enough to do that." The head coach responded, "If we're not paying you enough to do the job, then quit. But if you're taking the money, then you need to do the job."

Something else your employer has a reasonable right to expect from you is loyalty. That does not mean you cannot explore other career opportunities, nor does it mean you have to do everything your bosses demand of you, especially if it is unethical. Loyalty also does not mean you cannot express legitimate disagreements with your bosses, as long as you keep those disagreements in-house. You do not have to become an automaton to be loyal. What loyalty means in this context is that you will not denigrate the organization in front of outsiders and that you will not do anything to make the organization look bad (unless of course it has done something illegal, in which case you have an ethical obligation to report it). Otherwise, until the day you leave, it is your organization as much as anyone else's, and you should treat it that way.

Finally, speaking of ethics, your employers have a right to expect you to behave ethically and morally in every situation. Such behavior includes treating colleagues and coworkers fairly, but it also means you are willing to speak out when others—including your bosses—are behaving unjustly. As we discussed in the chapters on honesty and courage, people have a moral obligation to oppose genuine injustice, even if it costs them personally to do so. Leaders of a just or fair organization will be glad to have people on board who act as the group's conscience, even if they sometimes find the truth uncomfortable.

Just as your employer has a right to expect certain things of you as an employee, those who report to you have a right to expect certain things from you as a leader. They have a right to expect that, in making decisions, you will put the good of the unit or the organization above your personal good. They have a right to expect that you will not discriminate against them based on arbitrary criteria and that whatever criteria you use in decisions regarding hiring, promotion, and assigning raises will be clear and evenly applied. They have a right to expect you to share power, to the extent possible, so that they are able to play some role in the decision-making process when decisions directly concern them. They have a right to expect you to be as transparent as possible in your own decision-making and to communicate clearly and regularly. They have a right to expect you to tell them the truth, even if occasionally that truth is not pretty. They have a right to expect you to treat them as human beings, not robots or cogs in a wheel. Perhaps above all, they have a right to expect you to exhibit the same behaviors you demand from them.

Only when justice is a two-way street—when leaders have fair and reasonable expectations of those they lead, and the rank-and-file have fair and reasonable expectations of their employers, and both sides live up to those expectations—can an organization be just. Like the other virtues, justice is an individual characteristic. But unlike the others, it is also uniquely collective. In one sense, you can be honest or humble or loving or courageous all by yourself. But you simply cannot effect justice on your own. Justice, like leadership itself, is about relationships.

Trust and the Just Organization

To summarize our ideas in this chapter, the Just Organization, as with Plato's Just Society, will have certain defining characteristics. For one thing, it will be a place where individuals believe they are being treated fairly by their leaders and they can trust those leaders not to discriminate or show favoritism. It also is a place where staff members recognize the leaders have their best interests and the best interests of the organization at heart, rather than the leaders' own best interests.

Much has been written in recent years about the importance of trust within an organization. Trust is closely related to the Nine Virtues, especially honesty, wisdom, and justice. In fact, you could say it is a product of those three virtues. We tend to trust people not because they ask us to trust them—which is the approach too many leaders take—but because we believe they will tell us the truth and do the right thing for the right reason. As with justice, trust is a two-way street. For an organization to prosper, people must be able to trust their leaders, and leaders must be able to trust the people they lead. We believe this kind of trust is a natural side effect of people behaving justly.

We have noted, for instance, the importance of good communication within an organization and identified this as one of the basic expectations people ought to have of each other. But communication is useless without trust. If your leaders are always telling you things you do not believe, no genuine communication is taking place. In fact, this situation is worse than not being told anything at all because what is really being communicated is that leadership has no faith in or respect for those they lead. By the same token, leaders have to be able to trust the people who report to them, to rely on information they provide in order to make good decisions. Without trust on both sides—that is, unless all concerned act justly—what appears to be communication is nothing more than window dressing, designed to make the organization look good to outsiders.

Trust also has much to do with what we described earlier as equality of opportunity. If people believe the playing field is level and they have as good a chance as anyone of advancement and other rewards, they are much more likely to give their best effort to the organization. Again, this does not mean everyone is treated exactly the same, regardless of relevant factors such as education and experience. It simply means that, if you know a certain job requires an advanced degree or additional skills, then you might decide to do the extra work necessary to obtain that degree or acquire those skills. In that case, both you and the organization benefit. On the other hand, if you are convinced that no matter what you do, others will receive preferential treatment, at some point you are probably going to stop striving to achieve and start "phoning it in." That kind of attitude characterizes organizations in which there is no trust because there is no justice or expectation of justice.

Another important manifestation of trust has to do with self-interest or rather lack thereof. Go back to the situation we described in Chapter 9, in which Karl was consulting with an academic department that was, to put it mildly, mired in distrust. The chair did not trust the dean, the dean did not trust the chair, neither of them trusted the faculty, and the faculty had so much distrust of the administration that a good number of them were looking to leave. So why all the animus? Perhaps it was because each person was convinced that all the other members of the department were only looking out for themselves— that they were putting their own interests above their colleagues and above the organization. They may well have been right. Once you decide that nobody has your back, the natural reaction for most people is to look out for number one. Trust is indeed a two-way street, and when it shuts down, it shuts down in both directions.

This example represents the exact opposite of the Just Organization. As charity demands that we put others before ourselves, so justice requires that we consider the needs of all, not just our own. Few leaders are as disliked as those perceived as constantly using others to advance their own careers. No one trusts them, and with good reason: they can be trusted only to take care of themselves—at the expense of others if necessary.

Perhaps an even worse situation occurs when leaders who are concerned primarily with their own agendas begin cracking down in order to carry out those agendas, creating harsh new rules and issuing decrees designed to bring everyone else in line, even against their own interest or will. This action is a variation on the might-makes-right theme, and it is not the way leaders behave in a Just Organization. Justice requires some sharing of power, so that those who have to live by the rules get some say in what those rules are. When everyone has some input, the organization is much more likely to do what is best for all concerned.

Which brings us back to trust. When people genuinely believe their leaders have their best interests at heart, they are much more likely to trust those leaders and, in return, do their part to help the organization succeed. As a result, the leaders know they can trust those they lead to do their best. Creating a climate of trust and positivity in which everyone can agree upon shared goals and work together to achieve those goals is perhaps the most important effect the Just Leader has on an organization.

Justice and the Other Virtues

The just leader is one who exhibits all of the other eight virtues:

1. Without humility, the leader will not be inclined to listen to others, to share power, or to consider the concerns of others as equal to his or her own.
2. Without honesty, there can be no true justice. Lying, dissembling, obfuscating—these are all by nature unjust. The just leader tells the truth.
3. Without courage, the leader will not be inclined to stand up against injustice or to fight for those who have long been denied a voice.
4. Without perseverance, the leader will be unable to effect justice at all. A Just Organization does not spring to life fully formed. Pursuing justice requires patience, persistence, and sometimes lengthy suffering.
5. Without hope, what is the point of seeking justice? The ideal of justice posits that it is a better way—that people are likely to be happier and organizations more productive and responsive if they behave justly. Believing this, and striving to achieve it, requires hope.
6. Without charity, the leader may well see no need for justice. If there is no one greater than yourself, then justice is moot. Before a leader can treat people justly, he or she must have enough regard for others to believe they deserve such treatment.

7. Without balance, the leader will find it very difficult to base decisions primarily on reason. The leader who is ruled by appetites or emotions is by definition not balanced. Balance, in this sense, is informed by reason.

8. And without wisdom, justice essentially has no meaning, or at least that meaning is left for individuals to interpret as they see fit (which is really no justice at all). The just leader must first and foremost be wise, just as the wise ruler is by definition just.

Acquiring the virtue of justice means you are in the process of acquiring all the other virtues as well. Conversely, if you have internalized all the other virtues, then you cannot behave unjustly. This proposition is the one with which we began: you cannot have one virtue without having all of them; if you do not have one of them, you do not really have any because all work together and all must be developed simultaneously.

Practicing Justice

Throughout this book, we have used the word "practicing" as a heading for these brief exercise sections that conclude each chapter. We hope you have come to realize by now that the word has a double meaning for us. We certainly mean practicing in the sense of working at something in order to get better, the way you would practice a sport or a musical instrument. But we also mean practicing as in "practicing law"—that is, actually doing it on a regular basis.

The only way you can practice justice is in the second sense of that word, by behaving justly. That is because justice is unique among the Nine Virtues in another way: it is absolute. You can learn over time to be more humble or more courageous or more charitable, but with justice, either you are or you are not. There are no degrees of justice. If you are not behaving justly, then you are behaving unjustly.

We do not mean to imply that we cannot improve ourselves in this regard. Rather, improvement entails recognizing those areas in which we are not behaving justly and then striving to make the needed adjustments, regardless of the cost. This of necessity will be a lifelong pursuit, one inextricably linked to the other virtues. As we grow wiser, more honest, more humble, more charitable, and more balanced, we will become increasingly aware of those areas in which we fall short. As we gain courage, learn to persevere, and dare to hope, we will develop the strength of character necessary to address those areas of weakness.

But if you are still looking for an exercise as a place to start, here are some suggestions.

Read Plato. We have referenced many texts in this book without stating explicitly, "You ought to read this" (perhaps it was implied). In this case, however, we do want to challenge you to read Plato's *Republic* if you never have done so or reread it if you have. It is probably the definitive work on justice, and although it does not provide all the answers, it at least raises the right questions.

Take a personal "fairness inventory." Make a list of all the decisions for which you are responsible on a regular basis in your capacity as leader (or as many as you can think of), leaving lots of space between items. These may include tasks like evaluating subordinates, determining salary raises, deciding on promotions, assigning projects, and appointing people to committees or teams.

Next, make a list under each item of the criteria you typically employ when making that decision. Be as honest with yourself as you can; you may want destroy the list afterward because some of what you write may not be flattering. You may have to admit—if you are being really honest with yourself—that you have taken into account factors such as race, ethnicity, gender, or your personal like or dislike of an individual, even if you were unaware at the time you were doing so. We have an unconscious bias to favor people who are like us. Usually, we have to work hard to bring our biases into the light.

If you find your decisions have not always been as fair as they could be, resolve to eliminate irrelevant criteria from future decision-making. To the extent possible, without harming others or putting yourself in an awkward position, look for opportunities to make it up to people you have unintentionally mistreated, perhaps by giving them a bigger salary boost the following year or asking them to serve on a more prestigious committee.

Consider the proof in the pudding. If you want to know if you have been treating people in your organization fairly over the years, one simple (if potentially disturbing) way is to look at the results of your decisions. You can easily get data showing the salaries of all the people who report to you. Are the men in your office, for example, being paid significantly more than the women, with no legitimate reason for the discrepancy? Are whites paid more than blacks or Latinos? Are people who went to your alma mater paid more than those who attended the in-state rival? (Don't laugh. That happens.)

How about promotions and the best assignments? Can you look around the office and see that almost all your managers are women? Or men? Are the people given the best projects or put on the most prestigious assignments always your personal friends? Again, there may be a perfectly good explanation for any of those things—but if not, you may be acting unjustly.

Review policies. One of the biggest complaints employees have about their organization is that policies seem arbitrary or unfair. If you have ever heard those kinds of rumblings or observed them for yourself, appoint a committee to review the organization's policy manual. Be sure to make the committee as representative as possible, either by asking for volunteers or by holding an election (or both). Empower the committee to address any policy its members believe to be an issue and then to make substantive recommendations. Once the committee's review is completed, take the results back to the entire group for further discussion. The important thing is to make sure everyone has the opportunity to provide feedback.

Create an advisory group. In order to share power and thereby promote fairness, establish a group or committee whose charge is to advise you on matters important to the entire unit or organization. If the unit you lead is small enough, this could be what is known as a "committee of the whole." With a larger organization, you may need to identify subgroups or units and allow each equal representation. In either case, be sure to meet with the group regularly with two purposes in mind: 1) running your ideas by them, so you can get their feedback and advice; and 2) hearing their ideas about how to improve the organization.

As a leader, you must be humble and wise enough to recognize wisdom when you hear it and to accept advice or even criticism. You also must be courageous enough to act based on what you believe to be in the best interests of the entire organization. This balancing act is precisely what leaders are called upon to perform.

Ask your followers. One task you can assign to this advisory committee is to create a list of expectations for members of the organization. That is, what do they believe the group as a whole has a right to expect from its individual members? What emerges will be a document that represents not your own personal set of demands, but the expectations colleagues have for each other. You may be surprised to find that group members hold themselves and their peers to an even higher standard than you insist upon. As always, once you have a draft document, make sure those not on the committee have the opportunity to offer suggestions and criticism to inform the final version.

If you are really brave and want to take this concept one step further, you can ask the committee to create a list of expectations they have for *you* and perhaps for other leaders in positions similar to yours. Even if you are doing your best to be a good leader, you may make assumptions about what people expect of you based on the expectations you had for *your* leaders when you were farther down the organizational chart. Even though many of those assumptions may be true—because certain expectations are universal—others could be outdated or simply matters of personal preference. The bottom line is that you will never really know what the people you lead expect of you unless you ask them.

Cultivate trust. A great leader was once asked if it was more important for his followers to love him or respect him. "Neither," he replied. "What's most important is that they trust me."

Remember that justice, on a practical level, is all about trust. If you as a leader behave justly, the people who follow you will come to trust you. If they do *not* trust you, that should be a good indication you have treated them, on one or more occasions, in a way they regard as unfair.

Even if you have treated others unfairly, you can still change. You may need a while to earn (or earn back) someone's trust, but you can begin with something obvious and simple if not always easy: keeping your word. Is there something you promised to do for the people who work for you that you have not done yet? Something you promised to a particular individual? Figure out what that is and do it if it is within your power; if it is not, sit down with those people (or that person) and explain why you cannot. People will never come to trust you until they know you are going to keep your word.

Resolve to communicate. If you do not already have a means by which you regularly communicate with the people you lead, that is a lack you need to address immediately. Many leaders communicate with staff members through weekly or monthly e-mails or newsletters. Others call weekly meetings. Some do both. The point is that you have to let people know, on a regular basis, what is happening with the organization—even if the news is not good. Even bad news is better than what people will assume if they do not hear the truth from you. Worse, they will come to regard you as secretive and perhaps corrupt.

In these communications, be upbeat and positive, but also be candid. Explain what is happening in the organization, and if some of those things are challenging, tell them what you and others are doing to meet those challenges. Earnestly seek their input, put their good ideas to use, and give appropriate credit when it is due.

Finally, remember that communication, as with fairness and trust, is a two-way street. Little good is accomplished in communicating with people if you do not provide opportunities for them to communicate back and not just via return e-mail. If you do not already have an open-door policy, then institute one immediately: a *real* open door policy. Within the constraints of your busy schedule, make time for visits from people who care enough about the organization to come talk to you. You may even try creating or reserving office hours—times when, barring emergencies, you will always be in your office and everyone knows it.

All of these are steps you can take to make justice an integral part of the way you operate on a daily basis. As with all the other virtues, once people see you acting that way, they will be more likely to behave justly as well. Of course, there will be unscrupulous people who try to take advantage of you and use your desire to be fair to everyone against you. But such people will reveal themselves, and everyone in the organization will see them for what they are, as long as *you* remain steadfast in treating them and everyone else fairly.

Remember, you are never going to be perfectly just, any more than you are ever going to be perfectly wise or perfectly balanced. Nevertheless, you can resolve each day to treat everyone you come in contact with as fairly as possible and then do everything in your power to follow through on that commitment. Over time, you will find people are willing to overlook your imperfections because they know you are trying to do the right thing. Best of all, they will come to trust you—which, in the end, is really all you can ask.

14. The Virtuous Leader

IF YOU HAVE GOTTEN THIS FAR IN THIS BOOK, WE WOULD LIKE TO thank you for sticking with us. We hope we have been able to share our thoughts about virtuous leadership in a way that is helpful to you and your organization. We also hope you will go back and reread passages as you need refreshers and that you will recommend it to others. We realize that many of the concepts discussed may not have been new to you, and that is a good thing. Your familiarity means you have already engaged in trying to improve your leadership by reading and studying—which is exactly what we are advocating. Hopefully, our perspective on some of these concepts has been a little different and has thus led you to think about them in ways you have not before.

In any case, this book is plenty long enough, and we do not feel any need for a lengthy wrap-up chapter. We would, however, like to remind you briefly of some of the key points. These are the "take-aways" as conference presenters often say—the ideas that we most want you to internalize from this book, what we most hope you will remember.

Leaders are made, not born. Everyone has the potential to lead. True, some people are born with more potential than others in certain areas that relate to leadership, just as some people have more musical ability or athletic talent. However, the overwhelming majority of leaders, including some of our greatest ones, were simply people who worked hard to develop their abilities.

Becoming a virtuous leader is about nurturing what is natural. Virtue is about shaping your character through making the right choices so often that they become habits. Even if you lack extraordinary natu-

273

ral abilities, you can become an excellent, perhaps even a great, leader. All the virtues we discussed as characterizing effective leaders can be cultivated and developed. More important, they are developed through practice—because like any other abilities, they have to be used and used the right way, or they are worthless. Someone who is born with a great deal of musical talent but who never practices will never be as good a musician as someone with less talent who assiduously works at becoming a better musician. The same is true of leadership.

Our premise in this book is that the most effective way to become a better leader is to develop the virtues that all great leaders seem to exemplify. Whatever gifts you may or may not have been born with, if you work throughout your life to internalize and practice these virtues, people around you will assume that you are a natural leader—that you were born to lead. Only you will know the difference.

Leaders are lifelong learners. No one masters the Nine Virtues overnight. Internalizing, developing, and practicing those virtues must be, and is by definition, a lifelong pursuit. No matter to what degree you already possess these virtues, you can start working on them today. Over time, as you continue to practice incorporating the virtues into your life and into your leadership, you can become a virtuous leader.

The way you go about incorporating these virtues is by doing all the things we outlined in Chapter 3. Read. Study. Reflect. Seek advice and feedback. Read, study, and reflect some more. Seek more advice and feedback. Repeat as necessary, which may mean every day of your life from now on. Virtuous leaders must of necessity be lifelong learners, not merely because the pursuit of virtue is a lifelong endeavor, but because circumstances on the ground are constantly changing. Unless we continue to learn each and every day, we can never hope to gain wisdom. Without constant reminders of how much there is for us to learn, we will never attain humility. Without an ongoing appreciation for the situations of those around us, we cannot begin to understand what constitutes justice, much less pursue it. And so on. Lifelong learning is the *sine qua non* of virtuous leadership.

On a practical level, we also hope you work toward developing these virtues by doing the exercises at the end of each chapter. One word of caution, however—a reminder of something we discussed in Chapter 4: if you perform every one of these exercises but do so in a perfunctory way, as if merely checking items off a list, you will not achieve the desired results. Virtue is not nearly that clear-cut. To put it another way, there is no app for that. You must first of all truly desire to attain the Nine Virtues—all of them—not because you think doing so will impress someone or improve your chances of getting a promotion, but because you want to become a more virtuous person and leader. In other words, you must pursue virtue for its own sake, not as some stepping stone or tool.

All for one, one for all. Another key point about the Nine Virtues that we wish to emphasize is that although they are separate and distinct from each other, they are closely interrelated. Even though you have to work on each virtue individually, you also need to work on developing them all collectively because no one virtue by itself is worthy of the name. In a sense, it is impossible to embody any of the virtues unless you embody all of them.

To be sure, someone may appear to possess a virtue such as courage without also having charity. But in that case, is what appears to be courage really the virtue? What end does it serve, other than advancing the individual's own interests? Courage without charity is merely ruthlessness, just as wisdom without humility is arrogance, perseverance without hope is fanaticism, and honesty without justice is cruelty. An individual who appears to display one virtue—or even several of them—without displaying them all really has none of them. That person is not virtuous, whatever redeeming qualities he or she may possess.

The challenge, then, for anyone reading this book who wishes to incorporate its precepts and become a virtuous leader is to embrace *all* of the virtues. You may need to focus on one at a time initially, attempting to master it before moving on to the next. But our hope is that, as practicing these Nine Virtues becomes habitual, you will develop the ability to reflect on and regularly evaluate your behavior in terms of all nine.

Virtue is a habit. That last sentence is key: virtue is habitual. So is vice, for that matter. The distinction comes down to what you do on a daily basis. To paraphrase an old Chinese proverb, think of virtue and vice as a pair of ravenous wolves. Which ultimately will live? The one you feed every day, of course.

Please note the emphasis on *doing*. That is because virtue is not a feeling or a state of mind. Virtue is a state of character that develops through our behaviors. A virtuous person is one who consistently behaves virtuously. The inverse is also true: a person who consistently behaves virtuously is by definition a virtuous person. Remember the point we made several times, taking our cue from William James: if you want to develop a quality, behave as if you already have it. If you want to be brave, act brave. As you act out the attributes you wish to possess, two things will happen. Over time, you will become brave and charitable and wise and so on. Virtue is habitual. You develop a virtue as you practice it.

Virtue is contagious. Virtuous leaders have a responsibility not only to behave virtuously themselves, but to allow, enable, and encourage *others* to behave virtuously. The contagion of virtue does not happen naturally, the way an infection may spread. It is something leaders have to work at constantly. As they do so, they will see their virtuous habits spread throughout the organization; in that sense, virtue indeed is contagious.

Great leaders promote the spread of virtue in at least three distinct ways.

The first is by their own example. One of the defining features of all Nine Virtues is that they tend to stand out, to be immediately recognizable. People notice when someone is conspicuously honest or optimistic or charitable or wise—pick your virtue and insert it here. And while some may resent those who exhibit those characteristics, perhaps because they are afraid they will look bad by comparison, most are drawn to such people. Many even are inspired to imitate them. Just by behaving virtuously, a virtuous leader can have a powerful influence on the entire organization.

The second way a virtuous leader can spread virtue is by creating an environment in which such behavior is welcome. Many organizations make workers feel as if they have to behave unethically just to survive, not to mention get ahead. People see their peers exaggerating their own accomplishments, currying favor with management, and advancing their careers at the expense of colleagues—and they conclude that is what they need to do too. But an organization led by a virtuous leader will value charity over self-promotion, honesty over flattery, loyalty over careerism. In that way, the virtues ingrained in the leader will, over time, become ingrained in the organization as a whole.

Finally, virtuous leaders spread virtue by actively encouraging the people they lead to behave virtuously. Of course, this process assumes that those leaders are themselves behaving virtuously, which takes us back to our first point: leaders cannot very well ask people to trust them, for instance, if they do not show others that same trust or do not act trustworthy. Assuming they are setting the right example, leaders possess the moral authority to inspire others by pointing out what constitutes virtuous behavior in a given situation and by consistently rewarding virtuous behavior rather than its opposite.

A final assignment. So here is your last bit of homework: even if you do not share this book with someone, at least share what you have learned from it. Sharing does not necessarily require a formal setting—a workshop or training session, for example. Sharing can involve something as simple as chatting with a colleague over lunch about your pursuit of the Nine Virtues and what you hope to accomplish. No doubt you also can find opportunities, if you look for them, to weave bits and pieces of your understanding into your everyday conversations and communications. All this talk about the Nine Virtues would be useless if they did not become something you incorporate into your daily existence. In any case, feel free to quote us—or better yet, quote the many great thinkers we have cited.

Finally, resolve to set the kind of example we describe herein: to become someone who is known for virtuous behavior and who inspires others to behave in the same manner. Be ever mindful not just of the image you portray but of the kind of organization you lead and the kind of organization you *want* to lead. Does it reward and promote virtuous behavior, or does it do the opposite? Before you make any decision or set any policy, stop and ask yourself whether it will encourage others to think and act virtuously. As a leader, you have to give people an example to follow, but you also have to foster an environment in which they feel safe and valued as they strive to follow that example.

As you do all those things—as you strive to acquire and practice the Nine Virtues, set a good example, and invite others to follow that example—you will come to be perceived by everyone you encounter as a virtuous leader.

References

Adler, Mortimer J. *Six Great Ideas.* New York: Touchstone, 1997.

Adler, Mortimer J. *Syntopicon.* In *Great Books of the Western World* (vol. 3), eds. Mortimer

Adler and Robert Hutchins. Chicago: Encyclopedia Britannica, 1952.

Adler, Mortimer J. *We Hold These Truths: Understanding the Ideas and Ideals of the Constitution.* New York: Scribner, 1987.

Aristotle. *Nicomachean Ethics.* Trans. Terence Irwin. Indianapolis, IN: Hackett, 1984.

Blanchard, Ken and Phil Hodges. *The Servant Leader: Transforming Your Heart, Head, Hands, and Habits.* Nashville, TN: Thomas Nelson, 2003.

Bland, Archie. "Driven to the Distraction: Have We Lost the Ability to Focus on a Single Task?" http://www.independent.co.uk/arts-entertainment/books/features/driven-to-distraction-have-we-lost-the-ability-to-focus-on-a-single-task-8914010.html. Accessed: November 2, 2013.

Burlingham, Bo. "The Re-Education of Jim Collins." *Inc.com.* Inc. Magazine. September 26, 2013. http://www.inc.com/magazine/201310/bo-bulinghamo-burl/jim-collins-re-learns-leadership-at-west-point.html. Accessed: March 22, 2014.

Collins, Jim. *Good to Great: Why Some Companies Make the Leap, and Others...Don't.* New York: HarperCollins, 2001.

Coombs, P.H. *The World Crisis in Education: A View from the Eighties.* New York: Oxford UP, 1985.

Covey, Stephen F. *The Seven Habits of Highly Effective People.* New York: Simon & Schuster, 1989.

Csikszentmihalyi, Mihaly. *Flow: The Psychology of Optimal Experience.* New York: Harper, 2008.

Douglass, Frederick. *Narrative of the Life of Frederick Douglass, an American Slave.* Boston: The Anti-Slavery Office, 1845.

Frankl, Viktor. *The Doctor and the Soul.* Trans. Richard Winton and Sarah Winton. New York: Vintage, 1986.

Frankl, Viktor. *Man's Search for Meaning.* Boston: Beacon, 2006.

Franklin, Benjamin. *The Autobiography of Benjamin Franklin.* In *The Norton Anthology of American Literature, Vol. A,* eds. Nina Baym and Robert S. Levin. New York: W.W. Norton, 2011.

Freedman, Russell. *Washington at Valley Forge.* New York: Holiday House, 2008.

Gladwell, Malcolm. *Blink: The Power of Thinking without Thinking.* New York: Back Bay, 2007.

Gladwell, Malcolm. *Outliers: The Story of Success.* New York: Back Bay, 2011.

Gleiser, Marcelo. *The Island of Knowledge: The Limits of Science and the Search for Meaning.* New York: Basic Books, 2014.

Goleman, Daniel. *Emotional Intelligence.* New York: Bantam, 1995.

Greenleaf, Robert K. *The Servant as Leader.* Westfield, IN: Robert K. Greenleaf Center, 1982.

Haden, N. Karl. "Of Paradigms, Saints, and Individuals: The Question of Authenticity." *Dialogue,* October 1989, 7-13.

Hawthorne, Nathaniel. "Young Goodman Brown." In *The Norton Anthology of American Literature, Vol. A,* eds. Nina Baym and Robert S. Levin. New York: W.W. Norton, 2011.

Heilbrunn, Jacob. "Can Leadership Be Studied?" *Wilson Quarterly,* Spring 1994, 65-72.

Isaacson, Walter. *Steve Jobs.* New York: Simon & Schuster, 2015.

James, William. *The Principles of Psychology.* New York: Holt, 1890.

Jenkins, Rob. "A Song of Vice and Mire." *The Chronicle of Higher Education,* September 24, 2011, 27.

Jenkins, Rob and Beth Jensen. "How to Climb Down from Top-Down Leadership. *Academe,* 96(3), 24-27.

Johnson, Spencer. *Who Moved My Cheese?* New York: G.P. Putnam's Sons, 1998.

King, Martin Luther Jr. "I've Been to the Mountaintop." http://www. americanrhetoric.com/speeches/mlkivebeentothemountaintop. htm. Accessed: May 13, 2015.

King, Martin Luther, Jr. "Letter from a Birmingham Jail." In *50 Essays: A Portable Anthology (4th ed.),* ed. Samual Cohen. New York: Bedford St. Martins, 2013.

Kirkpatrick, S.A. Visionary Leadership Theory. In *Encyclopedia of Leadership,* eds. George R. Goethals, Georgia J. Sorensen, and James MacGregor Burns. Thousand Oaks, CA: Sage, 2004.

Lambert, Frank. *The Battle of Ole Miss: Civil Rights v. States' Rights.* Oxford: Oxford UP, 2009.

Locke, John. *Second Treatises of Government.* http://www.gutenberg. org/ebooks/7370. Accessed: July 28, 2010.

MacIntyre, Alasdair. *After Virtue: A Study in Moral Theory* (2nd ed.). Notre Dame, IN: Notre Dame UP: 1984.

Madison, James, Alexander Hamilton, and John Jay. *The Federalist Papers.* Clinton Rossiter, ed. New York: Signet, 2003.

Mezirow, Jack. *Transformative Learning: Theory to Practice.* New York: Wiley, 2002.

Paley, William. *The Principles of Moral and Political Philosophy* (8th ed). Boston: West & Richardson, 1815.

Plato. *Five Dialogues.* Trans. G.M.A. Grube. Rev. John M. Cooper. Indianapolis, IN: Hackett, 2002.

Plato. *Republic.* 2nd Ed. Trans. G.M.A. Grube. Rev. C.D.C. Reeve. Indianapolis, IN: Hackett, 1992.

Sashkin, Marshall and Shashkin, Molly G. *Leadership that Matters.* San Francisco: Berrett-Koehler, 2003.

Singh, Jai. "Dell: Apple Should Close Shop." http://www.cnet.com/news/dell-apple-should-close-shop/. Accessed: October 6, 1997.

Stockett, Kathryn. "Kathryn Stockett's 'The Help' Turned Down 60 Times before Becoming a Best Seller." http://www.more.com/kathryn-stockett-help-best-seller. Accessed: May 7, 2011.

Thoreau, Henry David. "Resistance to Civil Government." In *The Norton Anthology of American Literature* (vol. B), eds. Nina Baym and Robert S. Levin. New York: W.W. Norton, 2011.

Tolkien, J.R.R. *The Fellowship of the Ring.* New York: Ballantine, 1994.

Tolkien, J.R.R. *The Hobbit.* London: Harper Collins, 1998.

Wittgenstein, Ludwig. *Culture and Value.* Trans. Peter Winch. Chicago: University of Chicago Press: 1984.

Index

9 *Virtues* Development Opportunities from AAL

IMAGINE IF ALL YOUR LEADERS—FROM FIRST-LINE SUPERVISORS TO senior-level executives—had the opportunity to learn the life-changing principles revealed in this book. What kind of difference would that make in the daily operation and long-term success of your organization? The Academy for Academic Leadership (AAL) offers a broad spectrum of virtues-based development options tailored to meet your specific needs.

AAL began in 2005 with a focus on higher education, but has since expanded to work with for-profit companies as well as not-for-profits. AAL's highly qualified experts come from a wide variety of professional backgrounds, and are ready to help your organization unlock its leadership potential. We specialize in empowering current as well as aspiring leaders to grow and develop professionally and personally.

Below are some of the popular options for virtues-based development. Please keep in mind that AAL also can customize a program especially for your organization.

- **Three-day, onsite leadership training.** AAL will come to your site and work with members of your staff for three full days. This in-depth professional development, based closely on the book, will cover such topics as the principles of virtues-based leadership; the relationship between ethics, values, and the Nine Virtues; the importance of lifelong learning; and the role of leaders in promoting a virtues-based organizational culture. It also will cover each of the Nine Virtues in careful detail. This program is designed to be highly interactive, with group and individual activities aimed at helping attendees understand and internalize the Virtues. As part of the program, each attendee will receive a copy of *The 9 Virtues of Exceptional Leaders* well before the training is scheduled. Ideally, this will allow the entire group to read the book prior to the program and discuss it together using a study guide developed by Dr. Karl Haden and Rob Jenkins exclusively for this program.

- **Three-day executive leadership retreat (open enrollment).** AAL also offers its three-day executive leadership program in a relaxing retreat location. This program is aimed specifically at upper-level organizational leaders and is open to executives from any organization, although the number of participants is limited to ensure intensive attention to each person's development goals. In addition to the curriculum outlined in the first bullet above, attendees (and their guests, if they desire) will have the opportunity to socialize, play golf, hike, or visit some of the area's other attractions.

- **Three-day executive leadership retreat (organization-specific).** To best serve its clients, AAL also offers the three-day leadership program in the executive retreat format for individual organizations, at an offsite location of their choosing. The organization, in this case, will choose how many people may attend, restricted only by the site selected and the availability of accommodations.

- **One-day, onsite leadership program.** This experience is designed to accomplish some of the goals of the three-day program in a shorter time frame. Though the presenters will not be able to go into as much depth, the full-day program will take attendees well beyond the book to a deeper understanding of the Nine Virtues, showing them how they can develop the Virtues and incorporate them into their daily lives as leaders. Attendees will receive a copy of the book in advance.

- **Half-day, onsite leadership program.** The half-day program is designed to introduce organizational leaders to the fundamentals of virtues-based leadership. It will cover the Nine Virtues, the importance of lifelong learning, and the leader's role in promoting a virtuous organizational culture. This program is designed for upper-level managers, to introduce them to concepts they may wish AAL to share with the rest of their organization later, in a full-day or three-day training. Attendees will receive a copy of the book on the day of the session.

- **60-90 minute presentation.** An AAL consultant will come to your site and deliver a 60-90 minute presentation on the Nine Virtues and related concepts from the book. This option is ideal for organizations that wish to incorporate virtues-based leadership development into a larger program, such as a staff development day. Books can be purchased at a discount for attendees prior to the event, or they can be made available for individuals to purchase on the day of the program.

- **20-30 minute keynote address.** The authors of *The 9 Virtues*, Dr. Karl Haden and Rob Jenkins, are available to deliver a 20-30 minute keynote address at meetings, conferences, and other functions. If logistics allow, copies of the book can be made available for purchase on the day of the event. Book signings also can be arranged.

To schedule a program for your organization, obtain pricing information, or receive answers to any questions you might have, please visit **www.9virtues.com/programs** or call AAL at 404-350-2098.

CPSIA information can be obtained
at www.ICGtesting.com
Printed in the USA
FFOW03n1849010618
46990546-49256FF